Exploring the Spiritual in Popular Music

Bloomsbury Studies in Religion and Popular Music

Series editor: Christopher Partridge

Religion's relationship to popular music has ranged from opposition to 'the Devil's music' to an embracing of modern styles and subcultures in order to communicate its ideas and defend its values. Similarly, from jazz to reggae, gospel to heavy metal, and bhangra to qawwali, there are few genres of contemporary popular music that have not dealt with ideas and themes related to religion, spiritual and the paranormal. Whether we think of Satanism or Sufism, the liberal use of drugs or disciplined abstinence, the history of the quest for transcendence within popular music and its subcultures raises important issues for anyone interested in contemporary religion, culture and society. *Bloomsbury Studies in Religion and Popular Music* is a multidisciplinary series that aims to contribute to a comprehensive understanding of these issues and the relationships between religion and popular music.

Christian Metal, Marcus Moberg
Christian Punk, edited by Ibrahim Abraham
Mortality and Music, Christopher Partridge
Mysticism, Ritual and Religion in Drone Metal, Owen Coggins
Religion and Popular Music, edited by Andreas Häger
Religion in Hip Hop, edited by Monica R. Miller, Anthony B. Pinn and Bernard 'Bun B' Freeman
Sacred and Secular Musics, Virinda Kalra
U2 and the Religious Impulse, edited by Scott Calhoun

Exploring the Spiritual in Popular Music

Beatified Beats

Edited by
Mike Dines and Georgina Gregory

BLOOMSBURY ACADEMIC
LONDON • NEW YORK • OXFORD • NEW DELHI • SYDNEY

BLOOMSBURY ACADEMIC
Bloomsbury Publishing Plc
50 Bedford Square, London, WC1B 3DP, UK
1385 Broadway, New York, NY 10018, USA
29 Earlsfort Terrace, Dublin 2, Ireland

BLOOMSBURY, BLOOMSBURY ACADEMIC and the Diana logo
are trademarks of Bloomsbury Publishing Plc

First published in Great Britain 2021
This paperback edition published in 2022

Copyright © Mike Dines, Georgina Gregory and contributors, 2021

Mike Dines and Georgina Gregory have asserted their rights under the Copyright, Designs and Patents Act, 1988, to be identified as Editors of this work.

For legal purposes the Acknowledgements on p. xiii constitute an extension of this copyright page.

Cover design: Ben Anslow
Cover image © Sebastien Desarmaux / Getty Images

All rights reserved. No part of this publication may be reproduced or transmitted in any form or by any means, electronic or mechanical, including photocopying, recording, or any information storage or retrieval system, without prior permission in writing from the publishers.

Bloomsbury Publishing Plc does not have any control over, or responsibility for, any third-party websites referred to or in this book. All internet addresses given in this book were correct at the time of going to press. The author and publisher regret any inconvenience caused if addresses have changed or sites have ceased to exist, but can accept no responsibility for any such changes.

A catalogue record for this book is available from the British Library.

A catalog record for this book is available from the Library of Congress.

ISBN: HB: 978-1-3500-8692-0
       PB: 978-1-3501-9870-8
       ePDF: 978-1-3500-8693-7
       eBook: 978-1-3500-8694-4

Series: Bloomsbury Studies in Religion and Popular Music

Typeset by Integra Software Services Pvt. Ltd.

To find out more about our authors and books visit www.bloomsbury.com and sign up for our newsletters

Contents

List of Illustrations — vii
List of Contributors — viii
Acknowledgements — xiii

Introduction
Mike Dines and Georgina Gregory — 1

1. Beatified Beats, Ritualized Rhymes: Intersections of the Popular and the Sacred in Music
   Antti-Ville Kärjä — 8

Part One Personal Spirituality

2. Leonard Cohen, the 'Sufi' Mystic
   Jiří Měsíc — 29
3. Hank and Jesus: The Integral Roles of Religion and the History of Country Music in the Lives and Careers of Contemporary Country Artists
   Gillian Kelly — 48
4. Above the Clouds: Discourses of the Spiritual and the Religious in the Lyrics of Paul Weller
   Paul Spicer — 72

Part Two Christianity

5. 'Embracing the Divine Chaos': Transcending the Sacred-Secular Divide in the 1990s British Rave Church Movement
   Lucy Robinson and Chris Warne — 97
6. Pop Goes to Church: Pentacostal Evangelism and 'Chav' Christianity
   Georgina Gregory — 119
7. 'The Time Has Come, Exodus!': Congo Natty and the Jungle (R)evolution
   Shara Rambarran — 138

8 'Between Hipsters and God There is Sufjan Stevens': Sufjan Stevens and His Fans
Katelyn Medic   152

Part Three   Alternative Religions

9 'Save My Soul From the Poisons of This World': Straight Edge Punk and Religious Re-Enchantment
Francis Stewart   175

10 'Message From Thee Temple': Magick, Occultism, Mysticism and Psychic TV
Mike Dines and Matt Grimes   193

11 *I am God!* The Transference of Musical Fandom as Religion to Worshipping the Self
Javier Campos Calvo-Sotelo   209

Index   237

List of Illustrations

Figures

11.1	Esteemed importance of several elements, converted into percentage ratio	227

Tables

1.1	The popular/sacred grid	20
11.1	Use of earphones. Total figures and percentages	221
11.2	Sensations produced by the use of headphones. Total figures	222
11.3	Self-image of the participants. Total figures and percentages	222
11.4	Esteemed importance of several elements. Total figures and percentage ratio	226

List of Contributors

Javier Campos Calvo-Sotelo holds a double degree in History (Autonoma University of Madrid, Spain – UAM) and Music (Conservatory of Madrid). He received his PhD in Musicology from the Complutense University of Madrid (2008). Campos is Professor of Musicology at the Department of Music, UAM, and a member in the editorial board of the journal *Popular Music and Society*. He has formed part of several research projects on identity keys in popular cultures, alternative religions and Celtology, specializing also in some areas of systematic musicology. The results of his work have been published in a number of publications and conferences.

Mike Dines is a British musician, writer, scholar and publisher. He founded Itchy Monkey Press (http://itchymonkeypress.com) with the publication of the anarcho-punk novella *The Darkening Light* (2014), followed by *Tales From the Punkside* (2014), *Some of Us Scream, Some of Us Shout* (2016) and *And All Around Was Darkness* (2017) with Greg Bull. As a scholar he has written widely on subcultures and popular music, co-editing *The Aesthetics of Our Anger: Anarcho-Punk, Politics, Music* (Autonomedia/Minor Compositions, 2016); *Punk Pedagogies: Music, Culture and Learning* (Routledge, 2017); *The Punk Reader: Research Transmissions from the Local and the Global* (Intellect, 2019); *Punk Now!! Contemporary Perspectives on Punk* (Intellect, 2020); *Trans-Global Punk Scenes: The Punk Reader Vol. 2* (Intellect, 2020); and *Punk Identities, Punk Utopias: Global Punk and Media* (Intellect, 2021). He also has a chapter in *The Oxford Handbook of Punk* (2020), entitled 'Art School Manifestos, Classical Music and Industrial Abjection: Tracing the Artistic, Political and Musical Antecedents of Punk'. He is currently a Co-Pathway Leader of Popular Music at Middlesex University and is an avid supporter of Portsmouth Football Club.

Georgina Gregory teaches on the Film, Media and Popular Culture undergraduate programme at the University of Central Lancashire, which includes modules on American Cinema and Popular Music on Screen. Her research interests are centred around youth culture, subcultures, gender and popular music history. Recent works include the monographs *Send in the Clones*

(2012) and *Boybands and the Performance of Pop Masculinity* (2019). Georgina enjoys singing and is a member of Accord, an award-winning Manchester-based gospel group in the UK.

Matt Grimes is a senior lecturer in music industries and radio and the course director for the Music Industries BA at Birmingham City University. He is also a research member of the Birmingham Centre for Media and Cultural Research. Matt has recently completed his PhD, investigating the ideological significance of British anarcho-punk in the life courses of ex-scene participants. His previous publications include *Punk Now!! Contemporary Perspectives on Punk* (co-edited with Mike Dines [Intellect, 2020]), 'From Protest to Resistance: British Anarcho-Punk Fanzines (1980–1984) as Sites of Resistance and Symbols of Defiance' in M. Dines and M. Worley (eds), *The Aesthetics of Our Anger: Anarcho-Punk, Politics and Music, 1979–84* (Minor Compositions, 2016); 'Call it Crass, but "There is No Authority But Yourself": De-canonising Punk's Underbelly' in *Punk and Post-Punk* (special double issue 4.2/4.3, 2015); and 'Anarcho-Punk Webzines: Transferring Symbols of Defiance from the Print to the Digital Age?' (with T. Wall) in M. Worley (ed.), *Fight Back: Punk, Politics and Resistance* (Manchester University Press, 2015). Matt is general secretary of the Punk Scholars Network and on the editorial boards for the journals *Punk and Post-Punk* and *RIFFS: Experimental Writing on Popular Music*. He is also a lifelong supporter of Millwall FC.

Antti-Ville Kärjä is Professor of Cultural Music Research at the Sibelius Academy of the University of the Arts Helsinki, Finland. From 2008 to 2013 he was Chair of the IASPM Nordic branch; from 2016 to 2019 he was Chair of the Finnish Society for Ethnomusicology; and from 2017 to 2019 he served in the Executive Committee of the International Association for the Study of Popular Music (IASPM). He is a member of the editorial boards of *Perfect Beat* and the *Journal of World Popular Music*. His research interests include conceptualizations of popular music, postcolonial studies, historiography of music, music heritagization and audiovisual ethnomusicology. His latest publications include four ethnomusicological documentary films, both ethnographic and historical in orientation.

Gillian Kelly was awarded a PhD from the University of Glasgow in 2015 and her areas of academic interest include constructions of stardom and celebrity in the media, with a strong focus on male performers and masculinity. Her first monograph, *Robert Taylor: Male Beauty, Masculinity and Stardom in Hollywood* (University Press of Mississippi, 2019) was shortlisted for the prestigious BAFTSS (British Association of Film, Television and Screen Studies) Award for Best Monograph in 2020. The book investigates Taylor's star image and performance skills across his career, exploring both his filmic and extratextual personae within their industrial and socio-historical timeframes. She has contributed to several journals, including *Journalism and Mass Communication Quarterly*, *Historical Journal of Film, Radio and Television* and *Celebrity Studies* and her second book, *Tyrone Power: Gender, Genre and Image in Classical Hollywood Cinema*, will be released in 2021 as part of Edinburgh University Press's International Film Stars series.

Katelyn Medic is an ethnomusicologist focusing on relationships between popular culture, critical race studies, and lived religious experiences in the Americas. She holds a PhD in ethnomusicology from the University of Minnesota (Minneapolis, MN, USA). Her dissertation, 'The Politics of Sunday Worship: Millennials, Voice, and Performance' (2018), identifies performances of 'whiteness' in church communities in the Twin Cities, Minnesota, USA. Medic additionally holds a MM in ethnomusicology and a MM in performance from Florida State University (Tallahassee, FL, USA). Her master's thesis, 'City Church, Tallahassee: Blurring the Lines of Sacred and Secular' (2014), explores how church leadership recontextualizes current pop songs for communal worship and sermons.

Jiří Měsíc holds a PhD in English and American Literature from Palacký University, Olomouc, Czech Republic. His main interests are the mystical branches of Abrahamic religions (Christian mysticism, Kabbalah, Sufism) and their echoes in popular literature and song, especially in the work of the singer-songwriter Leonard Cohen. Besides this, he is a published poet and translator of John Pass, Ariana Reines and Gertrude Stein into Czech. Currently, he teaches ethics, anthropology, religious studies and modern language at ESIC University in Madrid, Spain.

Shara Rambarran is a musicologist, educator and speaker. Her research interests include contemporary music, digital technology, remixology, creative industries and education. She co-runs the Art of Record Production conferences and is on the editorial boards for the *Journal on the Art of Record Production* and the *Journal of Popular Music Education*. Shara is the co-editor of *The Oxford*

Handbook of Music and Virtuality (Oxford University Press, 2016) and *The Routledge Research Companion to Popular Music Education* (Routledge, 2020). More details can be found on her website, shararambarran.com.

Lucy Robinson is Professor of Collaborative History at the University of Sussex. She writes on popular music, politics and identity, feminism and punk pedagogy. Her book *Gay Men and the Left in Post-war Britain: How the Personal Got Political* was first published by Manchester University Press in 2007. Since then, she has worked on the Falklands War, charity singles, music videos, zine cultures, digital memory, protest and the politics of popular culture. As well as coordinating the Subcultures Network and the open access digital project Observing the 80s, she curates the Vivienne Westwood Intellectual Unite online book club.

Paul Spicer's research focuses on cultural history, with a particular focus on Japanese film, and popular music. He completed his doctoral thesis at the University of Portsmouth, UK, graduating in 2012. Currently, he is a lecturer in the Research Faculty of International Media and Communication, at Hokkaido University, Sapporo. In 2017, he was awarded a three-year JSPS Kakenhi research grant for a project entitled The Films of Kenji Mizoguchi, History, Tradition and Culture. This resulted in a number of international presentations and publications, as well as public outreach events across Japan. In addition to his academic work, he has written a number of articles and reviews on both British and Japanese artists for various music publications. Music is a huge part of Paul's everyday life. His favourite music includes mostly British: The Beatles, The Small Faces, The Creation, The Smiths, T-Rex, Oasis, Paul Weller; and Japanese artists: Kinoko Hotel, Chiyo Okumura, Apryl Fool, Shiina Ringo, and Seagull Screaming Kiss Her, Kiss Her.

Francis Stewart is the Implicit Religion Post-Doctoral Research Fellow and lectures in the theology department at Bishop Grosseteste University in Lincoln. A fellow of the HEA, she gained a Masters in Theology from the University of Glasgow before completing her PhD at the University of Stirling. Francis's PhD thesis was the first sociological overview of the UK Straight Edge punk scene and the first to explore the connections between religion and Straight Edge punk. Prior to joining BGU, she was a teaching fellow at the University of Stirling. Her research interests include punk and anarchy subcultures in Northern Ireland, Straight Edge punk, Sound and Noise, Curation and Memorialization, Marginalization, and Animal Activism. Francis is a steering group member of the Punk Scholars Network and editorial board member for the Intellect journal *Punk & Post-Punk*.

Chris Warne is Senior Lecturer in French History in the History Department at Sussex and has been at the university since September 1999. He worked previously in the Modern Languages Department at Keele University. Having completed PhD research in the field of nineteenth-century French historiography at the University of Birmingham, his research interests have moved to the area of contemporary French history, with a focus on the evolution of popular, material and everyday cultures since 1945.

Acknowledgements

First, we must thank those who have contributed to this volume, whose imagination, persistence and patience have ensured the publication of this project. Thanks must also go to staff at Bloomsbury Publishing who have helped to guide us through the process towards publication, notably Lily McMahon, Lucy Carroll, Camilla Erskine and Lalle Pursglove, all of whom have been very supportive throughout.

Mike Dines would also like to thank those who have supported him throughout this work, including colleagues within the Punk Scholars Network. He would also like to thank Sam, Spike, Sidney and Eric.

Georgina Gregory would like to express her gratitude to members of her 'second family' the Accord Gospel Choir and the inspirational work of songwriters Kadria and Tyndale Thomas.

Introduction

Mike Dines and Georgina Gregory

Music has always played a major role in religious practices – in paganism and the major world religions but also in the contemporary neo-religious movements more characteristic of postmodern culture. Regardless of where we live or what background we come from, listening to or creating music allows us to escape the constraints of our physical surroundings to articulate our spirituality and make contact with what we conceive of as sacred and divine. For some, this experience will be connected to an identifiable religious tradition, whereas for those who reject orthodox religions, popular music facilitates a highly personal and individualized route to spiritual awakening.

The use of music in religious practices helps bring people together to share their experience of the divine, and for many in today's increasingly secular society, popular music fulfills a somewhat similar role. In a fragmented contemporary landscape, where globalization and migration are eroding long-standing traditions, popular music lets us transcend physical dislocation and alienation while creating a sense of belonging. As Robert Walser (1993) demonstrated in his work on the heavy metal genre, for many fans, a shared love of music offers a quasi-religious experience and this is equally the case in such diverse gatherings as rock concerts, underground raves or a Northern Soul club night. These new forms of spirituality are related by Paul Heelas and Linda Woodhead (2004) to a wider 'subjective turn' in contemporary culture that eschews outward conformity to religious convention in favour of greater sensitivity to inner life. In this context, popular music can be likened to a religion because of the opportunities for communality it offers: devotion expressed towards artists, some of whom can take the place of spiritual leaders, draws forth an intensity of feeling that may be lacking in everyday life. Indeed, the reverence Beatles fans felt for the band during the 1960s was likened at the time to that experienced by religious believers by the late John Lennon, who said, 'We're more popular than Jesus now' and 'I don't know which will go first, rock 'n' roll or Christianity' (Cleave 1966). This controversial statement drew attention to the major significance of popular music in the lives of young people, at a time when church attendance in the UK was already on the wane.

Similarly, regular attendance at rock or pop concerts and continual enjoyment or reinterpretation of music texts creates opportunities for personal reflection and communal participation once reserved for religious observance by past generations. In today's increasingly secular societies, the importance of popular music artists, like the music itself, is magnified and key songs have come to acquire a canonic status; moreover, some are raised to a level of significance few would have envisaged in the early years of pop. For example, although Queen Elizabeth II is currently head of the Church of England, her Diamond Jubilee concert programme in 2012 was dominated by pop, rock and soul music, while references to God and divinity were kept to a minimum and slotted in at the end.[1] This illustrates the importance now attached to a medium providing a backdrop to everyday life, dismissed by some as little more than 'sonic wallpaper' – there to be heard, rather than listened to (Lanza 1995).

Although participation in traditional religion is declining in certain Western countries, new forms of religious identification are emerging to take the place of more conventional forms of religious observance. Here, popular music allows participants to make communication with divinity in all its diverse manifestations. Furthermore, in some cases, popular music artists have explored and shared their own newly found spiritual awakening via the medium of mainstream music. In 1970, for example, George Harrison helped to draw attention to his involvement with the emergent Krishna Consciousness movement in the song 'My Sweet Lord', which blended elements of Christianity, Vedic prayer, pop and gospel music. More recently, other developments blend popular music with religion and subcultural values as witnessed in the emergence of Krishnacore during the 1990s.

Conversely, mainstream religion has started to incorporate and appropriate popular music, partly as a response to the growing demand for pop songs at weddings and funerals, where its presence was once anathema. In the past, the meanings of sacred music were perceived as existing within the texts themselves, but there is a growing acceptance that members of the audience construct their own meanings when engaging with texts, secular or otherwise. Similarly, the divisions between popular and more elite manifestations of culture have been eroded significantly during the late twentieth and early twenty-first centuries. Music once reserved for sacred purposes is finding acceptance in the popular economy, whereas popular music is increasingly utilized in more lofty cultural settings, such as the use of 'Stand By Me' (a song originally sung by Ben E. King) at Prince Harry and Meghan Markle's wedding in 2018.

For musicians, too, popular music plays an important role in informing creative practice and accessing personal spirituality or facilitating access to the divine experience (e.g. John Maus uses the transcendent power of popular music to embark on a musical pilgrimage from Earth to Heaven and Hell). Popular music is also used by individual artists in the process of exorcizing demonic forces. For example, Daniel Johnston's lyrical preoccupation with the Devil in his efforts to gain psychological and spiritual relief by using music as a way of expressing his experience of bipolar disorder and schizophrenia.

This collection complements and adds to a growing body of work designed to tease out the function and meaning of religion within a wide range of cultural texts and practices: among others, Gilmour (2004) alludes to a proliferation of scholarly writing on religion and popular culture. The role played by religion and its articulation via the medium of popular culture is explored within journals such as the *Journal of Religion and Popular Culture* and the *Journal of Music and Religion*, both of which attempt to unravel what religion means in modern cultural life. More recently, *The Bloomsbury Handbook of Religion and Popular Music* (2017) examines the quest for transcendence in popular music, promoting enquiry around the medium's diverse manifestations of spirituality and the sacred. These include chapters on electronic dance music, goth and psychedelic music, while the wider relationship between religious ideas and popular music are unpacked, including Chinese religious music, paganism and Islam, and their distinctive relationships with popular music.

In Beethoven's view, music's unique capacity to articulate spiritual concerns made it 'the mediator between the spiritual and the sensual life' (Mazis 2008: 8). Although traditional Gospel hymns, devotional Vedic bhajan and African American spirituals were designed to express spirituality, secular popular music is equally capable of connecting us to that which we conceive of as divine. Similarly, almost all religions incorporate music within rituals, but spirituality cannot be limited strictly to the parameters of religious observance. Pop, rock, rap and folk songs are capable of transforming seemingly mundane day-to-day life events into deeply meaningful, sometimes transcendent, experiences. This is because music's inherently spiritual character is not defined or contained by religion, culture or genre.

Unlike religious music, the popular variety plays a major role in daily life – whether we are listening to it on the radio while driving, at home alone, in a nightclub or while out, popular music is our constant companion. Its omnipresence is unquestionable, but we seldom pause to question how it affects us and how much it informs our personal memories and personal quest. As a soundtrack to everyday living, the genre provides a deeply individualized sonic landscape linked mnemonically to important life moments.

Popular and sacred music do not necessarily have to be mutual exclusive categories. As William D. Romanowski points out, 'music serves different functions in the life of a community and is identified by thematic content, purpose, and physical location' (2000: 110); hence, we are conditioned not to expect an evening in a nightclub to be accompanied by hymns. Yet in certain circumstances, popular music provides an adjunct to participation in organized religion, blurring the division between the sacred and secular spheres. Song lyrics may or may not refer to recognizable religious symbolism, but their polysemic quality allows individuals and groups to negotiate the boundaries between religious observance and the secular. In other cases, it is used as a means of accessing alternative forms of participation in spiritual practices beyond mainstream religions. Furthermore, some artists deliberately 'crossover' the rigid binary between the secular and religious, thus leading to accusations of 'selling out'. Moreover, it is not uncommon for Christian artists to avoid being defined solely as such, preferring to be viewed primarily as musicians who are also practicing Christians; one such example being Ray Charles, who drew upon his church background to inform his song writing (the hymn 'Talkin' 'bout Jesus' was transformed into 'Talkin' 'bout You' and the gospel classic 'This Little Light of Mine' can be heard in Charles's 'This Little Girl of Mine').

The book aims to explore a range of themes, including the relationships of individual artists with their religious beliefs, whether or not the artists in question claim to be practitioners of a particular faith. For example, looking at how faith in the broadest sense is a fundamental component of popular music texts, many of which are imbued with vivid spiritual meanings and how these texts are put to use in personal and shared situations. Song lyrics regularly draw on religious metaphor and imagery, articulating existential questions, allowing musicians to tackle some of their deeply rooted fears and anxieties. The collection begins with 'Beatified Beats, Ritualized Rhymes: Intersections of the Popular and the Sacred in Music'. Here Antti-Ville Kärjä sets the theme and content of the book, exploring and unpacking how the popular and sacred are intertwined in the musical practices of institutional or otherwise organized religious movements. Kärjä recognizes the broader implications of the notions of 'sacred' and 'popular', examining how the intersection of both has a wider implication upon our understanding of popular music per se. Thus, the sacred may materialize in bodies, sounds, artefacts, practices and environments in the context of various ideological domains, whether these are primarily religious, political, nationalistic, economic or subcultural in nature.

Jiří Měsíc's chapter, 'Leonard Cohen, the "Sufi" Mystic', opens the book's first part on 'Personal Spirituality'. Although Cohen was not a Sufi adept as such (he was perhaps best known as a follower of Zen Buddhism and Kabbalah), Měsíc highlights how the musician often revealed an insight towards Sufi poetry and philosophy, especially in employing Sufi symbolism in his work. For Měsíc, Cohen found the same source of faith and instruction in Sufism that he found in Kabbalah, Christian mysticism and the work he was later to approach through Buddhist teachings. Proceeding the work of Měsíc, Gillian Kelly's 'Hank and Jesus: The Integral Roles of Religion and the History of Country Music in the Lives and Careers of Contemporary Country Artists' explores the integral role religion plays within the lives of country music artists. Nashville, Tennessee, home to the genre has been termed both 'Music City, USA' and 'The Buckle of the Bible Belt', alluding to its two main focuses: music and religion. Focusing on the work of Hank Williams, Alan Jackson, Brad Paisley and Eric Church, Kelly explores the intersection between the sacred, secular and commercial, opening up wider debates around the genre's place within popular music. Paul Spicer's chapter on the musician Paul Weller, entitled 'Above the Clouds: Discourses of the Spiritual and the Religious in the Lyrics of Paul Weller', examines Weller's consistent use of an Omnist perspective and examines how the musician applies this to transcend the constraints imposed by monotheism to accomplish a sense of spiritual freedom, expressing innermost thoughts and desires. Through a close textual analysis of specific songs, he uncovers a deep literary relationship between the content of Weller's songs and Buddhist and Christian doctrine.

Opening Part Two of the book, 'Christianity', Lucy Robinson and Chris Warne's chapter, '"Embracing the Divine Chaos": Transcending the Sacred-Secular Divide in the 1990s British Rave Church Movement', looks at the Sheffield-based Nine O'Clock Service (NOS). Robinson and Warne first read 1980s British evangelicalism as a series of interconnected subcultures, seeing NOS as the most visible expression of its complex of local activism, global networks and transnational exchanges. Secondly, they situate NOS within the global networks of rave culture, emphasizing the importance of the specific context, Sheffield, and of its localization of rave as a global party tribe. This chapter is followed by Georgina Gregory's chapter 'Pop Goes to Church: Pentacostal Evangelism and "Chav" Christianity', where the author explores ways in which music is used to articulate religious experience in Britain. Here, Gregory refers to Ignite Elim Pentacostal church in Lincoln, UK, where the pastor, Darren Edwards, uses drum and bass and mainstream pop songs to attract practitioners otherwise excluded from church; and thus examining how in some circumstances, popular music is becoming a medium for social inclusivity.

Shara Rambarran's chapter, '"The Time Has Come, Exodus!": Congo Natty and the Jungle (R)evolution', explores the relationship between the musical and cultural background of jungle and notions of spirituality. Drawing specifically upon the music of Congo Natty (and, in particular, his track 'London Dungeons'), Rambarran explores Natty's conversion to Rastafarianism and how this has informed his lyrics, sound and artistic sentiment. In '"Between Hipsters and God There is Sufjan Stevens": Sufjan Stevens and His Fans', Katelyn Medic explores the relationship between the American musician and his fans. Using social semiotics, Medic investigates the multimodal interactions of journalists, fans and Stevens to understand how these groups create meaning between Stevens and his hipster version of Christianity. Medic's findings suggest that scholars need to draw on new theories to understand how millennials blur the sacred and the secular within pop music, creating a new interpretation of Christian faith and practice.

Part Three, 'Alternative Religions', begins with Francis Stewart's '"Save My Soul From the Poisons of This World": Straight Edge Punk and Religious Re-Enchantment'. This chapter draws upon the work of Christopher Partridge, utilizing the punk subculture of straight edge in demonstrating how participants not only follow a strict moral code, but also seek to relocate religion, the sacred and individualized faith within popular culture and away from religious institutions. Through interview quotes, song lyrics and imagery, the chapter demonstrates that this is not a rearticulation of the secularization thesis but, instead, a new, deconstructed understanding of the concept of 'religion' in relation to music. Mike Dines and Matt Grimes's chapter, '"Message From Thee Temple": Magick, Occultism, Mysticism and Psychic TV', takes its title from the closing track on Psychic TV's debut album *Force the Hand of Chance* (1982). The chapter illuminates Psychic TV's past, and ongoing, relationship with magick, occultism, mysticism, paganism and, more specifically, how the ritualization of popular music through performance, lyrical content and production became a vehicle for the means of formulating broader philosophical, ritualistic and transgressive ideas around chaos magick, occultism and mysticism.

Javier Campos Calvo-Sotelo closes this collection with '*I Am God*! The Transference of Musical Fandom as Religion to Worshipping the Self'. Here,

Campos looks at the emergence of social media, and the subtle transference of the mechanisms of adoration toward the musical idol to worshipping the self on social media (like Facebook, MySpace or Instagram). This is examined through the framework of the creation of public profiles, through online gaming, adopting the culture of the *selfie* (broadly), with remarkable presence of concrete musical styles, and relying on performing practises and rites. In fact, for many adolescents the membership of their first social network becomes a true rite of passage.

Note

1   At which point the National Anthem was played, followed by Handel's 'Zadok the Priest', Holst's 'I Vow to Thee My Country', Elgar's 'Land of Hope and Glory' and Beethoven's 'Ode to Joy'.

References

Cleave, M. (1966), 'How Does a Beatle Live? John Lennon Lives Like This', *Evening Standard*, 4 March. Available online: http://www.beatlesinterviews.org/db1966.0304-beatles-john-lennon-were-more-popular-than-jesus-now-maureen-cleave.html (accessed 15 February 2016).

Gilmour, M. (2004), *Tangled Up in the Bible: Bob Dylan and Scripture*, New York: Continuum.

Heelas, P. and Woodhead, L. (2004), *The Spiritual Revolution: Why Religion is Giving Way to Spirituality*, Oxford: Blackwell.

Lanza, J. (1995), *Elevator Music: A Surreal History of Muzak, Easy-Listening and Other Moodsong*, London: Quartet Books.

Mazis, G. (2008), 'The Archetypal Alchemy of Technology: Escape and Return to Materiality's Depth', *Spring: A Journal of Archetype and Culture*, 80: 7–42.

Partridge, C. and C. Moberg, eds (2017), *The Bloomsbury Handbook of Religion and Popular Music*, London: Bloomsbury.

Romanowski, W. (2000), 'Evangelicals and Popular Music: The Contemporary Christian Music Industry', in B. D. Forbes and J. H. Mahan (eds), *Religion and Popular Culture in America*, 105–24, Berkeley, CA: University of California.

Walser, R. (1993), *Running With the Devil: Power, Gender and Madness in Heavy Metal Music*, Middletown, CT: Wesleyan University Press.

1

Beatified Beats, Ritualized Rhymes: Intersections of the Popular and the Sacred in Music

Antti-Ville Kärjä

Introduction

For many, it appears, the year 2016 represented the irrefutable loss of significant musical talent and objects of idolization. With the demise of megastars such as David Bowie and Prince and other significant artists like Pierre Boulez, Keith Emerson, Merle Haggard, Paul Kantner, Sir George Martin and Maurice White, music fans had good reason to mourn. A common consolation to all followers is nevertheless that 'his [sic] music will live forever', as demonstrable through a quick internet search (as of 29 November 2018). When combined with David Bowie or Prince, the phrase yields roughly 30,000 hits, while Haggard, White and Emerson get a tenth of this, Kantner exactly 170 and Boulez, well, five. The result for Sir George is 17,500, but the overwhelming majority of hits leads to another dead George and his fellow bandmates known as the Beatles.

Issues of idolization, megastars and the notion of investing music with eternal life connect the discussion to themes that are conventionally conceptualized as religious and linked to questions of transcendence, the otherwordly, the mystical, the numinous and the sacred. To spell this out: idols are, etymologically, (false) images or objects representing deities, while stars refer to heavenly phenomena, and the idea of eternal life, or life after death at least, is common to most major religions. At the same time, idols and megastars are by definition popular in that, like religions, they are favoured by a large number of people. Furthermore, most of the artists mentioned above represent 'popular music' in one form or another; even Pierre Boulez, who has been celebrated as one of the key figures of musical modernism, was known for his association with rock auteur Frank Zappa. Moreover, death is no stranger in the realm of cultural activity known as popular music, and as the rock 'n' roll cohorts are ageing, rebellious lifestyle as a cause of demise – or what Steve Jones (2005: 273) has called 'death by fame' – is being supplanted by natural deterioration.

It is evident that the deathly brushes in question – as well as any similar ones – foreground the ways in which the 'popular' and the 'sacred' become intertwined and inextricable. Yet, it is commonplace to treat the category of popular music as separate from and in many cases even antithetical to religious ideologies; but as Simon Frith (2001: 106–7) points out, 'even in these relatively Godless times most of us have sung hymns and carols at some stage of our lives … and the translation of gospel into soul shows how easy it is to love a man or woman musically in the same way that one loves God'. As this remark suggests, there very well may be more to the intersections of the popular and the sacred in music than that which is aroused by the quietus of one's favourite artist.

Thus, it is my aim to interrogate these intersections more carefully, by focusing on the multidimensionality of both denominators. On one hand, this entails asking: in the event one detects such an intersection, what definitions of the popular and the sacred are implicated? On the other, one may ask slightly more provocatively: what kind of definitions of the popular and the sacred would be operationalized in the event a 'popular' musical phenomenon was reconceptualized as 'sacred', or vice versa? In my treatment I will concentrate on conceptual issues and definitions of the two terms but also concretize the dynamics in question with selected examples. Hence, a broader aim of mine is to provide a general analytical framework that may be then tested and challenged with more varied examples.

Underlying my argument there is a frustration that stems from taken-for-granted utilization of the label 'popular', especially when used as an epithet for music or culture more generally. Certainly, to talk and write about 'popular music' may serve as a useful shorthand in order to secure that participants of the discussion are on the same page, as it were; yet, as a popular music scholar, I find it imperative and even fundamental to ask constantly, or at least to be mindful of the questions: 'what is popular', 'what is music', and 'what is popular music'? From this stance, a particular point of interest is how the sacred might be of aid in reconceptualizing the popular in the context of music.

Popular music and the post-secular postcolonial condition

The intersections of the popular and the sacred in music are of course implicated in various sets of broader cultural dynamics in the twenty-first century (according to the Gregorian Christian calendar). In very general terms, at issue here are the changes in the 'religious landscape' caused by global migration and cultural pluralism. As a consequence, the recent relatively Godless times may not be that Godless after all, albeit references to deities may not always be the most appropriate choice when discussing the change. This is to say that in addition to the continuing or re-emergent popularity of Christianity and other Abrahamic and monotheistic religions, there are various 'alternative spiritualities' available. One way to conceptualize this shift is constituted by the notion of post-secularization, which refers to the possibility of broadening the ethics and values of modern secular states through various religions and traditional cultural practices in the world (see James 2007).

Alongside alleged post-secular processes, the religious change can be associated with questions about multiculturalism and the so-called global postcolonial condition (see Young 2012). In fact, while the post-secularization thesis may be criticized as Eurocentric, the other two terms point to global dynamics in that no society, conceived no matter how, is culturally entirely homogenous, and the effects of the era of European colonialism and imperialism have scarred the world profoundly. It is nevertheless worth bearing in mind that when talking about multiculturalism here, what is at stake is the 'narrow' version of it. Simply put, in this version of multiculturalism, the notion of culture is equated almost exclusively with ethnicity, nationality and religiosity, with a particular emphasis on the effects of immigration and the 'ethno-religious mix' caused by it (Modood 2007: 2–8).

It is also important to recognize that the postcolonial condition manifests itself differently in different spatio-temporal contexts. Writing from and in, and maybe for, the north-eastern corner of 'Fortress Europe', one can start by noting how, boosted by the waves of both global migration and economic crisis, debates over multiculturalism and racism have increased tremendously in the region, accompanied occasionally (but increasingly frequently) by acts of extreme violence. There is a growing body of research where the role of Nordic welfare countries in colonial and postcolonial processes has been re-evaluated (Keskinen et al. 2009; Loftsdóttir and Jensen 2012), yet not often have these reassessments been done in an explicit connection to religious issues. Also, music is largely absent in these debates, despite racialized genre classifications, exoticism in cultural industries and the contradiction between strong associations with national traditions and the assumed ability of music to transcend cultural boundaries (cf. Born and Hesmondhalgh 2000; Radano and Bohlman 2000).

A particular area of inquiry in this respect is constituted by the position of Islamic communities in secular Western European societies. Despite this assumed secularity, however, the situation also gives grounds to explore more carefully claims about Christianity as one central part of Western European cultural heritage. Islam provides, in addition, a fruitful starting point with respect to cultural expression in that, depending on the interpretation of religious tenets and scripts, there may be severe restrictions on freedom of expression, especially in the realm of music and beginning with the definition of *mūsīqā* itself (see al-Farūqī 1985; Shiloah 1995). Furthermore, the cultural value of contemporary religious music has been recognized too, alongside its apparent economic dimension (Evans 2006). Moreover, this entails not only challenging conventional notions of popular culture as a secular sphere of activity on the basis of its apparent commercial framework, but emphasizing the economic imperatives of institutionalized religions in general. Thus, post-secular belief systems and musics provide a context for closer examinations of the denominator 'popular'.

The Music, itself, ingeniously

Music, for its part, constitutes a particularly pertinent realm of investigation of the popular/sacred dynamics. This is so not only because of etymological reasons that lead to the Greek mythology, but also due to what musicologists Susan McClary and Robert Walser (1990: 280) call '[a] choice between poetic or technical mystification' of music either through impressionistic vocabulary or graphic notation. To this, one can add the legacy of the Romantic aesthetic movement with its emphasis on ideas about the autonomy of Western art music, the ingenious artists and the spiritual origins of compositions, for example. In her analysis of the work of prominent Finnish composers, Milla Tiainen (2005: 52–145) points to the ways in which these ideas are closely connected and even implicated in Christianity most evidently through claims about the transcendent nature of music and composing, whereby the composers are invested with deific creative powers or, alternatively, subjected to the celestial 'will of music' itself. Such claims are by no means unique to music, but evince a broader and profound influence of Romanticism in the ways in which artistic geniuses become constructed and conceptualized as demi-gods 'with Protean powers to take on different forms and roles in the various ages and stages of historical development' and capable of bringing transcendent essences into existence (Battersby 1989: 14, 44).

Either divine geniuses or intermediaries for the transcendent, composers and other artistic geniuses remain the chosen ones whose work and works separate them from 'mundane materiality'. This separation is in turn heavily gendered; according to Christine Battersby (1989: 14), the genius 'is always a "Hero", and never a heroine, [nor] are his social duties consistent with those of fulfilling mundane domestic or reproductive tasks, nor of living a life of enforced, upper-class ease'. Instead of investing the notion of the genius with transcendence, or 'a naïvety about the relationship between facts and values', Battersby (1989: 156–7) suggests it be approached in pragmatic terms by evaluating and assessing cultural achievements 'against an appropriate background of artistic genres and traditions' where novelty and 'lasting value and significance' are the key criteria. Thus, for her, 'a female "genius"' is not a unique, élite individual but rather 'a woman who is judged to occupy a strategic position in the matrilinear and patrilinear patterns of tradition that make up culture'. As a result, ingeneity does not depend on types of personality or psychic processes but on influence and 'cultural "momentousness"', as determinable through situating individual creators within a series of collectives of tradition (Battersby 1989: 157).

The notion of a female genius, or a feminist notion of the genius to be more precise, remains contested nonetheless. Marcia Citron (1993: 225), in her excavation in the gendered aspects of canonization of music, fears 'that the label of genius would only hurt historical women: genius would inevitably be associated with transcendence'. Also Tiainen (2005: 75–8, 91–7) pays specific attention to the gendered aspects of constructing composers as godlike geniuses and argues that, on the basis of Einojuhani Rautavaara's writings in particular, women remain largely excluded from the construction of musical geniuses, either through emphasis on females as material creatures or a 'myth of martyrdom' hinging on the figure of Yeshua Ha-Nozri, better known as Jesus of Nazareth. Of course, Nazareth is also the name of a Scottish hard rock band, which, alongside such appellations as Black Sabbath, Judas Priest and HIM (a.k.a. His Infernal Majesty), clearly suggests that within the realm that is commonly referred to as popular music, references to and associations with religions and religiosity abound. The list can be augmented by a myriad of album or song titles attesting to the same. Intriguingly, there are extremely few female artists known for such acts of naming; within an online top thirty of 'Bands Named After Things from the Bible' (from ranker.com) there are but two with female members, namely Peter, Paul and Mary (Travers) and Teenage Jesus and The Jerks (led by Lydia Lunch).

From rescripting the sacred ...

Despite the abundance of bands and songs with religious names since the late 1960s – not to mention the significantly longer histories of gospel and spirituals as genres of popular music – a focus on the interrelatios between religiosity and the notion of popular culture is a very recent phenomenon indeed. Only during the first decades of the twenty-first century has there been a remarkable upsurge of studies focusing on different forms of religiosity and spirituality, and often discussed as popular culture. Alongside post-secularization, the rubrics used in this discussion include new religious movements, re-enchantment and occulture. This body of research attempting to 'rescript the sacred' (Santana and Erickson 2008), as it were, emanates especially from within anthropology and sociology of religion.

Within this field of study, a foundational argument is that until very recently popular culture in general has been shunned within the aforementioned disciplinary settings. According to Gordon Lynch (2005: 22), the shift from the study of abstract belief systems and practices of religious elites to exploration of everyday functions of religion has taken place primarily during the twenty-first century. Lynn Schofield Clark (2007: 19) in turn notes in a sarcastic fashion that 'conventional wisdom held that those in religious studies [and] theology should attain expertise in something suitably ancient and respectable, only to "dabble" in popular culture studies after tenure had been safely secured'.

The dabblings in question are noteworthy and commendable as they indisputably demonstrate the value and importance of religious and spiritual modes of thought in diverse contexts, but at the same time there are problems in this scholarship due to a trend towards taken-for-granted utilization of the notion of 'popular culture'. On one hand, there is a plenitude of unproblematized references to mass production, everyday life, consumerism, leisure and media in particular (e.g. Deacy 2009; King 2010; Pattison 2009), which in the end raises the question of whether there is anything that remains outside of 'popular culture'.

On the other hand, one can note an emphasis on what is labelled as 'everyday life', and while many scholars appropriately point to the problems in defining and conceptualizing both religion and popular culture (e.g. Lynch 2005: 2–17, 27–32), the dynamics and ambivalences inherent here tend to be subsumed and simplified into 'the shared environment, practices, and resources of everyday life in a given society' (Lynch 2005: 14). In other words, in these studies 'popular culture' is defined, yes, but not problematized in relation to its multidimensionality. Moreover, in deciphering the concept of everyday life, ethnographic approach has been given a virtually dogmatic status, with an emphasis on audiences and what they 'actually "do" with media and popular culture in their everyday lives', rather than subjecting rituals, texts and symbols to theoretical readings (Lynch 2007: 159).

David Morgan (2007: 26–7) advocates an approach that is practice centred and based on the idea of 'culture as circulation'. According to him, this entails examining 'what people do in addition to what they say they believe' and treating religion as 'neither a fixed essence nor a merely economic behaviour'. Furthermore, at issue are the ways in which given objects of study 'enfold … as a material reality into the ritual or routine or daily habit that puts [them] to work in the world-constructing and maintaining behavior'. For Morgan (2007: 27), the proper matrix of analysis is constituted by the interrelated fields of production, distribution and reception. Thus, while privileging reception, he stresses the importance of taking also institutional and commercial agents and factors into account. To the extent to which 'popular culture' is definable on the basis of commercial interests, this is a plausible addition to the methodology of investigating the intersections of the popular and the sacred.

… to retuning it

If attention to popular music and culture, however defined, within the study of religions is a recent phenomenon, within popular music studies the significance of religiosity has been recognized even more belatedly. For instance, an authoritative reader in the field from a decade ago (Bennett et al. 2006) does not include the headwords 'religion' or 'ideology' in its index, and all one can do is to check if such references as 'gospel', 'Hindi musicals', 'North Africa', 'Oriental Metal', 'straight edge', or 'prestige symbols' (under 'youth culture') lead to more elaborate discussion on the interrelations between the popular and the religious. In a similar fashion, in his collection of the key concepts of popular music culture, Roy Shuker (2012) does not afford 'religion' a key status, but has included entries on 'CCM (Contemporary Christian music)', 'gospel' and 'Rastafari', which are discussed explicitly in relation to religious issues. Also, on the basis of Tim Wall's book one might assume that religion is of no importance when studying popular music culture, except when noting the 'dramatic' increase in sales of the genre known as 'religious music' during the first decade of the twenty-first century (2013: 275).

Moreover, a textbook devoted to *Understanding Society Through Popular Music* (Kotarba and Vannini 2009) implies that in such a task, the only religion that matters is Christianity and then only marginally. In other words, the implication is that popular music is not really religious, and in the odd case it happens to be so, it has something to do with Christian religious belief systems. According to this logic, Muslim metal music for instance would be of no interest to popular music scholars.

However, the recent changes with respect to addressing popular music in the framework of the post-secularization thesis are evident in the second edition of the book, as it includes an entire chapter reserved for the topic (Kotarba et al. 2013). And, indeed, regardless of the lack of attention in constitutive readers and textbooks, the post-secular shift, as it were, has been evident also within popular music studies. Intriguingly for my topic, Rupert Till has approached the field through the notion of cult, emphasizing, for example, the importance of sex, psychedelia, death, stardom and locations. He introduces the notion of the 'sacred popular' by which he refers to the idea that in contemporary Western culture functions conventionally served by religions have been replaced by new forms of spirituality and religiosity based on popular culture and popular music in particular (2010: 169–72). In his estimation,

> Pop cults have provided for many a bridge across, or escape from, the crisis of ... having no rituals or trusted religious traditions to guide them into the transcendence and through the paradoxes of twenty-first-century life. ... [P]opular culture is reaching out to mend and replace the broken and lost rituals of community that have been allowed to fall into disrepair ... The religion of pop cults is a vital ritual technology for connection.
>
> (Till 2010: 175–9)

In addition, in a collection on *Religion and Popular Music in Europe*, the editors maintain that especially since the late 1960s hippie movement 'existential questions, ideology and religion have been negotiated and expressed' in the field of popular music. Importantly, in relation to global migration and postcoloniality, they also stress the links between changing religious landscape and changes in ethnicity (Bossius et al. 2011: 1–2). Moreover, interrelations between popular music and paganism have been subjected to critical scrutiny (Weston and Bennett 2013), and Christopher Partridge (2013: 3) has gone so far as to emphasize the importance of analysing 'the confluence of two of the principal dynamic forces shaping contemporary human life, popular music and the sacred'.

Yet, a common trait in these accounts is a tendency to celebrate the new forms of spirituality that participate in reconceptualizing the sacred.

Occasionally, the operationalized definitions of popular music are questionably broad, to the extent one may consider them as purpose-driven. A case in point is Partridge's somewhat circular inclusion of the output of 'the prolific avant-garde jazz musician' John Zorn in his idea of popular music, crucially on the basis of the artist's ideas about 'the creation of music as a sacred process' (2013: 33, 119). If it is sacred, it appears, it is also popular. While this kind of generic classification compels one to reconsider the epithet 'popular', there is not much help offered. Instead, in the above accounts this potential is drained by a reliance on conventional and even taken-for-granted ideas of what 'popular culture' is.

The popular multiplied by the sacred

Admittedly, regarding the notion of 'the popular', there is an abundance of academic accounts in which the ambivalence and multidirectionality of the denominator is acknowledged and addressed; yet, in many cases, especially in those that deal with a particular musical genre or scene, these issues are left untouched. In other words, heavy metal or hip hop or contemporary r 'n' b or straight edge are often treated as popular music by definition, rather than asking 'what does it mean if, and indeed when, hip hop for instance is conceived as popular music?' To a significant degree, at issue here, of course, is the way in which the notion of popular music is utilized in non-academic contexts, and in the music industry in particular. Nevertheless, on closer examination, crucial ambiguities may emerge.

Influential accounts on the multidimensionality of popular culture have been produced by John Storey (2003; 2009) in particular. In *Cultural Theory and Popular Culture: An Introduction* (2009: 5–12), he distinguishes between six different dimensions of the popular, the first of which is quantitative, referring to something that is favoured or well-liked by a relatively large group of people. Second, Storey notes the existence of an aesthetic dimension of the popular, which may be likened to conventional ideas about easyness, uniformity and simplicity. Third, there is the sociological dimension, indicating a stress on commerce and mass production and consumption, and implying a presence of working-class sensibilities. Fourth, Storey suggests that there is a folk dimension in conceptualizations of popular culture which is associated with vernacular expression and ideas about ethno-cultural or national authentic traditions. The fifth dimension explicated by Storey is the political one, whereby he refers to countercultural or subcultural aspects in particular. Finally, Storey mentions the postmodern dimension of popular culture, defining it as an inextricability of 'high' and 'low' forms of expression.

He also recognizes and discusses the global impact of especially North American and West European media products in terms of cultural identity formation (2009: 8–9). In other words, the cultural, economic and political effects of especially 'Western' forms of cultural expression worldwide should not be underestimated. In the realm of music, these are intimately tied with the activities of the transnational music industry, primarily in two ways: on one hand, the high level of conglomeration needs to be addressed especially in relation to questions about cultural homogenization and the viability of local cultural production (Hesmondhalgh 2007), and on the other, the pervasiveness of the marketing category of world music requires a closer scrutiny with respect to exoticizing tendencies and other imbalanced power relations between the Western centre and its peripheries (Guilbault 2001; Hutnyk 2000; Taylor 1997). With respect to the dynamics of the popular and the sacred in music, a pivotal outcome of these relations is the emergence of various religious or spiritual musics as virtually interchangeable forms of 'popular' world music. A case in point is the inclusion of Saami *joik* in a collection entitled *Sacred Spirit: Chants and Dances of the Native Americans* (1994), as if indigenous cosmologies from Northern Europe were indistinguishable from the Northern American ones (see Hilder 2015: 155). The case also foregrounds the diversity of conceptualizations of the denominator 'popular', as to label the collection as popular music necessitates an emphasis on industrial rather than aesthetic criteria.

Thus the question emerges: how to relate the multidimensionality of the popular to the sacred in the context of music? An obvious area of inquiry is constituted by the ways in which the popular and the sacred are intertwined in the musical practices of institutional or otherwise organized religious movements. As Till (2010: 184) points out, one aspect of this is the alternative worship movement within which Christian worship has been combined for instance with rock, ambient and electronic dance music. According to Till (2010: 184), however, the impact of these on Christianity has been limited, 'although they show how much similarity there is between pop cults and organized religions'.

A related example is the Metal Mass, organized by a coalition of Helsinki parishes in Finland for the first time in 2006, and run, or produced, nowadays by a registered association. It is maintained on the Metal Mass website that '[w]hen you come to a Metal Mass, you come to a service. It is not a concert, a spectacle, a gig. It is a service' (MM 2020). The website includes further information about this, explaining the peculiarities of a Lutheran mass and instructing potential participants that there are certain sections and progressions involved without which a mass would not be worthy of its name. In other words, in the Metal Mass the musical genre is secondary to a prescribed liturgy, and elsewhere on the website it is emphasized that the reasons for having such a mass do not pertain to 'artistic ambitions'; instead, for the organizers, metal music constitutes 'a means to bring the message forward'.

Yet, I am not entirely convinced the situation is best conceived in terms of primary and secondary aspects, as without either of them there would not be a thing called Metal Mass. I have only witnessed one, but on the basis of that experience and the fact that the mass constitutes something of a intra-church subculture of its own, I dare to maintain that it would be extremely difficult – and, more importantly, irrelevant and irreverent – to question or rank the participants' allegiance and commitment to either the religious or musical conventions involved. Furthermore, there are artistic ambitions at stake, and while the music performed at the mass is indeed hymnal, the arrangements leave very little room for doubts about the creativity and artistry of the executors. It also becomes important to recognize the broader implications of the notion of the sacred, especially in relation to identity construction. Here, I am heavily indebted to the anthropologist of religion Veikko Anttonen who defines the sacred as that which

> comes into being as a category in any value-laden situation to mark the inviolability of the boundaries of an entity in times of crises or in periods of transformations taking place in temporal or spatial categories of the society. The sacred forms a boundary that can either strengthen the inside against the dangers or impurities of the outside or it can just as well open up the inside in order to fuse into the outside.
>
> (2000: 204)

Anttonen (2000: 204) further stresses the importance of rituals as *the* cultural processes that deal with these boundaries and construct the sacred 'as a liminal space to bring up new connections between [the inside and the outside]'. In a similar vein, Kenneth Thompson (1998: 101) notes on the basis of his re-reading of Durkheim that the violations on an entity's boundaries may pertain just as well to 'the alien Other' as to 'the mundane/profane i.e. the world of everyday routine, particularly economic activity and its rationality'. It is worth emphasizing here that the rituals and routines at issue need not be religious, which is exactly why they serve as indicators of the sacred in the broader sense. Thus, in order to examine the sacred aspects of music, to centre on the ritualistic features of concert behaviour, music education and fandom may prove particularly propitious.

More recently, sociologist of religion Gordon Lynch (2012; 2014) has propagated 'an extended notion of the sacred' and its multiple forms. He defines the sacred as 'what people collectively experience as absolute, non-contingent realities which present normative claims over the meaning and conduct of social life' (Lynch 2012: 29; see also Lynch 2014: 32). Religions constitute a major arena of the sacred, but such an approach on the topic enables one also to consider how normative claims are prompted in a similar fashion with recourse to the allegedly absolute values of democracy, equality, justice and human rights. A particularly forceful dimension of the sacred centres in this sense around the notion of the national, as evidenced by the ubiquitous confluence of and confusion between nationality and citizenry, as well as by the extremity of punitive measures against breaching national security (see Lynch 2012: 37). On a less physical yet equally influential level, one may note how histories, notably those that focus on cultural traits such as music, tend to be demarcated on a national basis, and only rather recently has such construction of national canons become an object of critical scrutiny within the ranks of scholars of music history, with an emphasis of historical transnationalism and cosmopolitanism (see Kurkela and Mantere 2015: 7). Yet, among the general public and in mainstream media, discussion and output celebrating somehow uniquely national music histories proliferate.

In his extended definition of the sacred, Lynch (2012: 37, 48) also stresses the moral ambiguity involved and the harmful results it often yields. His examples in this respect deal primarily with the contingencies surrounding child abuse in religious contexts; in the realm of music, one can extend this line of enquiry to questions about extenuating violence against women when the ingenuity of male artists is at stake (Strong and Rush 2018). Likewise, musical practices of extremist groupings, whether religious or political from the outset, are connected to belief systems and ideologies based on forms of the sacred in their reliance on absolutes and normative conduct (see Shaffer 2017; Teitelbaum 2017). What is more, the stance towards the sacred as not exclusively religious is embraced in the landmark anthology in the study of religion and popular music, where it is maintained in the introductory chapter that a more inclusive conceptualization of the sacred might facilitate not only interdisciplinary research but also more delicate investigation of the historically contingent ideas of ultimate concerns and profound moral claims as they become exerted in and through musical expression (Moberg and Partridge 2017: 7).

The mundane materiality of multidimensionality

The emphases on rituals and routines foregrounds the material qualities of the sacred, whether they appear in the form of physical objects, human movements, sounds, images, scents, tastes or money. Moreover, this may be linked to the ideas deriving from classical sociology of religion where, following Durkheim (1965) and Éliade (1959: 11) in particular, the significance of different restrictive and even prohibitive measures and mechanisms, as well as *hierophany*, i.e. the physical manifestation of the sacred, is underlined. In addition, remembering the moral ambiguity of the sacred, a highly pertinent avenue of research opens up through physical violence and its legitimate justifications (see Girard 1977; also Johnson and Cloonan 2008).

Thus, the sacred may materialize in the bodies, sounds, artefacts and environments in the context of various ideological domains, whether these are primarily religious, political, national(istic), economic or subcultural in nature (see Angrosino 2004: 9). As a result of this, a grid (see Table 1 below) can be constructed to demonstrate the multidimensionality of both the popular and the sacred, and the possible intersections between them. However, as both include a political dimension, I have taken the liberty of renaming it as 'partisan' on the popular side, on the basis of Storey's (2009: 85, 225) explanation of this aspect as counter-cultural and subcultural in nature (the use of which would not solve the problem due to the existence of the 'subcultural sacred'). Likewise, for the sake of unambiguity, I have renamed the political or ideological dimension of the sacred as 'factional'; this is so also because there are always political and ideological dimensions involved when dealing with socio-cultural activity, inasmuch as politics has to do with power relations and ideology with more or less systematic clusters of ideas and value judgements (see Storey 2009: 2–4).

Table 1.1 The popular/sacred grid

		The sacred				
		religious	factional	national(istic)	economic	subcultural
The popular	quantitative					
	aesthetic					
	sociological					
	partisan (political)					
	folk					
	postmodern					

In terms of more detailed analysis, relevant points of interest include the protecting and distancing measures taken towards the sacred, for example in the forms of 'priesthood' and other 'sacred personage', sacred artefacts and emblems, 'shrines', rituals and 'cults', and environment (Angrosino 2004; Durkheim 1965; King 2010; Till 2010). In the context of music, then, these can be juxtaposed with

(a) how certain individuals, whether alive or dead, become and are hailed as guardians, gatekeepers, carriers, embodiments or revitalizers of tradition;
(b) how certain musical instruments, tunes, movements and performance styles are taken to represent something essential about a community;
(c) how an 'old/lost/imagined/mythological homeland' is looked upon and visited as a source of the authentic musical tradition;
(d) how seasonal and national holidays and festivals constitute occasions for culturally specific musical performances, especially in relation to religious feasts; and
(e) how the musical practices are conditioned by and in interaction with the material environment, for example in relation to performance venues and financial concerns.

Furthermore, as regards issues of postcoloniality and immigration, all these may be discussed in relation to the sacredness of collective commemoration on one hand and individual aesthetic expression on the other (Bendrups 2010). Indeed, regarding the years to come, it is rather certain that multiculturalism and other postcolonial processes will only increase the phenomena that can be analysed meaningfully through the conceptual dialectics of the popular and the sacred. As an aspect of this, it is already evident that the rise of (neo)nationalism, fascism and racism lead to destructive sanctification of 'race' and ethnicity. In the realm of music, I have witnessed situations where genres like rap have been degraded on racist grounds and the right to perform certain 'unofficial national anthems' has been claimed exclusively for the 'real' nationals (as opposed to 'immigrants').

Conclusion

It is likewise expectable that as the religious landscape continues to change, new forms of 'sacred popular' (or vice versa) music will emerge, whether these are linked to paganist re-enchantment or more traditional religious denominations.

One cannot exclude the impacts of religious fundamentalism from the discussion either, or the aesthetic and subcultural forms of extremism that are manifested in the pervasiveness of the ideas about the autonomy and authenticity of music. In this respect, it would be tempting to say that music really is worthy of its name as the mythologized art of the Muses, as, regardless of its ubiquity and universality as a cultural practice, there is a continuing tendency to sanctify or mystify it either technically or ideologically.

From a scholarly and methodological stance in particular, it is apparent that there is a need for further combinations of analytical approaches provided by religious studies and (popular) music studies. The popular/sacred grid I have offered thus represents merely a point of departure into more nuanced investigations, and in its two-dimensionality, is quite obviously insufficient to address, for example, temporal shifts in the intersections in question. And as can be learned from analytical geometry, more than three dimensions can easily be included in the coordinates; with respect to mundane materiality, for instance, to relate the grid to issues of technology and gender would undoubtedly yield additional insights. As long as there are people, there will be things that are popular and sacred, separately and simultaneously – and there will be music.

References

Angrosino, M. V. (2004), *The Culture of the Sacred*, Prospect Heights, IL: Waveland Press.

Anttonen, V. (2000), 'What Is It That We Call "Religion"? Analyzing the Epistemological Status of the Sacred as a Scholarly Category in Comparative Religion', *Method & Theory in the Study of Religion*, 12: 195–206.

Battersby, C. (1989), *Gender and Genius: Towards a Feminist Aesthetics*, London: The Women's Press.

Bendrups, D. (2010), 'Migrant Music in New Zealand: Issues and Concepts', in H. Johnson (ed.), *Many Voices: Music and National Identity in Aotearoa/New Zealand*, 30–8, Newcastle: Cambridge Scholars Publishing.

Bennett, A., B. Shank and J. Toynbee, eds (2006), *The Popular Music Studies Reader*, London and New York: Routledge.

Born, G. and D. Hesmondhalgh, eds (2000), *Western Music and its Others: Difference, Representation, and Appropriation in Music*, Berkeley, CA: University of California Press.

Bossius, T., K. Kahn-Harris and A. Häger (2011), 'Introduction: Religion and Popular Music in Europe', in T. Bossius, K. Kahn-Harris and A. Häger (eds), *Religion and Popular Music in Europe: New Expressions of Sacred and Secular Identity*, 1–10, London and New York: I.B. Tauris.

Citron, M. J. (1993), *Gender and the Musical Canon*, Cambridge: Cambridge University Press.
Deacy, C. (2009), 'Introduction', in C. Deacy and E. Arweck (eds), *Exploring Religion and the Sacred in a Media Age*, 1–22, Farnham and Burlington, VT: Ashgate.
Durkheim, É. (1965), *The Elementary Forms of the Religious Life*, New York: Free Press.
Éliade, M. (1959), *The Sacred and the Profane: The Nature of Religion*, San Diego, CA: Harcourt Brace Jovanovich.
Evans, M. (2006), *Open up the Doors: Music in the Modern Church*, London: Equinox.
al-Farūqī, L. I. (1985), 'Music, Musicians and Muslim Law', *Asian Music*, 17 (1): 3–36.
Frith, S. (2001), 'Pop Music', in S. Frith, W. Straw and J. Street (eds), *The Cambridge Companion to Pop and Rock*, 93–108, Cambridge: Cambridge University Press.
Girard, R. (1977), *Violence and the Sacred*, trans. P. Gregory, Baltimore, MD and London: The Johns Hopkins University Press.
Guilbault, J. (2001), 'World music', in S. Frith, W. Straw and J. Street (eds), *The Cambridge Companion to Pop and Rock*, 176–92, Cambridge: Cambridge University Press.
Hesmondhalgh, D. (2007), *The Cultural Industries*, 2nd edn, London: Sage.
Hilder, T. (2015), *Sámi Musical Performance and the Politics of Indigeneity in Northern Europe*, Lanham, MD: Rowman and Littlefield.
Hutnyk, J. (2000), *Critique of Exotica: Music, Politics and the Culture Industry*, London: Pluto.
James, H., ed. (2007), *Civil Society, Religion and Global Governance*, London and New York: Routledge.
Johnson, B. and M. Cloonan (2008), *Dark Side of the Tune: Popular Music and Violence*, Burlington, VT: Ashgate.
Jones, S. (2005), 'Better Off Dead: Or, Making It the Hard Way', in S. Jones and J. Jensen (eds), *Afterlife as Afterimage: Understanding Posthumous Fame*, 273, New York: Peter Lang.
Keskinen, S., S. Tuori, S. Irni and D. Mulinari, eds (2009), *Complying with Colonialism: Gender, Race and Ethnicity in the Nordic Region*, Aldershot: Ashgate.
King, E. (2010), *Material Religion and Popular Culture*, New York: Routledge.
Kotarba, J. A. and P. Vannini (2009), *Understanding Society Through Popular Music*, New York and London: Routledge.
Kotarba, J. A., B. Merrill, J. P. Williams and P. Vannini (2013), *Understanding Society Through Popular Music*, 2nd edn, New York and London: Routledge.
Kurkela, V. and M. Mantere (2015), 'Introduction', in V. Kurkela and M. Mantere (eds), *Critical Music Historiography: Probing Canons, Ideologies and Institutions*, 1–13, Farnham: Ashgate.
Loftsdóttir, K. and L. Jensen, eds (2012), *Whiteness and Postcolonialism in the Nordic Region: Exceptionalism, Migrant Others and National Identities*, Farnham and Burlington, VT: Ashgate.
Lynch, G. (2005), *Understanding Theology and Popular Culture*, Malden, MA: Blackwell Publishing.

Lynch, G. (2007), 'Some Concluding Reflections', in G. Lynch (ed.), *Between Sacred and Profane: Researching Religion and Popular Culture*, 157–63, London and New York: I.B. Tauris.

Lynch, G. (2012), *The Sacred in the Modern World: A Cultural Sociolocial Approach*, Oxford and New York: Oxford University Press.

Lynch, G. (2014), *On the Sacred*, London: Routledge.

McClary, S. and R. Walser (1990), 'Start Making Sense! Musicology Wrestles with Rock', in S. Frith and A. Goodwin (eds), *On Record: Rock, Pop, and the Written Word*, 277–92, London and New York: Routledge.

MM (2020), *Metallimessu*. Available online: http://metallimessu.com (accessed 20 October 2020).

Moberg, M. and C. Partridge (2017), 'Introduction', in C. Partridge and M. Moberg (eds), *The Bloomsbury Handbook of Religion and Popular Music*, 1–9, London: Bloomsbury.

Modood, T. (2007), *Multiculturalism: A Civic Idea*, Cambridge and Malden, MA: Polity.

Morgan, D. (2007), 'Studying Religion and Popular Culture: Prospects, Presuppositions, Procedures', in G. Lynch (ed.), *Between Sacred and Profane: Researching Religion and Popular Culture*, 21–33, London and New York: I.B. Tauris.

Partridge, C. (2013), *The Lyre of Orpheus: Popular Music, the Sacred, and the Profane*, New York: Oxford University Press.

Pattison, S. (2009), 'Deepening Relationships with Material Artefacts', in C. Deacy and E. Arweck (eds), *Exploring Religion and the Sacred in a Media Age*, 55–70, Farnham and Burlington, VT: Ashgate.

Radano, R. M. and P. V. Bohlman (2000), *Music and the Racial Imagination*, Chicago, IL: University of Chicago Press.

Santana, R. W. and G. Erickson (2008), *Religion and Popular Culture: Rescripting the Sacred*, Jefferson, NC and London: McFarland & Company.

Schofield Clark, L. (2007), 'Why Study Popular Culture? Or, How to Build a Case for your Thesis in a Religious Studies or Theology Department', in G. Lynch (ed.), *Between Sacred and Profane: Researching Religion and Popular Culture*, 5–20, London and New York: I.B. Tauris.

Shaffer, R. (2017), *Music, Youth and International Links in Post-War British Fascism: The Transformation of Extremism*, Cham: Palgrave Macmillan.

Shiloah, A. (1995), *Music in the World of Islam*, Aldershot: Scolar Press.

Shuker, R. (2012), *Popular Music Culture: The Key Concepts*, 3rd edn, London and New York: Routledge.

Storey, J. (2003), *Inventing Popular Culture: From Folklore to Globalization*, Malden, MA: Blackwell Publishing.

Storey, J. (2009), *Cultural Theory and Popular Culture: An Introduction*, 5th edn, Harlow and New York: Pearson Longman.

Strong, C. and E. Rush (2018), 'Musical Genius and/or Nasty Piece of Work? Dealing with Violence and/sexual Assault in Accounts of Popular Music's Past', *Continuum*, 32 (5): 569–80.

Taylor, T. D. (1997), *Global Pop: World Music, World Markets*, London and New York: Routledge.

Teitelbaum, B. (2017), *Lions of the North: Sounds of the New Nordic Radical Nationalism*, New York: Oxford University Press.

Thompson, K. (1998), 'Durkheim and Sacred Identity', in N. J. Allen, W. S. F. Pickering and W. Watts Miller (eds), *On Durkheim's Elementary Forms of Religious Life*, 92–104, London and New York: Routledge.

Tiainen, M. (2005), *Säveltäjän sijainnit: Taiteilija, musiikki ja historiallinen kesto Paavo Heinisen ja Einojuhani Rautavaaran teksteissä*, Nykykulttuurin julkaisuja 82, Jyväskylä: Jyväskylän yliopisto.

Till, R. (2010), *Pop Cult: Religion and Popular Music*, London and New York: Continuum.

Wall, T. (2013), *Studying Popular Music Culture*, 2nd edn, London: Arnold.

Weston, D. and A. Bennett, eds (2013), *Pop Pagans: Paganism and Popular Music*, Durham: Acumen.

Young, Robert J. C. (2012), 'The Postcolonial Condition', in D. Stone (ed.), *The Oxford Handbook of Postwar European History*, 600–12, Oxford: Oxford University Press.

Part One

Personal Spirituality

2

Leonard Cohen, the 'Sufi' Mystic

Jiří Měsíc

Introduction

Sufism is the mystical branch of Islam emerging in the Persian Empire during the eight century AD, but there are claims that the oral tradition had existed before (Burckhardt 2008: 4–5). Nowadays, Sufism is present practically in the whole world with spiritual and teaching centres (*zawiya*), which are often signalled with the words *merhaban* (welcome) and open to anyone who wants to undertake this spiritual path. Its main attraction lies in the fact that for Westerners, *zawiya* is more of a healing centre in which the adepts may reach higher states of consciousness and be closer to their selves while maintaining religious observances.[1] However, to be a Sufi, one needs to convert to Islam and then undertake an initiatory ceremony (*tasharruf*) into a religious order (*tariqa*) (Nicholson 1989: 21).

The main goal of Sufism is to approach the 'heart' which harbours the Divine and to perfect one's being.[2] The Sufi is obliged to attain seven spiritual 'stations' (*maqām*) on his way to perfection: repentance (*tawba*), watchfulness (*wara*), renunciation (*zuhd*), poverty (*faqr*), patience (*ṣabr*), trust (*tawakkul*) and acceptance (*riḍā*). The death of the ego/self (*fanā*) is a necessary step on this path. Only the perfected being and his purified soul can reach the 'heart,' open its gates and drink from the Divine source therein.

The Sufi is a person seeking such perfection. It is the perfection that the Muslims see in the Prophet and in G-d.[3] The adepts do not want to be completely like Them but rather to be immersed in Divine love. For this reason, Sufis are thought to be 'the spiritual elite' (*al-khāssa*) (Geoffroy 2010: 9) of Islam with the master (*sheikh*) handing down the knowledge to his disciples and instructing them in their evolution. The Sufi ethic modifies their character and makes them loving, truthful and respectful. Naturally, the adepts strive for mystical knowledge and a direct taste of Divine love (*dhauq*) and prefer it to any formal knowledge. They do not exclude, or forbid, other religions and it often happens that the adepts in Europe and the US also practice other spiritual teachings, such as Buddhism or Yoga. Some of the contemporary followers, often converts, have even learned how to live the Christian life through Sufism,[4] because Sufism embraces other religions and provides space for meditation and communion with G-d, which is the aspiration of most religions in general. Ibn Arabi (1165–1240), 'The Greatest Master' (Sheikh Al-Akbar), wrote in one poem dedicated to the Andalusian philosopher Averroes that his heart is universal and contains all religions and forms of worship. He even put love above religion and made it a creed itself:

> My heart can take on any form:
> a meadow for gazelles,
> a cloister for monks,
> for the idols, sacred ground.
> Ka'ba for the circling pilgrim,
> the tables of the Torah,
> the scrolls of the Quran.
> My creed is Love;
> wherever its caravan turns along the way,
> that is my belief,
> my faith.[5]

Sufism could, therefore, be termed a religion of love. The name, in addition, stands for the acceptance of the world and of one's own lot. The Sheikh Abd al-Hafidh Wentzel, whom I met on 22 June 2018 at Fes Café in Fes (Morocco), described Sufism as a way to perfection in the following narrative:

> One day one master was interviewed by one man from the newspaper. He asked him, 'What is Sufism?' and he replied, 'Sufism is a foot in shoe'. It is everything in its perfection, in its right place at the right time. It includes justice, giving everybody their rights. This is something we don't know anymore. We only want rights but we don't give rights to the others. Sufism means to respect everyone and to give everybody what is due to them. To the Creator, to the prophets and the saints, to the humanity, to the creation, to animals, to plants. That is Sufism.[6]

Evidently, Sufism is not only the mystical knowledge, but it is also an ethical system. It stems from love for everyone and everything, in particular, from love for everything in its perfection. To the question 'Who is the true Sufi?', the Sheikh replied as follows:

> The true Sufi, the first true Sufi was of course Mohammed, now there're probably ten million reports about him. Describing every different attribute of his being.

You should look for people who embody some of His attributes. One of the methods of discerning the true Sufi is whether his attributes; his actions; his words; his behaviour; his character fit with all these descriptions. But it's so difficult to find someone like that that we have to look for shortcuts. One of the shortcuts is to find someone who, when you look at him, reminds you of your Creator and you find that his words and actions are one thing and you're feeling at peace when you are in his presence. Bringing you closer to your purpose of being. This could be a Sufi.[7]

In the above citation, we see that the Sufi is not someone who is necessarily religious. It can be any loving person giving respect and right to others. The Sufis believe that G-d reveals Himself in concrete forms (*tajalli*) and that is because all that is beautiful in the world harbours the Divine, be it human beings or natural phenomena. Sometimes we see the Sufi worshipping a concrete person, sometimes a beautiful woman like in the story of Layla and Majnun[8] or Yusuf and Zulaikha.[9] It is because the beautiful girl or boy (or man or woman) represent the Divine and they are probably the 'shortcut' of which Sheikh Wentzel spoke. In Fes, I saw many Sufis kissing the hand of their brothers and the Sheikh during the incantation of G-d's name and praying (*dhikr*). I would argue that this was evidence of them recognizing G-d in the hearts of their brothers, and they were giving their love to one another. This impression was also strengthened by their ecstatic utterances (*shathiyat*) during the chant.

Sufism, the religion of love

Al-Junyad (830–910), a Persian mystic and saint, said that 'the essence of love is the replacement of the lover's attributes by the beloved's attributes so that the lover's actions are carried out by the beloved's attributes' (Abrahamov 2003: 33). This is the annihilation of the self, and Sufi literature is full of motifs of the searching lover for the perfect Beloved. The human lover is naturally the victim of his love but his suffering and solitude are necessary prerequisites of the mystical path.[10] The Beloved is often portrayed as cruel due to his unwillingness to be subdued by the human lover, which suggests the dichotomy between the Beloved (G-d) and his human lover. This dichotomy exists when the seeker commences his mystical path but disappears when the lover and Beloved become One. Quite naturally, the seeker looks for beauty (*jamal*) and G-d's majesty (*jalal*) in all places but cannot understand them before he finds them in his heart in the last step on his path, the revelation of the spiritual truth called *ma'rifa*.

As a religion of love, Sufis give preference to *'ishq*, a passionate form of love.[11] They further distinguish between *'ishq-i haqiqi* ('real love' directed to G-d) and *'ishq-i majazi* ('metaphorical' love directed toward other beings). Yet the bond between the Beloved and the lover is the bond between G-d and the soul and entails love for all things (see Vaughan-Lee 1993: xi). Some of the seekers have a natural inkling that G-d is present in their heart, others are discovering it step by step during their lives. The Persian poet Jalāl ad-Dīn Muhammad Rūmī (1207–73) calls them the 'sect of lovers' in the following verses: 'The sect of lovers is distinct from all others / Lovers have a religion and faith all of their own' (Rūmī 2008: 84). The lovers must be poor, not only spiritually but also materially because they will be filled with G-d's love. He also says that 'Lovers don't finally meet somewhere. / They're in each other all along' (Rūmī 2008: 84), which means that they are in their Beloved. Moreover, Sufi literature is full of references to the Beloved who needs us as we need Him (Vaughan-Lee 1993: 10).

Throughout history, the Sufis have been pursued and attacked by orthodox believers and many countries have even prohibited their teachings and practices.[12] In spite of drawing on the Holy Quran and Hadith of the Prophet (Waley 1993: 18), they have often been considered to be heretics within orthodox Islam and many of their greatest philosophers and poets were killed.[13] Their greatest 'sin' is that they strive to live in the oneness of the world, meaning that they do not see it as formed by opposing concepts. They go so far as to ignore the dichotomy between Heaven and Hell and prefer the direct/personal 'intoxication' with the love of G-d.[14] Some of them also interpret Quran in a more mystical fashion. Moreover, as there is no gender in Persian languages, their poems often refer not only to G-d but also to the Prophet, or concrete individuals and sometimes even to all of them. Often, they are erotic, which is seen as blasphemous. However, what is often erotic is the description of the soul searching for G-d before being annihilated in His love, the motif that also appears in the poetry of Leonard Cohen whose work may be read as a portrayal of the soul striving to come to the union with the Creator.

Leonard Cohen and Sufism

Leonard Cohen was not a Sufi adept, he was not initiated into any Sufi order and was best known as a follower of Zen Buddhism[15] and Kabbalah.[16] That said, he often revealed that he was studying Sufi poetry and philosophy and employing Sufi symbolism in his work.[17] Moreover, he acknowledged that the Jews were studying with the Sufi masters 'at a certain great period in our history' (Burger

2014: 388), which is true if we take into consideration the interrelation between Sufi and Kabbalistic teachings in the period of al-Ándalus on the Iberian peninsula and mutual borrowings and recompilation of the books and their rituals and beliefs (for a detailed analysis, see Block 2007–8; 2010). In Sufism, Cohen found the same source of faith and instruction that he found in Kabbalah, Christian mysticism and his studies of Zen Buddhist teachings. He also noticed that Sufi poems contain descriptions of the processes in which the soul comes into the communion with G-d.

Even before discovering Sufi poetry, it could be argued that songs like 'Joan of Arc' from the third studio album *Songs of Love and Hate* (1971) already resembled the passionate language of great Sufi mystics whose poetry reflects the symbolic marriage of their soul with G-d and annihilation of the self (*fanā*). The visual expression of this belief appeared earlier on the back cover of his first album *Songs of Leonard Cohen* (1967) which depicts a lonely soul surrounded by flames being purified by Divine love. In this instance, Cohen drew inspiration from the Christian tradition, but it is a motif that is common to all Abrahamic religions. Cohen must have thought that the purpose of the human being is to strive for such a purification as a necessary prerequisite to perfection, be it with the help of an official religion or its distillation into mysticism. This was the cure for his depression from which he was suffering and the way to mend his broken being.

At that time, in the early 1970s, Cohen was not a member of any religious or spiritual order, but he was already drawn to the idea that the spiritual path should be directed by a master.[18] *Songs of Love and Hate* also reflects the idea of stations through which he was passing and states he was experiencing, as well as, more importantly, portraying antitheses in mutual dependence of which the world of Sufi oneness is so meticulously composed. A very potent and intriguing motif is Cohen's understanding of the body and its unity with the soul. In the very first song of the album, 'Avalanche', Cohen presents a dialogue between the human being (Hunchback) and G-d. He speaks about the ugly body enveloping the soul. However, the 'hunchback' that Cohen mentions has got Beloved's 'flesh' (Divine body). Thus, 'hunchback' (ordinary human existence) is Divine according to Cohen because everything that constitutes him comes from G-d (body and soul).

Although the body is sacred, it is susceptible to sin (*shirk*), so the mystic's goal is to control its desires: not in the sense to avoid bodily pleasures but to see the body as a holy instrument which is to reconnect with other bodies and mediate the union of two souls with the Creator, such as was described, for instance, by Ibn Arabi in his treatise *'Anqâ' mughrib* (from the thirteenth century; see Elmore 1999). That is why Cohen writes: 'You who wish to conquer pain, / you must learn what makes me kind', as if to say that we have to learn what appeases the body. After such a union, the mystic lives in a spiritual state and his body, naturally, does not need anything more than food and water to maintain it. On the third track, 'Dress Rehearsal Rag', Cohen speaks about the sacrifice of the body: 'Just take a look at your body now, / there's nothing much to save' and suggests suicide: 'That's right, it's come to this, / yes it's come to this, / and wasn't it a long way down, / wasn't it a strange way down?' However, the death of the body is just a rehearsal for something that is to come later: 'it's just the dress rehearsal rag, / you know this dress rehearsal rag, / it's just a dress rehearsal rag'. Here he implies that the death of the body, or, rather, of bodily needs, is the result of the annihilation of the ego, ultimately leading to the transformative experience of living Divine existence. This explains why the track is followed by 'Love Calls You by Your Name', since Divine love only comes when the soul is purified and the 'heart' prepared to receive it. It is exactly this experience that puts the adept onto the station of repentance and seclusion (*tawba*) as described in the 'schizophrenic' track 'Famous Blue Raincoat', which portrays a divided being, a worldly man and a 'mystic' representing himself liberated from his ego. *Tawba* is a necessary precondition of the mystic to reach the stage called *haquiqa* (truth) in which the soul obtains a direct knowledge of G-d. At this stage, the seeker is able to see his self and make a clear distance from it thanks to his proximity to the Divine.

Haquiqa is also supported by an infinite number of mystical states (*aḥwāl*) granted by G-d which shape the adept's path. Sheikh Wentzel commented on states as follows:

> Our aim is not to target only one state, we have to pass through various states. We don't know one state without another, we don't know black without white, we don't know sweet without bitter, love without disgust, we know only the states that have to be in this world. Because we're being tested and if you look at the source of everything, at the reality of everything, the states, we can't avoid them. But don't look for them, let them come. The states that come are given to you by the Creator. Accept them. There's nothing better than what He is giving.[19]

Each of us has different predispositions, some may bear and cope with manifold states, while others can bear only a few. The Sheikh Wentzel goes on to point out that we are under no obligation to bear more weight than we can carry:

> Whatever level you reach is what you can reach, there is no obligation to do more than you can. You do only what you can. This is divine justice. It's like carrying buckets with water. Some carry only a few buckets but other people are

stronger so they can carry more, they can carry universes, they exist, they might be rare but they exist. We strive to be like ants who can carry twenty times their weight. This is magic! The ant![20]

Each of the states is given by the Creator and at the end of the path, the seeker (*tâlib*) becomes a gnostic (*'arif*), the lover and Beloved simultaneously (Nicholson 1989: 22). Cohen speaks in 'Sing Another Song, Boys', about lost contact with the outside world and a girl who wants to seduce him without any knowledge of the notion of mystical love. She is described as waving 'a Nazi dagger' in her advances. He suggests the 'station' *zuhd* (renunciation) because succumbing to her love would be like renouncing the spiritual path. The song ends with the verses: 'But let's leave these lovers wondering / why they cannot have each other, / and let's sing another song, boys, / this one has grown old and bitter.' It is then followed by the portrayal of greater love, the union of the soul with G-d, of the lover with the Beloved in the song 'Joan of Arc',[21] which uses the passionate language of love directed to G-d (*'ishq-i haqiqi*).

It would be futile to enumerate all the songs that present the idea of stations and states in Cohen's work but we could perhaps highlight the song 'Passing Through' from the album *Live Songs* (1973), in which all of the characters Jesus, Adam, George Washington and Franklin Roosevelt represent stations through which the singer is passing. However, the total annihilation of the self (*fanā*), which is necessary on the Sufi path, is revealed in the song 'Please, Don't Pass Me By (A Disgrace)' from the same album. Here, Cohen begs his audience to lose themselves and go home as 'someone else'. In the song, he also proclaims that he cannot stand his self and describes his personality as a master and tyrant:

> Ah, I'm not going to be. I can't stand him. I can't stand who I am. That's why I've got to get down on my knees. Because I can't make it by myself. I'm not by myself anymore because the man I was before he was a tyrant, he was a slave, he was in chains, he was broken.

Lover, lover, lover

The loss, or annihilation of the self, is a necessary prerequisite to engage in a dialogue with the immanent power of the heart that Sufi believers call G-d. In Cohen's lyrics, we encounter such dialogues, often without understanding who the characters are or who is speaking to whom: a good example being the song 'Lover, Lover, Lover' from the album *New Skin for the Old Ceremony* (1974) which emerged during the Yom Kippur War in 1973.[22]

The song presents a dialogue between the singer (lover) and his Beloved (Father G-d). The lover begs the Beloved to change his name because it is 'covered up with fear and filth and cowardice and shame'. This begging suggests repentance demanded at the first station on the Sufi path (*tawba*), an initial step towards abandoning corporeality. The Beloved then urges the lover to return to Him in the lines: 'Yes and lover, lover, lover, lover, lover, lover, lover come back to me', which resemble the chanting of the first creed of Islam 'La ilaha ilallah' (with words saying: *la* [there is no], *ilaha* [G-d] and *ilallah* [except Allah]); in common translation: 'There is no god except Allah'. Similarly, the repetition of the word 'lover' invokes the practice of *dhikr* (remembrance), where constant repetition of Allah's name creates a mantra designed to heighten consciousness. Within more esoteric branches of Sufism the word Allah is believed to be compound of the article 'al' and the word 'lâh' meaning ('Nothing') thus it can be understood as an incantation of nothingness (Vaughan-Lee 1993: 118).

G-d ('the Nothing') responds to the singer that he made his body as a 'kind of trial', suggesting we have two choices in this life: we can liberate our soul from the body, purify it on the mystical path, or we can nourish it through bodily pleasures. For the Sufis, G-d is always loving. He has never turned away from people but was idolized and then shunned by the Jewish people. In Cohen's song, the voice of G-d is heard to say: 'I never turned aside ... I never walked away ... it was you who covered up my face'. Thus, accusing the Jews of covering His face and Name with their Temples in Jerusalem and their official religion.[23]

In the last stanza, Cohen dedicates the song to the soldiers fighting on both the Israeli and Arab sides, and uses it as a shield against the enemy,[24] with the sleeve-notes of the live album *Field Commander Cohen: Tour of 1979* (2001), on which the song was later also released, giving credits, among other people, to the Persian poet Rūmī (1207–73) who always addressed G-d as the Lover or Beloved.[25] Sometimes it is difficult to discern whom he is addressing because his poetry often portrays the experience of *ma'rifa* when the lover and Beloved become One and it is this idea of oneness which appears to influence Cohen's work. Rūmī was also the founder of Sufi rituals honouring music and dance which gave him the impetus to establish the order of Whirling Dervishes in Konya (today's Turkey). It is said that while walking through the goldsmithing section of Konya he was struck by the sound of hammering so suddenly that he started dancing in 'surrender and yet with great centered discipline' (Barks and Rūmī 2004: 277). By imitating this 'original' dance, Whirling Dervishes believe that human and Divine can meet in the empty space created by turning (Barks and Rūmī 2004: 277). This idea of emptiness is in close relation with the loss of the individual's self on which Sufism is based. According to the scholar of Islamic literature, R. A. Nicholson, '[t]he whole of Sufism rests on the belief that when the individual self is lost, the Universal Self is found, or, in religious language, that ecstasy affords the only means by which the soul can directly communicate and become united with God' (Nicholson 1989: 42).

Although not intended for Dervish ceremony the song certainly uses a rhythmic pattern used for *sama*, where the drum dictates the rhythm of their heart and breathing, in a ritual designed to invoke loss of consciousness and fusion with the Creator on the vertical axis. In their rotation, the participants resemble stars and planets dancing around the sun while incanting *Al-lâh* (Nothingness), in reality, inhaling *al* and exhaling *lâh*. The song also suggests a loss of the self on the battlefield, where lovers die and are born again, perhaps explaining why Cohen often speaks about himself as a soldier.[26] A battlefield is an apt symbol because the human and Divine existence are in constant tension with the self preventing the soul from reaching Divinity and the Divine rejecting the soul for its imperfection.

Take this waltz

It could be argued that Cohen returned to the idea of whirling later on, in 1988, when he released the song 'Take This Waltz' on the album *I'm Your Man* (1988), where he looks at the consummation of desire in the Garden of Eden transferred to a rather Gothic Viennese setting. The lyrics are the adaptation of the poem by the Andalusian poet Federico García Lorca (1898–1936) 'Pequeño vals vienés', translated by Cohen himself. His goal is obvious, he is aiming at the dissolution of the flesh and purification of the soul through the sexual union: 'Oh I want you, I want you, I want you / On a chair with a dead magazine / … / Take this waltz, take this waltz / Take its broken waist in your hand.' Here, waltz is just a personified desire for two intertwined bodies sweating in thrusts between major and minor notes like Dervishes dancing in the circle and thrusting their head from side to side with the aim to lose consciousness in the climax of the ritual. Cohen wants to 'yield to the flood of [the woman's] beauty' to become the martyr of love dying as a result of his desire. It is no longer repentance and solitude preparing his 'heart' to receive love or maintaining a mystical state but lust.

In this song, the Sufi whirling is exchanged for secular waltzing, which is not an intimate dance between a mystic and the Creator but a dance between two human partners with openly sexual connotations. Nowadays, we may not realize it, but according to the musicologist Mark Knowles, when the dance was first introduced 'genteel society was shocked by the intimacy implied by the waltz's embracing position' (Knowles 2009: 17). It could have been a coincidence, or perhaps a certain manifestation of the age, but the roots of waltz appeared approximately at the same time as the Dervish-like whirling in the medieval Occitan dance called *volta*, whose etymology connotes notions of whirling.[27] Moreover, it is believed to be a reflection of the troubadour idea of Courtly Love (Knowles 2009: 19) and an expression of proper decorum between two partners fulfilling social expectations (Knowles 2009: 189). Through this song, Cohen might have wanted to get rid of the overly religious language of the previous albums and to adapt his music to the more secular taste. Although the song presents a very surreal and modernist language, I would argue that it can be read as an allegory of the passionate love *'ishq* at the end of the twentieth century, when religion was practiced not in temples and shrines but in bedrooms, and what was once so distant became suddenly close through the union of two bodies.

The guests

In 1979, Leonard Cohen released the album *Recent Songs* which contains the most notable Sufi statement of his career. In the first track, 'The Guests', he describes a banquet attended by many souls where they have the opportunity to meet their Beloved (Host). When asked in the documentary *The Song of Leonard Cohen* (1980) directed by Harry Rasky about the song's imagery, Cohen revealed that Rūmī's poetry was a source of inspiration:

> The Persian poet Rūmī uses the idea of the guests a lot, the festival, the feast and the guests. It's almost impossible to talk about that seed moment of when a song begins. It could be the soul comes into the world. There is some notion that the soul has, that there is a feast, that there is a festival, that there is a banquet. It strives to experience the hospitality of the world. It doesn't achieve it. It feels lonely, this is everybody's experience. It feels lost. It stumbles around on the outskirts of the party. If the striving is deep enough or if the grace of the host is turned towards the seeking guest, then suddenly the inner door flies open and he finds himself or the soul finds himself at that banquet table. Although no one knows where the night is going, and no one knows why the wine is flowing. No one actually understands the mechanics of this grace except that we experience it from time to time. (Rasky 2010: 90)

Here, Cohen's statement is consistent with Sufi philosophy which speaks about grace being given to some of the souls who achieve perfection by it. The song also suggests that the experience does not last and that it originates a new cycle: a new cyclical rebirth of the soul which will be thrown over the 'garden wall' and invited to the banquet once more. In Rūmī's symbolism, the guest house can be the heart which is being approached and which contains Divine power.

In addition, the song's portrayal of a nocturnal journey is a frequent theme in Sufi rituals, such as in *lila derdeba*, a night ritual of the mystical group of Gnawa from Morocco. The ritual is accompanied by music and dance and nourished by sensory perceptions, such as wearing colourful dresses, smelling incense and spices, listening to music and observing or participating in dance. The practitioners often fall into a trance in which they lose their self and temporary control of the body (Dieste 2013: 266). Often, it resembles an epileptic seizure, with other adepts needing to support the struggling body of the practitioner. By this, it is thought that individuals can be spiritually healed and attain union with the Creator. Cohen's song portrays a similar night journey of the soul being healed and reborn into the world once again; evidenced by Cohen's claim in 1988 that one Sufi community practiced their Whirling Dance while listening to the song because 'it has the spirit of Rūmī in it'.[28] In other words, the Sufi community practised their sacred ritual to the words and music of a Western singer-songwriter.

The window

On *Recent Songs*, Cohen also presents the process in which the soul gets separated from the body and comes to the final union with the Creator. He now sees the soul as lingering in the 'window' – on the threshold between the physical and spiritual worlds. It is '[a]bandoned to beauty and pride', to the temptations of the body and therefore prepared to come to the union with the Creator. In the track 'Window', Cohen sings how the soul is 'Lost in the rages of fragrance / Lost in the rags of remorse / Lost in the waves of a sickness / That loosens the high silver nerves' which implies a ritual. It could be a ritual like *lila derdeba* that I described above during which the adepts burn fragrant spices and plants, or the Havdalah ceremony, which marks the end of the Jewish Sabbath and the loss of the extra Sabbath soul *neshamah yetayrah*. The soul is repenting, which means that it regrets the sins of the body and bodily pleasures (*tawba*). It is still attached to the physical world and worldly pleasures, but the singer begs the Saviour in the chorus to gentle the soul.

In this song, Cohen does not call G-d his Beloved nor Lover, but 'darling', offering an explanation in an interview with Harry Rasky that to many the word can stand for the Christian Saviour, for others, it may be G-d Himself, but for the Sufis, it is the immanent G-d harboured in their hearts.[29] Furthermore, Cohen exhorts the soul 'come forth from the cloud of unknowing' which is a reference to a fourteenth-century book of Christian mysticism in which the author instructs his disciple – a 24-year-old boy – to 'Lift up [his] heart towards God with a humble stirring of love' (Spearing 2001: 21). But when he does, that he will find between him and G-d 'only darkness, and as it were a cloud of unknowing' (Spearing 2001: 22). His only hope is to 'remain in this darkness as long as [he] can' (Spearing 2001: 22), and 'beat on that thick cloud of unknowing with a sharp dart of longing love, and not to give up, whatever happens' (Spearing 2001: 28). This cloud, therefore, is a place of communion with G-d and represents the station of *tawakkul* (trust), a complete surrender to His will. However, Cohen wants the soul to return after its sojourn in the cloud. He exhorts it to 'kiss the cheek of the moon' and then consecrate Israel as a nation in which the New Jerusalem is 'glowing' thanks to the fulfilment of the old promise – restoration of the original human being (Adam) of the feminine and masculine poles, a complete being which may again enter the Garden of Eden and live in the proximity of G-d.

In the next verse, he may also be referring to another book of English mysticism, *The Ladder of Perfection* written by the Augustinian monk Walter Hilton (1340/45–96). Climbing on the 'ladder of thorns' would then mean nourishing the desire for Jesus in one's heart in silence and contemplation, which is an interesting point of intersection with some Sufi orders, such as the Naqshbandi, known for contemplating G-d as an immanent power. Then Cohen, the mystic, instructs us to take the purified soul and lay it on fire and merge with the Creator, entering 'the arms of the high holy one' and thus conforming ourselves to the fact that the soul belongs to G-d and that it is Divine (*ridā*). In the last verses of the song, the singer reminds us that the Creator constantly recreates us, that is why the 'continuous stutter' is mentioned. The letter – logos – the Word of G-d – is being born every single instant in our selves.

The album *Recent Songs*, therefore, presents the willingness of the singer to put his life into the hands of G-d and complete his *fāna* to 'die before one dies'. Cohen later continued with zeal in the *Book of Mercy* (1984), a collection of psalms portraying inner dialogues with G-d. In the very first psalm, he speaks about asking the Beloved for his love and the Beloved's consent of his love to the lover in the act of revelation of the mystical truth sustaining Leonard Cohen as a singer:

> I bargain now. I offer buttons for his love. I beg for mercy. Slowly he yields.
> Haltingly he moves toward his throne. Reluctantly the angels grant to one

another permission to sing. In a transition so delicate it cannot be marked, the court is established on beams of golden symmetry, and once again I am a singer in the lower choirs, born fifty years ago to raise my voice this high, and no higher. (*Book of Mercy*, Psalm no. 1)

Conclusion

In the commentary to the songs above we have seen that Cohen, in spite of not being initiated into any Sufi order, employs the specific idea of stations and states and maps his spiritual progress as the mystical adept with the aim to suppress/annihilate his self (*fāna*) and achieve submission to the will of G-d (*riḍā*). Indeed, I would contend that this hints at Cohen perhaps following Sufi teachings in his personal life while simultaneously observing Jewish and Buddhist religious practices. The analysis also helps to clarify his religious perspective, revealing that Cohen does not invoke symbolism from one unique school of thought, but employs motifs from various sources to portray the unique experience of Divine love.

There are many other songs which substantiate Cohen's influences of Sufi thought, such as the well-known verse 'There is a crack in everything / that's how the light gets in' from the song 'Anthem' (*The Future*, 1992), which contains the echoes of a verse from Rūmī about Divine light in the wound.[30] Nevertheless, the work that shows a profound submission to the Sufi concept of *riḍā* and the complete acceptance of the fact that one's fate depends on the will of the Lord is the last album *You Want It Darker* (2016) and its title song in which Cohen sings 'Hineni Hineni / I'm ready, my Lord'. Here he is echoing the call to Abraham to kill his son Isaac (Gen. 22:1) or Moses who was ready to comply with Divine orders when G-d called upon him from the burning bush (Exod. 3:4). Cohen uses the biblical phrase to proclaim he is ready to fulfil Divine will to reach the ultimate goal of the Sufi path (*ma'rifa*). It could also be argued that the lyrics were drawn from the prayer of the Ashkenazi *musaf* service held on the Jewish new year Rosh Hashanah which starts with the Hineni prayer: 'Here I am, devoid of deeds, trembling and afraid, from the fear of the one who sits upon the prayers of Israel', which resembles the Sufi surrender to the Lord as described in a poem by Rūmī: 'As a pen I lie / Before my scrivener' (Chittick 2005c: 75).

Moreover, Cohen's posthumous collection of poems *The Flame*, published in October 2018, contains the work 'Listen to the Hummingbird' in which Cohen bids his reader not to listen to him, as a person, 'Leonard Cohen', but rather to listen to G-d and the natural world manifesting Divine love (*dhauq*). Through this poem, once again he aligns the Sufi ethic that one does not nourish one's ego with striving for the complete realization in G-d's perfection (Cohen 2018: 70).

Notes

1. As an example, I suggest reading about the Sufi community in the mountains of Sierra Nevada in Spain. See Sánchez Alonso (2015) about the influence of the Sufi mystic Rūmī in the US who is described as 'the best selling poet' there. See also Ali (2017). The last article even mentions how the Sufi poetry helped Chris Martin, Madonna and Tilda Swinton to overcome crises.
2. Like in the Quranic verse: 'God is with those who search for excellence' (Quran 29:69). But we should not be confused because it is not the physical heart but the 'Heart of Hearts' which receives the spiritual energy of which our heart is merely a symbol.
3. All throughout the text, I use the spelling of 'G-d' with a hyphen, which is a traditional Jewish practice showing reverence for the Hebrew G-d in English. Moreover, since any printed text is liable to be discarded or destroyed soon or later, the Jewish authors prevent the desecration of the Name by writing it as 'G-d', by which they avoid mentioning the Unutterable Name completely. I keep the same spelling when speaking about G-d of Abrahamic religions (Judaism, Christianity and Islam) for much the same reasons.
4. See Sánchez Alonso (2015).
5. Translated by Michael Sells and reprinted in María Rosa Menocal, *Shards of Love: Exile and the Origins of the Lyric* (1999: 71). Here we may easily notice the similarity with Dante's school of love *Dolce stil novo* that operated basically with the same motif of love lying dormant in the heart.
6. Jiří Měsíc and Abd al-Hafidh Wentzel. Personal interview during an event entitled 'Spiritual Evening of Zikr and Sufi Songs', 22 June 2018.
7. Ibid.
8. See Nizami (1997, 2011), which also inspired Eric Clapton to write his song 'Layla' (1992).
9. The story was retold by the poet Jami (1414–92) in *Haft Awrang* ('Seven Thrones'), the compilation of seven books containing Sufi teachings, translated into English and edited by Charles Horne in 1917.
10. It is exactly this motif which made me think of the medieval Occitan poetry as influenced by Sufism and Kabbalah in my doctoral dissertation: about the suffering lover and his unconsummated love. See Měsíc (2016).

11 'It is precisely this notion of *'ishq* as a passionate and extreme variety of love which was the subject of the first text written on love in Persian, the *Sawanih* of Ahmad Ghazali (d. 1126).' See Safi (2003).

12 One of the countries that have wanted to get rid of the Sufis is, for instance, Turkey where the reforms of 1925 banned the Sufi orders. However, Sufism has survived as an underground movement in Turkey defended by the well-known philosopher and spiritual leader Fethüllah Gülen who is residing in the US and whom the Turkish government accuses of being behind the coup in 2016.

13 One of the first known Sufis who was executed for his beliefs was Mansur Al-Hallaj (*c.* 858–922) known for his saying 'I am the Truth' ('Ana 'l-Ḥaqq') which was misinterpreted as claiming that he was Divine, instead of proving that he annihilated his self and discovered the Divine in his heart. He is one of the three well-known Sufi martyrs, together with Ayn al-Quzat Hamadani (1098–1131) and Shahab al-Din Yahya ibn Habash Suhrawardi (1154–91).

14 The female saint and mystic from Iraq, Rabia Basri (717–801), renounced the concepts of Heaven and Hell straightforwardly. Moreover, she claimed that 'the concepts' prevent her from the attainment of the love of G-d. 'O God! If I worship You for fear of Hell, burn me in Hell / and if I worship You in hope of Paradise, / exclude me from Paradise. / But if I worship You for Your Own sake, / grudge me not Your everlasting Beauty.' See Chittick (2005b: 59). Another Persian mystic and philosopher Ayn al-Quzat Hamadani (1098–1131), the disciple of Ahmad Ghazali, spoke even about incinerating the Islamic creed and religion and searching directly for G-d: 'I will incinerate this creed and religion, and burn it. / Then I will put your love in its place. / How long must I hide / this love in my heart? / What the traveller seeks / is not the religion / and not the creed: / Only You.' See 'Ayn al-Qozat Hamadani (2004: 23).

15 There are two books specifically dealing with Zen Buddhism and Leonard Cohen. The first was written by the French author Christophe Lebold, *Leonard Cohen: L'Homme qui voyait tomber les anges* (2013) while the other one has been recently published by Alberto Manzano, *Leonard Cohen y el zen* (2018).

16 I wrote about Cohen's Jewish mysticism in the essay 'Leonard Cohen, The Priest of a Catacomb Religion' (Měsíc 2015: 29–47). A summary of Cohen's Jewish belief was presented by the Rabbi Mordecai Finley who was a close friend of Cohen before his death. See Finley (2016).

17 In an interview with Robert Sward and Pat Keeney Smith that appeared in *The Malahat Review*, No. 77 (1986) and was reprinted in the Spanish magazine *El Correo del Sol* in January 1988, Cohen speaks about the poetry of Rūmī and Attar and presents some of their motifs on his album *Recent Songs* (1979), particularly in the text 'The Guests' and 'The Window'.

18 Listen to Leonard Cohen, 'Master Song' (*Songs of Leonard Cohen,* 1967), in which he presents a dialogue between himself and G-d.
19 Jiří Měsíc and Abd al-Hafidh Wentzel. Personal interview during an event entitled 'Spiritual Evening of Zikr and Sufi Songs', 22 June 2018.
20 Ibid.
21 I devoted a specific essay on the ascent of the soul to the Creator as portrayed in the work of Leonard Cohen through Sufism, Kabbalah, Christian Mysticism and Zen Buddhism. See Měsíc (2018).
22 Yom Kippur is the holiest feast for the Jews. It takes place on the tenth day after the Jewish New Year in the month *Tishrei* (meaning a new beginning). It is said that on Rosh Hashanah, G-d opens *the Book of Life* into which he inscribes fate of a person for the upcoming year according to their deeds. Afterwards, the person has ten days to repent for his sins trying to influence a negative verdict. The end of Yom Kippur seals it. During the war, Cohen met Sholomo Semach, who employed him as a volunteer in an entertainment group for the air force.
23 This accusation appears also in the Quranic verse 2:63: 'And remember, Children of Israel, when We made a covenant with you and raised Mount Sinai before you saying, "Hold tightly to what We have revealed to you and keep it in mind so that you may guard against evil." But then you turned away, and if it had not been for Allah's grace and mercy, you surely would have been among the lost. And you know those among who sinned on the Sabbath. We said to them, "You will be transformed into despised apes." So we used them as a warning to their people and to the following generations, as well as a lesson for the God-fearing.'
24 The idea of the shield is suggested in *hadith* and Sufi prayers with the shield being Mohammad protecting the believers. The religious observances are also understood to be a shield. Such as fasting: 'Fasting is a shield from the Hellfire just like a shield of yours in battle.' See Hadith no. 1639 from the colection *Sunan Ibn Mājah.* Available online: https://muflihun.com/ibnmajah/7/1639.
25 The word 'lover' is of a Quranic provenance. In Quran and Hadith, records of the sayings of the Prophet, Allah is often described as *wudud* (the One Who Loves). See also Chittick (2005a: 31).
26 See the song 'Field Commander Cohen' (*New Skin for the Old Ceremony,* 1974) as an example.
27 'The word volta was used in both Italian (*volta* – to turn) and French (*volte, voltare* – to turn).' See Knowles (2009: 187).
28 See the interview 'Dinner with Leonard' conducted by Elizabeth Boleman-Herring, reprinted in Burger (2014: 225–35).
29 According to Cohen, 'the word darling now, has a lot of resonance. You know if you're interested in that sort of thing, which I don't expect anybody to be except craftsmen and technicians in the trade itself, but, *Charlie is My Darling,* that song

Charlie is My Darling. It's not just a term of endearment between men and women. It has other resonance. So, darling of angels, demons and saints, and the whole broken-hearted host means that one which is beloved and cherished by the whole, all the inhabitants of the whole cosmos, that is the arisen one. That is the Christ, or that is the Messiah, or that is the Redeemer, that is that highest aspect of one's own being that has the regenerative capacity.' See Rasky (2010: 94).

30   Rūmī speaks specifically about the wound to which enters Divine light. 'Let a teacher wave away the flies and put a plaster on the wound. / Don't turn your head. Keep looking at the bandaged place. / That's where the light enters you. / And don't believe for a moment that you're healing yourself.' See Barks (2016: 149–50).

References

Abrahamov, B. (2003), *Divine Love in Islamic Mysticism*, New York, NY: Routledge Curzon.

Ali, Rozina (2017), 'The Erasure of Islam from the Poetry of Rūmī', *The New Yorker*, 5 January. Available online: https://www.newyorker.com/books/page-turner/the-erasure-of-islam-from-the-poetry-of-rumi.

'Ayn al-Qozat Hamadani (1994), *Tamhidat*, ed. 'Afif 'Usayran, reprint edn, Teheran: Kitabkhana-yi Manuchihri.

Barks, C. (2016), *Rumi's Little Book of Love and Laughter: Teaching Stories and Fables*, Newburyport, MA: Hampton Roads Publishing.

Barks, C. and Jalāl Ad-Dīn Rūmī (2004), *The Essential Rūmī: New Expanded Edition*, New York: HarperCollins.

Block, T. (2007–8), 'The Question of Sufi Influence on the Early Kabbalah', *Sophia: The Journal of Traditional Studies*, 13 (2), 69–86.

Block, T. (2010), *Shalom Salaam: A Story of a Mystical Fraternity*, Louisville, KY: Fons Vitae.

Burckhardt, T. (2008), *Introduction to Sufi Doctrine*, Bloomington, IN: World Wisdom.

Burger, J. (2014), *Leonard Cohen on Leonard Cohen: Interviews and Encounters*, Chicago, IL: Chicago Review Press.

Chittick, W. C. (2005a), *Ibn 'Arabi: Heir to the Prophets*, Oxford: Oneworld Publications.

Chittick, W. C. (2005b), *Sufism: A Short Introduction*, Oxford: Oneworld Publications.

Chittick, W. C. (2005c), *The Sufi Doctrine of Rumi*, Bloomington, IN: World Wisdom.

Cohen, L. (2018), *The Flame*, Edinburgh: Canongate.

Dieste, J. L. M. (2013), *Health and Ritual in Morocco: Conceptions of the Body and Healing Practices*, Leiden: Brill.

Elmore, G. T. (1999), *Islamic Sainthood in the Fullness of Time: Ibn Al-'Arabi's Book of the Fabulous Gryphon*, Leiden: Brill.

Finley, M. (2016), 'Being Leonard Cohen's Rabbi', *Jewish Journal*, n.p., 16 Nov. 2016. Available online: http://www.jewishjournal.com/religion/article/being_leonard_cohens_rabbi (accessed 6 July 2018).

Geoffroy, E. (2010), *Introduction to Sufism: The Inner Path of Islam*, trans. Roger Gaetani, Bloomington, IN: World Wisdom.

Knowles, M. (2009), *The Wicked Waltz and Other Scandalous Dances: Outrage at Couple Dancing in the 19th and Early 20th Centuries*, Jefferson, NC: McFarland.

Lebold, C. (2013), *Leonard Cohen L'Homme qui voyait tomber les anges*, Rosières-en-Haye: Camion Blanc.

Manzano, A. (2018), *Leonard Cohen y el zen*, Barcelona: Luciérnaga.

Menocal, M. R. (1999), *Shards of Love: Exile and the Origins of the Lyric*, Durham, NC: Duke University Press.

Měsíc, J. (2016), 'Leonard Cohen, The Modern Troubadour', PhD diss., Department of English and American Studies, Palacký University, Olomouc. Available online: https://theses.cz/id/ksff70/Leonard_Cohen_The_Modern_Troubadour.pdf (accessed 15 November 2020).

Měsíc, J. (2018), 'The Nature of Love in the Work of Leonard Cohen', *Journal of Popular Romance Studies*, 7. Available online: https://www.jprstudies.org/2018/10/the-nature-of-love-in-the-work-of-leonard-cohenby-jiri-mesic/ (accessed 15 November 2020).

Měsíc, J. (2015), 'Leonard Cohen, The Priest of a Catacomb Religion', *Moravian Journal of Literature and Film*, 6 (1): 29–47.

Nicholson, R. A. (1989), *The Mystics of Islam*, London: Penguin.

Nizami ([1997] 2011), *The Story of Layla and Majnun*, trans. Rudolf Gelpke, New Lebanon, NY: Omega Publications.

Rasky, H. (2010), *The Song of Leonard Cohen: Portrait of a Poet, a Friendship and a Film*, London: Souvenir.

Rūmī (2008), *The Masnavi*, trans. Jawid Mojaddedi, vol. 2, Oxford: Oxford University Press.

Safi, O. (2003), 'On the "Path of Love" Towards the Divine: A Journey with Muslim Mystics', *The Journal of Scriptural Reasoning*, 3 (2). Available online: http://jsr.shanti.virginia.edu/back-issues/vol-3-no-2-august-2003-healing-words-the-song-of-songs-and-the-path-of-love/on-the-path-of-love-towards-the-divine-a-journey-with-muslim-mystics (accessed 15 November 2020).

Sanchez Alonso, Fernando (2015), 'Conversos sufies, los misticos del islam', *El País*, 21 January. Available online: https://elpais.com/elpais/2015/01/21/eps/1421845208_671813.html.

Spearing, A. C. (trans.) (2001), *The Cloud of Unknowing and Other Works*, London: Penguin.

Vaughan-Lee, L. (1993), *The Bond with the Beloved: The Mystical Relationship of the Lover and the Beloved*, Inverness, CA: Golden Sufi Center.

Waley, M. I. (1993), *Sufism: The Alchemy of the Heart*, San Francisco, CA: Chronicle Books.

Discography

Cohen, Leonard, *Songs of Leonard Cohen*, [CD], Rec. Aug. 1967, John Simon.
Cohen, Leonard, *Songs from a Room*, [CD], Rec. Oct. 1968, Bob Johnston, 1969.
Cohen, Leonard, *Songs of Love and Hate*, [CD], Rec. Sept. 1970, Bob Johnston, 1971.
Cohen, Leonard, *Live Songs*, [CD], Rec. 1970, 1972, Bob Johnston, 1973.
Cohen, Leonard, *New Skin for the Old Ceremony*, [CD], Rec. Feb. 1974, Leonard Cohen, John Lissauer, 1974.
Cohen, Leonard, *Death of a Ladies' Man*, [CD], Rec. June 1977, Phil Spector, 1977.
Cohen, Leonard, *Recent Songs*, [CD], Rec. Apr. 1979, Leonard Cohen, Henry Lewy, 1979.
Cohen, Leonard, *Various Positions*, [CD], Rec. June 1984, John Lissauer, 1984.
Cohen, Leonard, *I'm Your Man*, [CD], Rec. Aug. 1987, Leonard Cohen, Roscoe Beck, Jean-Michel Reusser, Michel Robidoux, 1988.
Cohen, Leonard, *The Future*, [CD], Rec. Jan. 1992, Leonard Cohen, Steve Lindsey, Bill Ginn, Leanne Ungar, Rebecca de Mornay, Yoav Goren, 1992.
Cohen, Leonard, *Ten New Songs*, [CD], Sharon Robinson, 2001.
Cohen, Leonard, *Old Ideas*, [CD], Rec. 2007–11, Patrick Leonard, 2012.
Cohen, Leonard, *Can't Forget*, [CD], Rec. 2012–13, Mark Vreeken and Ed Sanders, 2015.
Cohen, Leonard, *Popular Problems*, [CD], Rec. 2014, Patrick Leonard, 2014.
Cohen, Leonard, *You Want It Darker*, [CD], Rec. 2015–16, Adam Cohen and Patrick Leonard, 2016.

3

Hank and Jesus: The Integral Roles of Religion and the History of Country Music in the Lives and Careers of Contemporary Country Artists

Gillian Kelly

Introduction

Religion and country music's own history are consistently entwined within the genre, a style of popular music which perpetually sits on the cusp of the secular and the sacred. Indeed, this has remained an ongoing dichotomy in the imagery and music of commercial country music performers for the past century. This chapter focuses on artists Hank Williams, Alan Jackson, Brad Paisley and Eric Church in order to examine how the commercial and secular repeatedly infiltrate the sacred within the genre and what this tells us about country music as a cultural medium. Moreover, exploring the central links between religion and country music's history through these artists opens up wider debates concerning country music's place within popular music and popular culture.

To contextualize and inform these key arguments, I begin with a brief history of the genre, although the main focus is the paradoxical nature of masculine renditions of mainstream country music as evidenced by the artists I have chosen to focus on. Collectively (and derogatorily) labelled 'bro-country', in response to their assemblage of songs about beer, trucks and objectifying women, male artists are often dismissed as shallow and misogynistic, thus feeding into the genre's ubiquitous patriarchal associations. Yet, an exploration of their back catalogues unearths a rich array of songs covering a sundry of social issues (including poverty, war and abortion) as well as dominant or subordinate religious themes reflecting the individual artist's beliefs and background as well as the genre's history. Additionally, country music's past is closely linked to religion, through the legacy repertoire of historical artists and the extensive references made to them in the music of today's artists. Although country music has become more secular in its focus over the decades, many mainstream artists remain deeply embedded in Christian culture. Using textual analysis to 'read' both the song lyrics and artists' images, this chapter draws on methodologies developed across studies of popular music, gender, stardom and religion in popular culture. Although there remains a lack of scholarly texts on modern country artists, existing academic writings on the genre's history and its relationship with religion help inform this chapter.

Before commencing, I include a short disclaimer that, as in Sheila J. Nayar's work, the terms sacred, holy and spiritual are used here interchangeably, as this is how country music tends to employ them. As Nayar points out, and as I am fully aware, these terms have 'independent, nuanced intellectual histories of their own', but here they are treated 'as fairly synonymous' (2012: 5). Nayar continues that these concepts are 'highly resistant to meaningful definition because they can be so personal and mean so many things', resulting in them becoming 'less things than *thresholds*', thus making them extremely challenging to unpack in writing (2012: 6). Similarly, Christopher Partridge notes that 'the sacred' and 'religion' are often taken to mean the same despite their not being interchangeable terms. He suggests that the term 'sacred' relates to absolute ideas understood to be set apart from the rest of social life and which exert a profound moral claim over people's lives, whether embedded within religious discourses or not (2015: 39). Nevertheless, these terms do tend to be used interchangeably within country music so this is how they will be employed here.

In the beginning (Genesis 1:1)

Country music sensibility is interwoven in both biography and history, and while religious and historical tropes will be explored primarily through the lens of modern commercial country music, a historical overview of the genre's key moments and performers helps to identify when these tropes began emerging and how they inform the positioning of the genre today. Of particular importance is the early commercial success of Jimmie Rodgers and the gospel-influenced The Carter Family almost 100 years ago, and later Hank Williams, who, 65 years after his death, still remains the genre's most referenced artist.

The history of country music is deeply rooted in Celtic folk and Appalachian mountain music: its heritage can be traced back to 1800s travelling shows, European settlers in America and, most importantly for this study, gospel and church music of the early 1900s. In 1922, the first country music recording, 'Sallie Gooden' by fiddle player 'Eck' Robertson, coincided with the advent of the South's earliest radio station, WSB in Atlanta, which began broadcasting in March of the same year. By the close of the 1920s, the commercialization of country music had led to the success of recording artists Rodgers and The Carter Family (Joyner 2009). David Lee Joyner suggests that, while Rodgers's music encompassed a more heterogeneous 'blues and pop-orientated southwestern style', The Carter Family's leaned towards a 'moralistic and traditional south eastern conservative style' (2009: 133), thus forging two distinctive paths still evident in today's country music: the secular and the sacred. Jocelyn R. Neal slightly disagrees with this notion, proposing that although The Carter Family's image embodied 'homespun, wholesome goodness' of 'regular folks' who came down from the mountains singing gospel songs and treasured old ballads, this was not entirely the case (2009: 8). However, it did prove to be a substantial element of how country music began to build its image commercially.

As Maxine L. Grossman points out, although the 'religious core' of commercial country music dates back to this founding generation, The Carter Family actually performed both secular and religious songs with 'the same intonations and stylings, which erased many of the differences of content' (2005: 278). Likewise, Rodgers's background also has strong ties to religion since he married a minister's daughter and several of the songs he recorded were written by his sister-in-law, a church organist (Neal 2009: 6). Furthermore, when Rodgers came to record the 1927 session that launched his career, it was in the famous Studio 1 in Camden, New Jersey, formally a Trinity Baptist Church (Neal 2009: 10). Also, Neal's labelling Rodgers as 'the avowed Father of Country Music' (with a capital F), also brings into play religious connotations which evoke God/the Heavenly Father (2009: 2). Thus, although The Carter Family have been viewed as an exclusively religious band and Rodgers as grittier and secular, this all suggests that country music's linking of the secular and sacred has been present since the genre's formation, while being paradoxically embodied by individual acts.

Further alluding to the artists' backgrounds, Neal compares popular music to religion in that they both need to establish conception stories, 'those explanations of origination that contain the most valued seeds of ideology and that take on mythical proportions among followers' (2009: 8). For country music this was the commercial recordings The Carter Family and Rodgers made in Bristol, Tennessee in 1927, which were then distributed nationwide. On 16 August 1971, a monument was erected in Bristol honouring this event, thus cementing its key importance in the genre's history, proving these artists to be 'seminal in the history of the genre' and acting as 'a touchstone for country music's retelling of its own history' (Neal 2009: 7). Monuments also have strong connotations to religion and the past in that they have a similar function to shrines or tombs, while helping to preserve the past in the present and for the future.

Despite his death in 1933, the 1950s reappearance of Rodgers's 1928 song 'In the Jailhouse Now' fashioned Rodgers as 'an important figurehead in the industry's rush to canonize its own past' (Neal 2009: 174).[1] Indeed, the song continues to be sampled by contemporary artists such as Brad Paisley, a key figure in this chapter. On his 2007 album *5th Gear*, the guitar solo which concludes the track 'Mr. Policeman' fades into Paisley's reimagined version of Rodgers's earlier song. Neal suggests that no one embodied country's new approach more than Paisley, since he 'laced his debut album with retro sounds: western swing, honky-tonk two-steps, an unabashedly sincere gospel tune, and his own blistering performance on the pink paisley Fender guitar, itself a throwback to the 1960s' (2009: 116).

Virinder S. Kalra declares that the strong link between the sacred and the secular in music results in the sacred quality of a song being subjective. Thus, while some may view a particular song as sacred, others might find it 'disrespectful or even actively despise it' (2015: 8).[2] Kalra's theory can be applied to countless country songs,[3] perhaps none more so than Paisley's controversially titled 'Those Crazy Christians'. As a singer-songwriter, Paisley is known for lyrics that provoke a response from his listeners, making them re-evaluate their actions and life choices (for example, see the controversy over his duet with LL Cool J titled 'Accidental Racist'). Thus, even before hearing a word of the song, the title arouses the audience's curiosity, and in the Christian centric world of country music this seems to be quite a risk. Uploads of the song onto the internet site YouTube garnered mixed reviews[4] but, as in the case of the controversy over Little Big Town's 'Girl Crush', it is obvious that many of the commenters have failed to listen to the words of the song and instead have based their review exclusively on the title. Although beginning with what at first appears to be the protagonist's criticisms of traditional Christian practices (loud church bells on Sunday mornings, praying before eating or sleeping, and so on) it is, in fact, an extremely pro-Christian song commenting on the strength of Christians who 'risk their lives in Jesus' name' and have a proclivity for forgiveness. Obviously, this is a simplistic, and perhaps stereotypical, view of the Christian faith, but here it helps to get an important message across to a mainstream audience. Equally, as Tia DeNora suggests, music can serve as 'a kind of template against which feelings, perception and social situation are created and sustained' and can be used as a reference for clarification of identity (2000: 44), which can certainly be applied to Christians embracing the ideas in Paisley's song. Besides, the country community obviously did not object to Paisley's track since it features on the compilation album *Country Faith Volume 1* (an aural tie-in with Deborah Evans Price's 2015 book of the same name). Interestingly, the album features mainstream artists known for recording religiously themed songs, and yet the tracks included are primarily secular (Carrie Underwood's 'See You Again' and Craig Morgan's 'That's What I Love About Sunday' for example).[5] Moreover, on Amazon UK the CD is listed under the category 'religious and gospel', thereby further blurring the lines between the secular and the sacred in contemporary country music.

Sing for the joy of the Lord (Psalm 95:1)

In 2005, Michael Gilmour noted a marked increase in the study of religion and popular culture. Indeed, academic studies on religion within film studies has exploded over the last fifteen years and, in terms of popular music, several journals and monographs explore expressions of religion within genres such as rock music and heavy metal (Cope 2010). As evidenced by this series from Bloomsbury, this increase has not only continued to mount in the subsequent decade or so since Gilmour's original assertion, but proves that there is a stronger emphasis on religion within popular music than ever before (Brown and Hopps 2018; Joyner 2009; Kalra 2015). That said, there remains a lack of scholarly studies on how religion works within country music, especially contemporary country music. This is surprising given the fact that the genre is, and always has been, ingrained with religious tropes and symbolism.

While popular music in general is often derided as unworthy of academic study, as highlighted by Simon Frith throughout his influential monograph *Taking Popular Music Seriously* (2007), country music in particular is prone to scorn and ridicule more than many other popular music forms (Washburne and Derno 2004).[6] Even today, almost a century since its inception as a commercial musical form, country music continues to be discussed in terms of its being simplistic, backward and corny.[7] It is often spoken about by those outside the genre in outmoded terms such as 'country and western',[8] and is enacted parodically via line dancing and moribund tropes of wives leaving and dying dogs.[9] Although these themes do continue to emerge every so often,[10] artists are increasingly recording tongue-in-cheek songs parodying these stereotypes, which in turn acts as a sort of in-joke for those aware of the genre's history. This reflexive awareness allows artists to tap into the genre's historical context, turning these tropes on their head by presenting them in innovative and self-knowing ways. Songs such as Paisley's 'I'm Gonna Miss Her (The Fishing Song)' and 'Little Boys Grow Up and Dogs Get Old' by Luke Bryan feature a leaving wife and a dying dog respectively, while Jake Owen's 'Yee Haw' offers a satirical take on the most overused phrase connected to the genre. Thus, country music's own history plays a key role in the output of today's artists, influencing their interaction with this stereotypical history.

As an important thread in this dialogue, country music seems both proud of and able to project that history into its current values and beliefs, as in Paisley's 'This is Country Music' and Bryan's 'What Makes You Country'. Along with many other acts such as Blake Shelton, Florida Georgia Line and Jason Aldean, these artists can be filed under a recently coined subcategory of country music labelled 'bro-country'.[11] The country equivalent of 'cock rock' (see Frith and McRobbie [1978] 1990), 'bro-country' connotes the genre's aggressive male domination while also suggesting homosocial bonds between (apparently) heterosexual men, thus complicating the overt straightness of the genre. Moreover, the output of these artists is a heterogenous blend of comedic songs, soaring ballads, drinking songs, songs referencing the genre's past and songs with religious themes, combinations of which often feature on the same album. So, what does this eclectic mix tell us about these artists individually and, more importantly, about the present state of the genre more generally?

As an example, Paisley's sophomore album *Part II* (2001) opens with 'I'm Gonna Miss Her', a comedic song about choosing between fishing and his wife (he chooses fishing). It is then followed by 'Two People Fell in Love', a ballad considering the fragility of human life and our truly arbitrary probabilities of ever existing by problematically (but that is for another study) suggesting that everyone exists because 'two people fell in love'. Given controversial issues such as rape or the illegality and risk of abortion we know that this is not true, but with the romantic demeanour and the childlike innocence of this suggestion (even though he was, at the time, a man in his thirties) we are asked to suspend our disbelief for the duration of the song, similar to escapist plays and movies. Concluding the album are 'Too Country' and 'The Old Rugged Cross'. The former ponders the state of country music in the millennium, highlighting the difficulty writers of more traditional country music face when trying to get their songs played on country radio. Legendary performers Bill Anderson (who co-wrote the song), Little Jimmy Dickens and George Jones join Paisley on the track.

The concept of country songs being *too* country for *country* radio is an ongoing and interesting debate,[12] although not one I have time to go into here, but it allows Paisley to be linked to artists and concepts of the past. The song also taps into religious themes by asking if the grace is too amazing or the steeple too tall. Finally, the album concludes with a live version of the traditional hymn 'The Old Rugged Cross', recorded by Paisley at the Grand Ole Opry, known as the 'Mother Church' of country music. Given this label, alongside the Opry's vast historical importance to the genre and its original location at the Ryman Auditorium (a converted church), it seems a particularly fitting setting for Paisley's rendition of this classic hymn.[13] Its location in Nashville, known as both 'Music City, USA' and the 'Buckle of the Bible Belt' also allows it to play an integral role within country music's changing but consistent identity.

The paradoxical nature of Paisley's music becomes most obvious when we compare his recordings of traditional hymns (several of which he uses to close his albums), as well as 'New Again' (with Sara Evans) and 'When I Get Where I'm Going' (featuring Dolly Parton) with the more comedic, co-written 'Long Sermon' (which suggests that 'ain't nothin' that'll test your faith like a long sermon on a pretty Sunday') or 'Those Crazy Christians'. Although different in form and nature, they help to link Paisley, and by extension modern country music, to religion by interweaving tradition with new modes of hearing and understanding the sacred in twenty-first-century America.

Christopher Partridge suggests that in Western culture, ideas of Christian theology are 'central to constructions of the sacred, the profane and mortality', further elaborating that mortality in popular music occulture is 'theologically nuanced' and contains overt links between sex, sin and death (2015: 38).[14] In Paisley's case, this is never more obvious than in 'Whiskey Lullaby', a duet with bluegrass artist Alison Krauss, which tells the story of a man drinking himself to death after discovering his wife cheating on him. Feeling guilt and remorse, she subsequently does the same until they are buried together below a willow tree as 'the angels sang a whiskey lullaby'. This line seems quite paradoxical, but one which strongly links the earthly to the ethereal and explores the idea of rest and peace following death. In the song's music video, we are introduced to a soldier returning from World War II to find his wife in bed with another man. As the track plays, images of the singing Paisley and Krauss are interjected by disjoined scenes of the man drinking heavily, which display the deterioration of his health and, ultimately, his death. As Krauss begins her verse, the point of view changes to the woman's and we are presented with a repeat performance, this time involving the wife, as she also succumbs to alcoholism. The historical wartime positioning of the video makes her behaviour perhaps more understandable for the viewer, and we even get the privileged view of seeing the regret on her face as she watches her husband walk out. Thus, the song overtly links sex, sin and death, while allowing the story of their painful earthly lives and violent, untimely deaths to be juxtaposed with the melodic harmonies of angels singing and promises of a better life in heaven through forgiveness and redemption.

Krauss duetted with another popular country musician, Alan Jackson, on the similarly titled 'The Angels Cried', a song with a very different theme and one relaying the birth of Jesus Christ. As a youth, Jackson primarily listened to gospel music, and at twelve began singing in church, a common theme running through the biographies of country musicians.[15] Since the start of his recording career in 1989, he has remained a key figure in country music's trajectory, recording both secular and sacred songs, as well as songs which unite the two.[16] In 2006, Arista record label convinced Jackson to commercially release an unpolished album of gospel songs he had recorded as a Christmas gift for his mother (Jackson 2007). Given the title *Precious Memories*, it reached number one in the Billboard country charts and was certified platinum, illustrating both a need and audience for this kind of recording. The album's cover art features a sepia image of a small church with Jackson sitting on the steps, holding a guitar. Almost merging with the front door, he could easily be missed, which suggests that he is not using his star image or status to sell the album. Indeed, Jackson is almost rendered invisible and at one with the church, signifying the integral part that religion plays in his life (a fact reinforced by his wife Denise Jackson in her 2007 book *It's All About Him*). The size difference between man and building, made more apparent by the photograph's low angle, further demonstrates the power of the church and Jackson's embodying the 'little man' he often sings about, consequently alluding to the David and Goliath bible story.[17] The album contains a range of his mother's favourite hymns, including 'What a Friend We Have in Jesus', 'The Old Rugged Cross' and 'In the Garden', all of which were also recorded by Paisley.

Jackson's twentieth, and latest, studio release, *Angels and Alcohol* (2015), encompasses several of the genre's key themes. Notably covering both the secular ('Mexico, Tequila and Me') and sacred ('When God Paints'), there is also a reference to Hank Williams ('Jim and Jack and Hank'). The latter song alludes to both the genre's and Jackson's own past since his single 'Midnight in Montgomery', released twenty-three years earlier, which communicates the story of a protagonist's possible interaction with Williams's ghost on the anniversary of the singer's untimely death. It is not until the song's final line that Williams is named, but several tropes used throughout guide the (knowing) listener. The 'Montgomery' of the title refers to Williams's burial place of Montgomery, Alabama, and although Jackson first sings about visiting a 'friend' there, the elaboration that he 'found his name' strongly implies his friend is deceased. Jackson's travelling to play a New Year's Eve show parallels Williams's final journey, since he too was on his way to play just such a show when he died in the backseat of his Cadillac. Additionally, Jackson's abstract description of travelling in a 'silver eagle' is evidently a reference to his tour bus, but it correspondingly provides a link to Williams by connoting the silver casket the latter's body was transported to Montgomery in, as well as suggesting the spiritual final journey to the afterlife. Thus, connecting life and death, as well as the past and the present. Moreover we are given an apt description of Williams when the protagonist is startled by the sudden and silent appearance of a drunken man wearing a Stetson, a Nudie suit,[18] shiny boots and 'haunted haunted eyes'; while later one of Williams's most famous songs is referenced when Jackson proposes that the whistle of a midnight train appears to be singing 'I'm So Lonesome I Could Cry'. Williams is indirectly referenced through the personification of the train, but in a two-fold way implying that Williams's vocals were as haunting and uneasy as a midnight train whistle. Co-written by Jackson, 'Midnight in Montgomery' is loaded with metaphors and poetic language while demonstrating his extensive knowledge of Williams's life, career, and the circumstances surrounding his death.

Creating a sense of authenticity, a widely discussed element of the genre (Peterson 1999), the song's music video features Jackson shining a torch on Williams's gravestone and concludes with the shadow of a man resembling the late singer moving across the grave after Jackson has returned to his bus. Further alluding to the past, the video was shot in black and white and we are given a close-up shot of the engraving on Williams's gravestone, which reads 'Praise the Lord – I Saw the Light', alongside the plaque featuring his pseudonym: Luke the Drifter, under which Williams recorded the majority of his gospel songs. This suggests that both men are buried here: the secular *and* sacred singers, embodied in one complex human being who died extremely young but continues to be celebrated today.

House of God (Genesis 28:19)

Since religious music is so fundamental to the lives of rural southerners, Bill C. Malone feels that it probably shaped secular songs and their performances as well. Noting that most southerners learn how to sing in church, he feels that 'country music has been subjected to no greater influence than southern religious life' (1985: 10). Grossman notes that 'the earliest training ground for many country singers is the church' with hymns and gospel songs historically providing 'a common pool of shared knowledge for country artists' (2005: 278). Indeed, as mentioned, most country musicians' biographies include details of their learning how to sing in church. Teresa L. Reed notes that 'music and religion are inextricably bound together ... so much so that it is impossible to imagine one without the other' (2003: 4), while David Fillingim explains that, 'because of the prominence of religious faith' of the people in this area, it has become known as the 'Bible Belt' (2003: 29). The fact that Nashville is known as the '*Buckle* of the Bible Belt' adds centrality and importance to religion's place in the city, while also connoting traditional cowboy attire though the notion of the belt buckle.

Performing or attending a show at Nashville's Grand Ole Opry, known as 'the home of country music', is regularly described as comparable to a religious experience for artists and fans alike. Described by Malone as 'the most important country music institution in the world' (1985: 470), between 1943 and 1974 the Opry was housed in the Ryman Auditorium, a converted tabernacle. The Ryman's official Instagram account overtly displays the iconography of country music by featuring a church emoji under its name, while regularly posting photographs of the building's stained-glass windows, pews and altar, alongside performers past and present. Furthermore, its tagline unites tradition, music and religion: 'Mother Church of Country Music. Where Bluegrass was Born. Where Johnny met June. Where artists dream to play'. The construction of the original Tabernacle is discussed in the Book of Exodus (Exodus 25–31 and 35–40), and when the Ryman was completed in 1892 it was originally called the Union Gospel Tabernacle, the lettering of which is still visible outside the building today. While Malone notes that many people view 'the historic old building ... as almost sacrosanct' (1985: 369), Charles K. Wolfe highlights the problems the Ryman faced as the genre became ever popular. The construction only held 3,500 people and, being an old church, it was cold in winter, hot in summer and required audiences to sit on 'hard wooden pews' for the duration of performances (1980: 280). In 1974, when the Grand Ole Opry House was built, it was created to resemble the Ryman but with more modern comforts added, such as cushioned pews. Using religious language to discuss the Ryman, Joyner suggests that the building 'still holds a mystique', with 'many country music pilgrims still flock[ing] to the old nineteenth-century tabernacle, and young artists still desir[ing] to perform and shoot videos there' (2009: 157). Joyner's words highlight the sustained importance of the building's history for fans and musicians, and the concept of the country music pilgrim is a fascinating one, given that the Bible is full of stories of pilgrims' journeys to find moral or spiritual significance and quests for the homeland.[19]

Since just after his death to the present day, Hank Williams has been the most consistently cited musician in country music history. His centrality to the genre cannot be overstated. Aside from this fact, he is also the artist most often associated with religion (alongside, perhaps, Johnny Cash). Significantly for this chapter, Williams wrote and released a number of both sacred and secular songs in his brief career, thus embodying the genre's most fundamental paradox, as will be discussed presently. The most enduring is also the one cited on his gravestone: 'I Saw the Light', which is frequently performed by a diverse range of artists at the Grand Ole Opry. Fittingly, Alan W. Bock declares Williams 'in some measure an evangelist, a witness to the faith, a teacher and a preacher' (2014: 183), strongly paralleling the description of Christ in the Bible passage Ephesians 4:11 which reads 'Now these are the gifts Christ gave to the church: the apostles, the prophets, the evangelists, and the pastors and teachers.'

(Hank and) God saw the light (Genesis 1:4)

While Barney Hoskyns feels that Hank Williams began his career as a 'backwoods gospel Roy Acuff-imitator (1987: 36), Charles Reagan Wilson notes that 'death-obsessed rock musicians who seem to court death do not typically write gospel music, but Hank Williams did' (1992: 117). Introduced to religious music through his mother, a church organist, Williams 'always loved and performed the hymns and gospel tunes which he heard in the Fundamentalist Baptist churches of his childhood' (Malone 1985: 239). Retaining much of this gospel singing throughout his career, Williams distinctively combined it with honky-tonk (Joyner 2009), thus highlighting his intense and lifelong struggles between the sacred and the secular and sin and salvation.

Partridge suggests that when well-known celebrities die, especially those with untimely deaths, people turn to mythic narratives to make sense of their passing. He proposes, for example, that there are two versions of Elvis Presley: 'Dead Elvis' and 'historical Elvis' which he compares to 'Christology['s] kerygmatic Christ (the proclaimed Christ of faith) [and] the Jesus of history' (2015: 137). Within country music, this concept is most fully realized through the figure of

Williams, whose untimely death at the age of twenty-nine, after a long battle with drug and alcohol abuse (partly due to his lifelong chronic pain from an undiagnosed case of spina bifida occulta), has helped him to obtain legendary status.

Although undoubtedly due in part to his premature death, the voracious interest in Williams that continues to this day cannot be exclusively put down to this since other artists have died young and failed to receive such unwavering attention. Nor is it exclusively due to his musical recordings – although, again, they play a significant role in his durability – since many of the genre's young fans know *of* Hank Williams but are unfamiliar with the titles of or lyrics to any of his songs. It is more obviously a combination of these factors, alongside the consistent references made to him in the music of other artists, that has aided in introducing Williams to subsequent generations of country music fans, while keeping him at the forefront of the genre more than sixty-five years after his passing.[20] Since his death, a deluge of songs citing Williams have been released, with an unprecedented fifteen recorded by friends and colleagues in 1953 alone (the year of his death). Some of these link Williams to religion ('Singing Teacher in Heaven', 'That Heaven Bound Train', 'There's a New Star in Hillbilly Heaven'), while others connect him with deceased predecessors ('Hank Williams Meets Jimmie Rodgers') or eternal life and immortality ('Hank Williams Will Live Forever').

As David Inglis notes, art has taken the place of religion in the lives of many people, with artists replacing 'prophets, saints and other religious figures as a character to admire and venerate' because of their 'privileged insights into "spiritual" affairs and matters that were out of the ordinary' (2005: 91). Likewise, Chris Rojek discusses hero worship and the birth of stars as the result of a longing for 'larger-than-life versions of ourselves, or superhuman gods' through our need for 'elevated, transcendent forms of meaning' (2012: 180). In their pioneering work on stardom, Edgar Morin (1969) and Richard Dyer (1979) suggest that with stars of silent cinema being depicted as gods and goddesses they achieved divinized status, a term strongly associated with Christian theology. This divinized status was largely due to the fact that performers' voices were not heard in early cinema, resulting in an ethereal aura around them and an otherworldly presence that was superhuman, but this is clearly not the case with recording artists. Michael Williams, who has written about stardom in relation to myth and classicism (2013), recently queried what has happened to the elevated, divinized form of stardom which was so compelling in the silent era (2017: 15). His book *Film Stardom and the Ancient Past: Idols, Artefacts and*

Epics concludes that this divinization does, in fact, still exist, only in an altered form that works for the sound era. The term idols, in the book's subtitle, has its origins in religious worship, but has often been used to describe cinematic and, more recently, sport and music stars.[21] Although predominantly focusing on film stardom, Williams's study does expand to music stars, most notably Beyoncé, a performer often depicted as a modern-day goddess and prone to hero worship from fans. Moreover, in her costuming and performances Beyoncé has depicted several goddesses of the past, including deity Oshun (the Yoruba goddess of fertility), Hindi goddess Durga, Yemoja and The Virgin Mary. Therefore, having a singing star, known primarily for her voice, both performing as past goddesses and being known as a modern goddess herself is significant in the development of modern stars being divinized.

In terms of fandom as a form of worship, Partridge suggests that commitment to a dead musician 'need not, and often does not, lead to transfiguration and the construction of mythic narratives' because, as studies of fandom as popular devotion indicate, 'a person can still organize his or her life around a commitment to a celebrity without the commitment becoming, in some sense, *religious* devotion' (2015: 139). Although he does suggest that such commitments can have similarities to religious ones, he also acknowledges that they do not progress much beyond fandom. Understanding this distinction is important, since not to do so can lead to a common confusion between fandom and religious conviction, supported by a mythic narrative.

When Williams unexpectedly died, his funeral was held 'amid a background of gospel singing' by fellow country artists Roy Acuff, Ernest Tubb, Carl Smith, Red Foley and the Statement Quartet, a gospel quartet from Georgia (Malone 1985: 243). At the time of his death, Williams's 'I'll Never Get Out of This World Alive' was in the charts, posthumously reaching number one, with his name and legacy remaining ubiquitous within the genre ever since through the music of others. After the initial releases from his peers after his death, the 1970s saw the next generation of artists bringing further tributes and references, most famously Waylon Jennings's 'Are You Sure Hank Done It This Way?'. It was during this decade that Williams's namesake son, Hank Williams Jr, also began his singing career.[22] He references Hank Sr in several songs, either as 'Hank' ('The Ballad of Hank Williams', 'Whiskey Bent and Hell Bound'), or 'my father' ('Family Tradition', 'All My Rowdy Friends (Have Settled Down)'). The latter cites several of his contemporaries (including Jennings), and referring to Hank Sr simply as 'my father' implies both strong religious connotations and the anticipation that listeners have prior knowledge of their relationship. Likewise, in order to understand George Jones's later release 'Who's Gonna Fill Their Shoes' knowledge of country music history is vital since it references Hank Sr as both 'Hank' and his lesser-known alter-ego Luke the Drifter (the pseudonym under which Williams recorded most of his gospel songs).

In 1999, almost fifty years after his death, The Hank Williams Museum opened in Montgomery, situated close to the earthly remains of Williams in the nearby Oakwood Cemetery Annex. The museum houses a range of Williams's clothing, photographs and other apparel, along with perhaps the ultimate artefact: the 1952 Baby Blue Cadillac in which he died. As the museum's centrepiece, the car symbolizes both Williams's life and death, acting as a shrine to the musician, particularly since the museum's rules state that it is prohibited to touch the car 'in which he made his final journey'.[23] Discussing community museums, Sarah Baker proposes that items often become part of a collection 'because they make a connection in a materialised form to the people they represent and can even stand in for the people themselves' (2015: 59); and this is certainly true of Williams's car (alongside other 'death cars' which are on display to the public). The small museum is the realized lifelong dream of dedicated fan Cecil Jackson, who met Williams several times in childhood and kept a selection of ephemeral material from the 1940s onwards which is now housed in the museum. Brandellero, Hoeven and Janssen suggest that DIY popular music-archiving such as this is 'representative of a shift from sacred to vernacular in collecting' (2015: 31), while Baker notes that the space of these archives and museums allow popular music's past to become enacted in the present (2015: 3). Baker's words are almost echoed by the official Hank Williams Museum website which states that the museum is 'a visit into the past, a past that continues today', implying Williams's omnipresence. It calls him 'one of the most powerful iconic figures in American Music', and with thousands of fans visiting his grave and the museum every year it gives a strong sense of pilgrimages by fans and followers.

With each subsequent generation of country artists, songs mentioning Williams continue to appear, thus keeping him ever present and ubiquitous. Recent songs citing him in the title include 'Hank Williams' Ghost' (Darrell Scott), 'Hank's Cadillac' (Ashley Monroe) and 'Hank Williams Lonesome' (Gord Bamford). However, the artist whose oeuvre most overtly links religion and the genre's history (including frequent references to Williams) is Eric Church. The following section conceptualizes Church's work as part of the larger concerns informing the genre in terms of artistic output, religious references and the affirmation of its own history.

On this rock I will build my church (Matthew 16:18)

Sheila J. Nayar proposes that, within human experience, the sacred 'implies a perceptual and affective set-apartness from everyday or ordinary experience', therefore 'pertaining less to religion than to an experience long identified with religion – and ergo, the philosophy of religion' (2012: 17). She further suggests that if the sacred is something separate or set apart from other things, then the profane is about the ordinary or the everyday (2012: 17). Within the oeuvre of many country music artists, the dichotomy of sacred and secular is ever present, even those earning the labels 'country-rock' or 'tough guys' such as Eric Church and Brantley Gilbert. While not all country songs focus on religion, many still address the topic in terms of faith, holy love, the afterlife/heaven, redemption or contrasting notions of sin and salvation. Most commonly, as with early commercial artists like The Carter Family, country albums continue to straddle the sacred and secular. This is usually achieved by including at least one religious song as an album track alongside some radio-friendly singles alluding to the artist's beliefs, though not a predominantly sacred song, such as Blake Shelton's 'God Gave Me You' or Chris Young's 'The Man I Want to Be' which tie the artist's love of God to romantic love.

This concluding section concentrates on the aptly named Eric Church as a final case study of the dichotomy between secular and sacred in the work of contemporary male country artists; but I could have chosen from the wealth of virile 'tough guys' who sing about an amalgamation of trucks, guns, women, Jesus and God. For example, the songs of the extremely masculine Tyler Farr range from 'Redneck Crazy' and 'C.O.U.N.T.R.Y.' to 'Raised to Pray' and 'I Should Go to Church Sometimes', while Brantley Gilbert's 'One Hell of an Amen' and 'Faith in You' conflict with his drinking songs 'Kick it in the Sticks' and 'Bottoms Up', and his most recent album title, *The Devil Don't Sleep*. Likewise, Blake Shelton's 'God Gave Me You' contrasts with the hypermasculine 'Kiss My Country Ass', while Justin Moore's macho tunes 'I Could Kick Your Ass' and 'Outlaws Like Me' strongly juxtapose with 'If Heaven Wasn't So Far Away' and 'Small Town, USA'. Thomas Rhett's chilled, youthful vibe of 'Crash and Burn' and 'T-shirt' is also present in 'Beer with Jesus', a song written by his father Rhett Akins, also a successful recording artist who released 'If Heaven Wasn't So Far Away' prior to Moore. Moreover, in Australian country singer Keith Urban's recent single 'John Cougar, John Deere, John 3:16' he declares that he learned everything he needs to know in life from John Cougar (a John Mellencamp album), John Deere (a tractor brand), and John 3:16 (the Bible passage which reads 'for God so loved the world, that he gave his only begotten Son, that whosoever believeth in him should not perish, but have everlasting life' [King James version]). However, given the consistently dominant themes of music and religion in Eric Church's work, alongside his rather fitting surname and the clever marketing of it, he provides the perfect example for discussing how modern male country artists can seamlessly weave dominant themes of religion and the genre's history into their work, while also remaining tough, modern and relevant for a diverse range of audiences.

Dave Urbanski quotes Johnny Cash as saying, 'Being a Christian isn't for sissies … it takes a real man to live for God – a lot more man than to live for the devil' (2003: xxii). Church is a modern 'tough guy' who regularly sings about both Jesus ('Like Jesus Does', 'Country Music Jesus') and country legends, including Cash ('Lotta Boot Left to Fill', 'Country Music Jesus'), Merle Haggard ('Pledge Allegiance to the Hag'), Willie Nelson ('Record Year'), Waylon Jennings ('Lotta Boot Left to Fill', 'Like Jesus Does') and Hank Williams 'Lotta Boot Left to Fill', 'Like Jesus Does', 'Record Year'), thus signifying that his music is steeped in tradition while exhibiting an overt awareness of its legacy. Similar to the artists of the 1970s Outlaw Movement (whom he often references), Church's star persona is anchored in his self-proclaimed position as an 'outsider' of the present-day Nashville scene, while paradoxically being a successful recording artist for EMI Nashville. Church opened the 49th annual Country Music Association Awards show (which is televised to millions of viewers), alongside Hank Williams Jr on the track 'Are You Ready for the Country?' Church's first line: 'talking to the preacher, said God is on your side' immediately links him to religion, while the song overall comments on the state of the music industry. Written by Neil Young for his 1972 album *Harvest*, Waylon Jennings later used it as the title track for his 1976 album, therefore it appears that the criticisms made about the industry then still apply in the new millennium. Church's album *The Outsiders* includes other songs questioning the ethics of the present-day country music industry, while correspondingly linking music to religion. In 'Devil Devil' Church proclaims that 'The Devil walks among us and Nashville is his bride', while the blasphemous 'That's Damn Rock and Roll' mentions a preacher, a shepherd boy and the infamous image of Cash giving the middle finger to a photographer while performing at Folsom Prison. Furthermore, the track's harmony vocals are reminiscent of a gospel choir. Linking with Joe L. Kincheloe's suggestion that we are currently being sold a 'new and improved Jesus', one who is both Americanized and 'a macho, kick-the-heathens'-ass savior' (2009: 15), in 'Country Music Jesus', Church stresses the genre's desperate need for a second coming: a 'long-haired hippie prophet preaching from the book of Johnny Cash'. The song, which alludes to revivals, revelations, the divine, believers and God, also features the sound of a gospel choir alongside hand clapping which add to the sacred nature of the song, while instruments such as the banjo retain the music's authentic 'country' feel. This reflects Robin Sylvia's suggestion that belonging to a musical subculture 'provides as all-encompassing an orientation to the world as any traditional religion' (2002: 4), as well as Partridge's belief that popular music has the ability to operate at the boundary of the sacred and the profane (2015: 39).

Church's 'Boot Left to Fill' plays on the words of Jennings's earlier track by commenting on current country music with: 'I don't think Waylon done it this way, and if he was here he'd say "hoss, neither did Hank"'. While a similar theme to Jones's 'Who's Gonna Fill Their Shoes', the boot allegory allows the footwear of choice to be 'countrified' while likewise suggesting that it is a much larger vessel that now needs filled, and hints at the arduous task that that will be.[24] The title of 'Like Jesus Does' alludes to the protagonist's realization that he is loved equally, and unconditionally, by both Jesus and his wife, no matter what sins he has committed. In this song, Church uses several metaphors to firmly integrate himself into both the legacy of country music ('I'm a long-gone Waylon [Jennings] song on vinyl') and religion ('I'm a back-row sinner at a tent revival'). These lines seamlessly blend into each other, demonstrating the creative ways in which Church's music repeatedly connects the sacred and the secular. It also indicates country music's dilemma as a cultural medium and Church's dilemma as a mainstream artist. Often alluding to his place as an 'outsider' of the current Nashville scene, Church reinforces this both via the title track of his album *The Outsiders* and 'Devil, Devil'. In the latter, which mentions a diverse range of country songs and artists of the past, he suggests, as quoted above, that the Devil and Nashville are intimately connected, before he tells Satan to 'go screw yourself, and then go straight to hell'. However, demonstrating his confusion and position as an earthly sinner, the song concludes by suggesting that the Devil is also part of him, and prays for an angel (i.e. a woman) to love the Devil out of him.

'Love Your Love the Most' is one of the most unromantic love songs, in which Church compares his love for his wife to several other things he loves, such as NASCAR, football, cold beer, fishing and Jack Daniels with Coke. In 'Pledge Allegiance to the Hag', he proposes that country music legend Merle Haggard is worthy of the same amount of respect as the US flag. Similarly, in 'A Man Who Was Going to Die Young', the song's protagonist, who has made countless bad decisions in his life, awakens on his thirty-sixth birthday wondering how he miraculously managed to outlive the two most referenced figures in country music: Hank and Jesus. This track is important for the ways it displays both the edgy and rebellious hypermasculinity side of Church's star persona with the more tender side showing quiet reflection as he expresses his unconditional, but completely heterosexual, love for Williams and Jesus, two men who died extremely young. Given the religious tropes present in Williams's life and music, along with the mythical notions still associated with him in death, the song powerfully demonstrates ways in which religion and popular culture continue to intertwine in country music, permitting the commercial to seep into the secular. Moreover, the fact that Church was thirty-six years old when recording the song gives it a sense of authenticity and autobiography, two more dominant themes in country music.

As demonstrated, Church's strong links to both religion and the genre's history are consistently anchored within his song lyrics. The title of his live album, *61 Days in Church*, plays on the fact that he shares his surname with the Christian building of religious worship, while his fan club is knowingly called The Church Choir. His official website sells 'Church Choir' merchandise, including T-shirts and guitar plectrums; however, although the website is accessible to all, the Church Choir page features a banner declaring that access is for 'members only', connotating a cult, private club or religious congregation. Moreover, as a youth Church's first job was in the furniture business, and he has recently released a line of furniture, with some pieces featuring lyrics to his songs. One particular piece, the Joanna Ottomon, reads: 'good girls never miss church', a rather tongue-in-cheek slogan with religious connotations while referring to Church's live concerts and the devotion of his female fans. Furthermore, these pieces made by hand out of wood allow Church a further, somewhat unusual, link to Jesus, who was a carpenter.[25] Common themes of a conflicted man wishing to repent, and the paradox of the sacred and secular are also strongly evident in 'Like Jesus Does', 'A Man Who Was Going to Die Young' and 'Devil, Devil', allowing Church to stand as a blueprint for other contemporary artists with a similar musical output and image, as discussed above.

Conclusion

This chapter examined the interplay between the thematic concerns of religion and country music's own history throughout the development of the genre as a commercial musical form over the past century, as well as exploring how the work of modern male country artists provides us with paradoxical yet interwoven examples of these notions today. As demonstrated, from its inception to the present-day, country music has established consistently strong ties to both religion and its own history, with imagery from the Bible, references to God, Jesus, Satan, the church and struggles between sin and salvation being evident at every phase of the genre's existence. While this may appear at first to manifest more overtly in the work of early commercial acts such as The Carter Family and subgenres like bluegrass, this chapter confirms how religion remains central today. Indeed, the genre has consistently tread a fine line between the secular and the sacred, while managing to appeal to a broad range of audiences including both Christians and atheists. Recent arguments in academia suggest that popular music has become a substitute for the ever-depleting institutional forms of religion (Kommers 2011) but, as this chapter has proven, country music is a popular genre which has successfully managed to combine the two seamlessly, and commercially, for almost a hundred years.

Given its mainstream appeal, contemporary country music's synthesis of the sacred and secular allows listeners to engage with, and perhaps find inspiration from religion in their everyday lives ('I Saw God Today' by George Strait, 'The Family Bible and the Farmer's Almanac' by Randy Travis), as well as in more traumatic situations when people often turn to, or against, God ('Concrete Angel' by Martina McBride, 'Alyssa Lies' by Jason Michael Carroll, 'Go Rest High on that Mountain' by Vince Gill), thus making religion more inclusive, accessible and acceptable to a wide demographic. As shown, religion is a key trope in the oeuvre and images of particular artists, present in their songs, music videos and album artwork. In addition, since country sensibility is interwoven into both biography and history, the genre's continuous development and deferential relationship with its own past has resulted in deceased artists such as Hank Williams, Waylon Jennings and Merle Haggard being introduced to a new generation of fans and followers through the work of contemporary artists. Thus, in conclusion, country music is a genre which has consistently been bound with religious discourse, tradition and knowledge of its own history, with themes portrayed in rhetorically religious and/or historical tropes. Despite its long, tangential and complex history, the entwining of the sacred and the secular has always been intrinsic to country music and remains so today.

Notes

1. Likewise, even in the twenty-first century contemporary country music is reiterating the importance of historical artists, with songs like Sunny Sweeney's 'Mama's Opry' referencing both Jimmie Rodgers and The Carter Family. The song also names several of their tracks including The Carter Family's rendition of the traditional hymns 'Rose of Sharon' (mentioned in Isaiah 35:1, Song of Solomon 2:1 and Ephesians 5:2) and 'Abide With Me', as well as The Carter Family's own composition 'Gospel Ships', thus connecting contemporary artists with historical ones through both music and religion.
2. In modern country music, Brad Paisley's controversially titled but strongly religious 'Those Crazy Christians' might fall under this category. The song is discussed in this chapter.
3. See, for example, Paul Brandt's 'Virgil and the Holy Ghost'.
4. Although no official YouTube video exists of this album track, a video uploaded by userLyricsHelp101 on 27 April 2013, https://www.youtube.com/watch?v=-wGPxSwqIl8 (accessed 15 November 2018), has had almost 2,000 views at the time of writing (including 1,300 likes and only 106 dislikes). Comments are mixed between non-Christians and Christians saying they love the song, and others saying they despise the song and, as a result, also despise Paisley.
5. Underwood, in particular, is known for religiously themed songs from her debut single 'Jesus Take the Wheel' to the more recent 'Something in the Water' and 'Church Bells', but these are also songs about everyday people in extraordinary circumstances who turn to God for help when they truly need it.
6. However, there have been recent shifts in the status of prominent country artists Taylor Swift and Blake Shelton. While Swift has moved fully into the genre of pop, Shelton is currently a judge on television talent show *The Voice*, was recently voted 'Sexiest Man in the World' by *People* magazine and is now half of a celebrity couple with pop singer Gwen Stefani (following his divorce from fellow country artist Miranda Lambert). Thus, these artists have progressed from country/subgenre artists into international stars, gaining a new set of listeners in the process, but also inviting some unwanted attention as 'sell-out' artists. Although Shelton's music is still deeply rooted in country, his 'Hollywood lifestyle' does not reflect the kind of life he sings about in recent single 'I Lived It' or similar tracks, although this song is supposed to be a reflection of his humble upbringing.
7. Labels that many contemporary country songs have poked fun at in their music.
8. This did not appear until much later in the genre's history (Neal 2009).
9. Some contemporary country songs which mention dying dogs are 'Tough Little Boys' by Gary Allen, 'The House that Built Me' by Miranda Lambert and 'Little Boys Grow Up and Dogs Get Old' by Luke Bryan.

10 Contemporary songs about wives leaving include comedic ones such as 'I'm Gonna Miss Her (The Fishing Song)' and 'Oh Yeah, You're Gone', both by Brad Paisley, as well as more soulful ballads including 'Tomorrow' by Chris Young and 'She Wouldn't Be Gone' by Blake Shelton.

11 Andrew Baker, in the article 'Despite Detractors, Bro-Country May Be a Bellwether of Nashville's Future' for *Variety* suggests that 'No one can quite agree where "bro-country" started, and most of its primary practitioners are hesitant to embrace the label' (26 November 2014). Available online: https://variety.com/2014/music/features/despite-detractors-bro-country-may-be-a-bellwether-of-nashvilles-future-1201364802/ (accessed 29 October 2018). While Jon Bream of the *Star Tribune (Minneapolis)* called it a 'new wave of mindless party songs – dubbed "bro-country" – [that] has prompted some frustrated country fans to change stations', while dubbing Luke Bryan its 'poster boy' (the full article is available on the *Commercial Appeal* website: https://web.archive.org/web/20140602052353/http://www.commercialappeal.com/news/2014/mar/09/luke-bryan-is-the-poster-boy-for-the-new (accessed 29 October 2018). *Time* magazine included an article by Adam Carlson in October 2014 titled '"Bro Country" Is Still Thriving, Even If Everyone Hates It', available online: http://time.com/3502546/florida-georgia-line-bro-country/ (accessed 29 October 2018). Even earlier than this, *Entertainment Weekly* published an article written by Grady Smith from 13 October 2013 that sought to list 'Every truck, beer, and "girl" reference on the current country chart' complete with links to the videos of said songs and a 'bro-rating' out of ten for each; available online: https://ew.com/article/2013/10/18/bro-country-beer-trucks-lyrics/(accessed 29 October 2018).

12 In 2012, Erin Duval wrote an article for the popular online country music news site *The Boot* titled 'This is Country Music?' which discusses the sound of the genre over the years, and also quotes various contemporary artists and their disapproval of the direction in which the genre is going. One such artist is Gary Allen, who suggests that country radio is to blame for the lack of variety in the genre as the key demographic for the genre is now 'soccer moms' and the strategy of big businesses to appeal to the masses. The article is available online: http://theboot.com/controversial-country-music/ (accessed 29 October 2018).

13 This song fades out at the end of Paisley's album and fades back in at the start of his subsequent release, *Mud on the Tires* (2003), released two years later. The pattern of his album tracks continues and ends with a fade out of the traditional Southern gospel song 'Farther Along' arranged by Paisley, thus more fully integrating him into both the music and religion.

14 See Florida Georgia Line's 'H.O.L.Y' and Kane Brown's 'Heaven' for examples of contemporary country songs that sound religious but are actually based on sexual pleasure.

15 Country singers mentioning they got their start singing in church include Vince Gill and Carrie Underwood, as well as Ronnie Dunn of the duo Brooks and Dunn, who almost became a preacher before becoming a musician.
16 Other popular artists to release albums composed solely of religious songs include Dolly Parton and Hillary Scott from the group Lady Antebellum.
17 See, for example, Jackson's songs 'Small Town Southern Man', 'Little Man' and 'Little Bitty'.
18 Nudie was a famous Nashville designer who created unique, usually bejewelled, suits.
19 Country musician, historian and former son-in-law of Johnny Cash, Marty Stuart named his 1999 album *The Pilgrim* and Helen Morale's recent book *Pilgrimage to Dollywood* (2014) captures the essence of fans' almost spiritual journeys to sites of interest relating to their favourite artists.
20 The recent biopic *I Saw the Light* (2015, dir. Marc Abraham) starring Tom Hiddleston as Williams also brought his life story and music to a wider audience.
21 Moreover, as is the case with the title of the television talent show *American Idol*, this may even include people who are not (yet) famous, such as country artist Carrie Underwood who became a star after winning the contest in 2005 and who remains one of the genre's most successful artists today.
22 Alluding to his own musical style, Hank Williams Jr released the autobiographical song 'Blues Man', which was later covered by Alan Jackson.
23 The Hank Williams Museum: http://www.thehankwilliamsmuseum.org/ (accessed 21 November 2018).
24 In this song Church also discusses modern performers who sing about Johnny Cash, adding 'The Man in Black would have whipped your ass'. Since Jason Aldean had released a song called 'Johnny Cash' two years previously, listeners are left to speculate who Church is referring to.
25 Furthermore, Jesus as manual labourer aligns him with the working-class country community, and is an occupation often associated with him in country songs, such as 'It Wasn't His Child' (which was recorded by both Sawyer Brown and Trisha Yearwood), and James Bonamy's 'Jimmy and Jesus'. One of the original 'young country' performers of the 1990s, Bonamy released two mainstream albums, which including the religiously themed songs 'When God Dreams', 'Little Blue Dot' and 'Daddy Never Had a Chance in Hell' before leaving the business. He later became a Worship Pastor at Christ Fellowship in Florida.

References

Baker, S. (2015), 'Affective Archiving and Collective Collecting in Do-it-Yourself Popular Music Archives and Museums', in S. Baker (ed.), Preserving Popular Music Heritage: Do-it-Yourself, Do-it-Together, 46–61, London and New York: Routledge.
Bock, A. W. (2014), 'Excerpt from I Saw the Light: the Gospel Life of Hank Williams (1977)', in P. Huber S. Goodson and D. M. Anderson (eds), *The Hank Williams Reader*, 181–3, Oxford: Oxford University Press.
Brandellero, A., A. Hoeven and S. Janssen (2015), 'Valuing Popular Music Heritage: Exploring Amateur and Fan-Based Preservation Practices in Museums and Archives in the Netherlands', in S. Baker (ed.), *Preserving Popular Music Heritage: Do-it-Yourself, Do-it-Together*, 31–45, London and New York: Routledge.
Brown, D. and G. Hopps (2018), *The Extravagance of Music*, London: Palgrave Macmillan.
Cope, A. L. (2010), *Black Sabbath and the Rise of Heavy Metal Music*, Farnham: Ashgate.
DeNora, T. (2000), *Music in Everyday Life*, Cambridge: Cambridge University Press.
Dyer, R. (1979), *Stars*, London: British Film Institute.
Fillingim, D. (2003), *Redneck Liberation: Country Music as Theology*, Macon, GA: Mercer University Press.
Frith, S. (2007), *Taking Popular Music Seriously*, Oxon and New York: Ashgate.
Frith, S. and A. McRobbie ([1978] 1990), 'Rock and Sexuality', reprinted in S. Frith and A. Goodwin (eds), *On Record: Pop, Rock and the Written Word*, 371–8, London: Routledge.
Gilmour, M. J. (ed.) (2005), *Call Me the Seeker: Listening to Religion in Popular Music*, New York and London: Continuum.
Grossman, M. L. (2005), 'Jesus, Mama, and the Constraints on Salvific Love in Contemporary Country Music', in M. J. Gilmour (ed.), *Call Me the Seeker: Listening to Religion in Popular Music*, 267–98, New York and London: Continuum.
Hoskyns, B. (1987), *Say It One Time for the Brokenhearted: The Country Side of Southern Soul*, Glasgow: William Collins Sons and Co.
Inglis, D. (2005), *Culture and Everyday Life*, London and New York: Routledge.
Jackson, D. (2007), *It's All About Him*, Nashville, TN: Thomas Nelson.
Joyner, D. L. (2009), *American Popular Music*, 3rd edn, New York: McGraw-Hill.
Kalra, V. S. (2015), *Sacred and Secular Musics: A Postcolonial Approach*, Oxford, New York, New Delhi and Sydney: Bloomsbury.
Kincheloe, J. L. (2009), 'Selling a New Improved Jesus: Christotainment and the Power of Political Fundamentalism', in S. R. Steinberg and J. L. Kincheloe, *Christotainment: Selling Jesus Through Popular Culture*, 1–22, Boulder, CO: Westview Press.
Kommers, H. (2011), 'Hidden in Music: Religious Experience and Pop Festivals', *Journal of Religion and Popular Culture*, 23 (1): 14–26.
Malone, B. C. (1985), *Country Music U.S.A.*, rev. version, Austin, TX: University of Texas Press.

Morale, H. (2014), *Pilgrimage to Dollywood: A Country Music Road Trip Through Tennessee*, Chicago, IL and London: University of Chicago Press.

Morin, E. (1969), *The Stars: An Account of the Star System in Motion Pictures*, New York: Grove Press.

Nayar, S. J. (2012), *The Sacred and the Cinema*, London and New York: Bloomsbury.

Neal, J. R. (2009), *The Songs of Jimmie Rodgers: A Legacy in Country Music*, Bloomington, IN: Indiana University Press.

Partridge, C. (2015), *Mortality and Music: Popular Music and the Awareness of Death*, London and New York: Bloomsbury.

Peterson, R. A. (1999), *Creating Country Music: Fabricating Authenticity*, Chicago, IL and London: University of Chicago Press.

Price, D. E. (2015), *Country Faith Christmas*, Washington, DC: Regnery Faith.

Reed, T. L. (2003), *The Holy Profane: Religion in Black Popular Music, Kentucky: Religion in Popular Music*, New York and London: Continuum.

Rojek, C. (2012), *Fame Attack: The Inflation of Celebrity and its Consequences*, London: Bloomsbury.

Sylvia, R. (2002), *Traces of the Spirit: The Religious Dimensions of Popular Music*, New York and London: New York University Press.

Urbanski, D. (2003), *The Man Comes Around: The Spiritual Journey of Johnny Cash*, Lake Mary, FL: Relevant Books.

Washburne, C. J. and M. Derno (2004), *Bad Music: The Music We Love to Hate*, New York and London: Routledge.

Williams, M. (2013), *Film Stardom, Myth and Classicism: The Rise of Hollywood's Gods*, Basingstoke: Palgrave Macmillan.

Williams, M. (2017), *Film Stardom and the Ancient Past: Idols, Artefacts and Epics*, London: Palgrave Macmillan.

Wilson, C. R. (1992), 'Digging Up Bones: Death in Country Music', in M. A. McLaurin and R. A. Peterson, *You Wrote My Life: Lyrical Themes in Country Music*, 113–29, Philadelphia: Gordon and Breach.

Wolfe, C. K. (1980), 'Modern Country', in P. Carr, *The Illustrated History of Country Music*, 276–339, New York: Dolphin Books.

4

Above the Clouds: Discourses of the Spiritual and the Religious in the Lyrics of Paul Weller

Paul Spicer

From political sniping to prophecies of social apathy and hopelessness, Paul Weller has continually offered us shrewd observations of and an empathetic take on British life. His lyrics have had a profound effect on his audience, evoking the stresses and strains of the present, and their hopes and dreams for the future. This chapter will explore Paul Weller's relationship with religion and spirituality through his lyrics, drawing primarily on late-period Jam recordings and his earlier solo work (1991–5). A great number of Weller's songs contain rich spiritual meanings. Writing primarily from an omnist[1] perspective, he is able to transcend monotheism,[2] combining various strands of doctrine which allow a sense of spiritual freedom and avoids his words being confined to one particular religious outlook. This is an area of his work which has remained constant from the late 1970s but has thus far been largely unacknowledged. Yet faith is a crucial component of Weller's more mature songwriting and is something he has relied on heavily, particularly during the early years of his solo career. It is also important to question the axiological characteristics of the artist's personal values as represented through the lyrics, with a view to addressing how they represent his inner thoughts and spiritual desires.

It is generally acknowledged that Weller is a skilful social observer, whose work can be likened to that of earlier writers such as the Kinks's Ray Davies and the Beatles's John Lennon. He has commentated on the volatility of 1970s life in songs such as 'Bricks and Mortar' (1977), 'Down in the Tube Station at Midnight' (1978), 'Saturday's Kids' (1979) and 'Man in the Corner Shop' (1980); offered faint hope in the lyrics of 'When You're Young' (1979) and 'The Gift' (1982); and warned against negativity and apathy in '"A" Bomb in Wardour Street' (1978), 'Scrape Away' (1980) and 'Running on the Spot' (1982). With his band The Style Council, Weller changed direction rather radically, replacing indirect wordplay and metaphor with unmistakeable vitriol aimed at government policy and voter apathy. The 'Council' era could be viewed as a call to arms for all with whom Weller identified during his Jam days: in particular, those suffering oppression under Prime Minister Margaret Thatcher and her war against the working classes. Paradoxically, despite the polemic of the Style Council songs, its broader frame of musical reference lacked the directness of The Jam's uncompromising sound, and for some Jam fans this musical transformation diluted the meaning behind Weller's words. As broadcaster and Jam fan Gary Crowley notes, the band 'confused and infuriated their fans to the point of apathy … too many views for the politically fatigued public to keep up with' (2006).

Weller's early solo years saw a reinvention, not just musically but also in terms of his lyrical style. This period also witnessed a change of perspective, from social critique to introspective reflection. The transformation was chronicled through songs such as 'Into Tomorrow' (1991), 'The Weaver' (1993) and 'Has My Fire Really Gone Out?' (1993): self-critical observations, which questioned morals, drive, vision and passion. The aforementioned examples exemplify the lyrical content of the first three solo albums; *Paul Weller* (1992), *Wild Wood* (1993) and *Stanley Road* (1995). The recordings not only contain some of Weller's finest words, as he began to explore personal issues formerly given little credence, they represent him at his most open, and soul-searching. Notably the lyrics were deeply spiritual confessions, drawing on religious imagery and metaphor and thus combining self-doubt with questions of being. These recurring lyrical motifs became an integral component of his songwriting and can clearly be heard in songs such as 'Above the Clouds' (1992), '(Can You Heal Us), Holy Man' (1993) and 'The Changingman' (1995).

To explore in depth the themes set out above, contemporary sources drawn from the popular music press, broadcast interview material, religious publications and journals will be used. This chapter will identify the relationship between Weller's early solo work and the incorporeal by using a number of key themes and songs to establish a connection between the artist, his life and spirituality. Close textual analysis of 'Above the Clouds' and 'The Changingman' will expose a profound literary relationship to Buddhist and Christian doctrine respectively.

Such a study is not without its challenges. In a recent XS Manchester interview with the musician and DJ Clint Boon, Boon asks 'Are you a religious type of man or not?', to which Weller replies, 'No, no I'm not, not really, no, not any kind of organized religions, no. It's a more spiritual thing. I'm up for being part of the earth and part of the universe as well, we're just part of a cycle really' (2017). These ideas, as the chapter will show, is a view that has been considered (and rejected), by various music writers, and even by Weller himself over the years. But as this chapter will discuss, there is a deep connection with religion and spirituality which resonate profoundly in his later lyrics. The intention of this chapter is not to argue that Weller is a Christian, or a Buddhist, but to establish how much Weller, consciously or unconsciously, draws upon various aspects of religious thought and spirituality, and how this manifests through his words.

Time for truth – axiology, The Jam and The Style Council

When Paul Weller appeared on *Later with Jools Holland* in July 1993, many had thought they had seen the last of the ex-Jam and Style Council frontman. As it has been well documented, the latter part of the 1980s proved a trying time for Weller, both professionally and personally. In the UK, the cultural and personal impact of The Jam cannot be overstated; throughout the five years of the band's professional existence, they connected to their audience through the music, but arguably and more importantly, through Weller's lyrics. The lyrical content of songs such as 'Saturday's Kids' (The Jam 1979) and 'That's Entertainment' (The Jam 1980) came from a place that was instantly recognizable to many. Such was the integrity of these lyrics, that they could have only have been written by someone who understood the hopes, fears, desires and, most importantly, the lives of his audience. This honesty drove Weller's lyrics into the heart of the fans, connecting on both a social and emotional level. Gilbert and Pearson note that such honesty is crucial if an artist is to be considered authentic, and that when writing, they 'must speak the truth of their (and others') situations … [the singer's] fundamental role was to represent the culture from which he comes' (1999: 164–5). I would contend that Weller did this throughout The Jam period, and while many other popular bands of the period were singing about far distant beaches, mysterious European capital cities and cocktail bars, Weller chose to convey emotive issues with an ethical social conscious. He wrote about people and for people, using his working-class experiences as a foundation for his words. Examples of this kind of writing are identifiable in songs across all five Jam studio albums. With the exception of a handful of the earlier lyrics, Weller does not position himself as the central focus. Lyrics such as those found in 'Going Underground' (1980), explore the judgement of others; 'Some people might say my life is in a rut … Some people might say that I should strive for more' (Weller 1980). Other songs, such as 'Thick as Thieves' (1979), highlight the strength and fragility of teenage friendship and begin with hope by expressing the strength of formative relationships: 'Times were ... tough', he sings, 'we were ... close and nothing came between us or the world'. However, by the song's final verse the protagonist's personal ideologies and passions have changed. Weller is ambiguous, leaving us to fill in the gaps in this crushing finale. Highlighting how 'something came along' that changed his/her mind, Weller concludes how 'we seemed to grow up in a flash of time / While we watched our ideals helplessly unwind'.

Friendship is also explored in The Jam's 1980 hit 'Start!' of which John Reed, in his book *Paul Weller: My Ever Changing Moods*, notes deals with 'the importance of human contact – of connecting socially – and whether that could be achieved in a pop record' (1996: 106). In addition to these themes are the kitchen-sink observations on the mundane, in 'Private Hell' (1979), a lyric which explores a housewife's personal demons and her downward spiral into depression through 'Valium hazes ... catalogues, and coffee', and 'The Planner's Dream Goes Wrong' (1982), a stark and uncompromising commentary of contemporary architecture, social housing and urban decay. Here, Weller talks of the dream of building communities, but in reality, with 'the piss stench hallways and broken down lifts ... the planners dream went wrong'.

These songs are rooted in celebratory and often plaintive expressions of the everyday, expressing the reality of a lived experience. In the documentary *Highlights and Hang Ups* (1994), Billy Bragg considers how this kind of writing helps to form a bond between fan and artist. Discussing Weller's lyrics, he contends: 'if you want to write stuff that connects with a lot of people, you need to touch their experience pretty deep ... you do it by going as deep as you can in your own experience, because inside, we have all experienced similar sorts of things' (1994). Such socially conscious writing in popular music can shape individual's lives and has done much to cultivate and sustain loyal fan subcultures. Whether it be Bob Dylan, John Lydon or Morrissey, the power of the lyric is capable of marshalling empathy and self-identification. Weller's best writing – poetic, deeply emotive, spiritual – is presented with commitment and belief, which is crucial to its power to communicate. The directness of his lyrics is also vital, and Weller does not waste the space he has to express his thoughts: an approach promoted by the philosopher Samuel Hart who writes: 'We detest plethoras of words, redundant expressions, metaphysical excursions in a realm of essences, and reject any truth which remains a private, intuitive experience' (1971: 34). Directness, honesty and a profound use of language identify Weller not only as a seasoned wordsmith, but also indicate a strong concern for others, and a principled stance on cultural issues.

For Weller, the importance of artistic integrity has remained a key component of his creative process. As Vic Garbarini notes in *Musician*, 'he [Weller] realises that he's got to live his ideals before he can preach them' (1984: 38). This is a matter which has been of great importance to composers for centuries. The idea of integrity – or the honest artist as spokesperson – has been discussed from Aristotle debating the role that the musician plays in formalizing a citizen's *ethos* (Mathiesen 1984: 264–79), to Tom Cox highlighting the lack of emotional veracity in the music of the Smashing Pumpkins (1999: 24). Weller's beliefs, his single-mindedness and his spiritual honesty moves and influences his audience in a moral way redolent of Albrecht Riethmüller who, in *Music Beyond Ethics*, posits that the *ethos* of music is multifunctional, firstly allowing an individual to question their own morals, and secondly to help them to understand an era, a culture or community (2008: 169–76). Although Riethmüller's position is a historical one, the ethical question is raised consistently by Weller through his lyrics. For example, 'To Be Someone' (1978) questions the writer's reaction to fame and its perils, as well as the fear of loss – a topic Weller revisits during his early solo career, and one explored later in this chapter.

When Paul Weller split from The Jam in 1982 many were confused as to why – only five years and six albums into their career, at the height of their powers and with an army of dedicated fans behind them – they had disbanded. Talking of the split during the documentary *Thick as Thieves: Personal Situations with The Jam* (2012), fan John Abnett recalls how it was like the 'world had come to end'. Elucidating further, he notes how the band had 'been [his] life for five years … everything was based around The Jam'. However, Weller wanted to reinvent himself artistically and went on to form The Style Council, an antithesis to The Jam in every respect. The Style Council's early releases had been met with general positivity across the music press but some dissenters found Weller's new project a very difficult listening experience. Such was the eclecticism of the initial Style Council offerings it appeared, musically at least, that Weller was in a state of confused transition. In a 1984 *NME* review of *Café Bleu* (1984), Hector Cook wrote: 'One minute I hear "Strength Of Your Nature" and think Paul Weller's cracked it, next I'm hearing some snippet of Blue Note clone-work and I can't fathom what he wants or expects out of such faceless music …' (1984). But what had really alienated fans was his complete rejection of The Jam, a band in which many had invested so much personal and spiritual currency.

In an interview with Dean Chalkley of *Mojo*, Weller notes that although he did care how the fans felt, to move on in life he had to be selfish (2010: 83). This represented a 'no looking back policy' and total rejection of The Jam, alienating fans who had given the band a voice. However, on The Style Council's debut album *Café Bleu,* Weller had performed not just a musical, but also a lyrical volte-face, and the album's themes were as varied as the music. Love songs such as 'You're the Best Thing' ('Your love is all I need, baby … come and rock my dreams') and 'The Paris Match' ('Empty nights with nothing to do … sit and think every thought is for you') sat alongside anti-American sentiment in 'A Gospel' ('Hands clasped tight / To shut out the victims' screams of ol' Uncle Sam fights / He sweats and he strains as his boney frame comes – into the womb of an innocent one') and the provocatively titled instrumental, 'Dropping Bombs on the White House'.

This was a world apart from songs about council estates, youth angst and everyday struggles. It is a different politics, one that reaches out to larger issues that affect lives, opposed to the close societal and domestic problems which are faced on a daily basis. Weller had moved from looking at identity politics to focusing more on global issues, which shifted his writing away from the deeply personal issues which fans could share. For Jam fans there seemed to be no honesty, no authenticity and lyrical distance. In addition, this new music seemed ethically sterile and musically naïve. David Quantick highlights the problem, noting that 'Weller's intended plans to create a great big furnace of burning soul passion and socialist power have often resulted in very ordinary records onto which a sparky brass section has been tacked' (1984). But despite the criticisms and the lack of spiritual overtones in the lyrics of this period, the music did contain a strong fusion of white and black soul, something lost on reviewers such as Quantick. Musically, at least, this was, as Garbarini notes, 'a necessary, therapeutic step towards the formulations of new values' and that Weller had 'extended his search back beyond Motown to black pop's real roots, gospel music', finally adding that it is this very music that 'finds a resonance in Weller's own soul' (1984: 38).

The demise of the Council in the late 1980s was, as Weller himself admits, 'a bad time, a low time' (1993), as Polydor dropped The Style Council and ended a twelve-year association with Weller himself. However, there had been earlier warning signs. Even by 1987's *The Cost of Loving*, there was a feeling that Weller had become too insular, too far removed from both his musical roots and, more importantly, his audience. Of this, Steve White notes that 'everything became too "in" … the whole kind of outlook of the band became very inward and the humour was very insular. I think a lot of the fans basically didn't understand it. Which is fair enough' (*Highlights and Hang Ups* 1994). *The Cost of Loving* proved to be the beginning of the end for the Council. Reviewers, who had always been tolerant of the band, began to question not just the musical content, but the one thing that had always been a key part of Paul Weller – his authenticity, the ethical quality of the work. A scathing review by Simon Reynolds in a February 1987 edition of *Melody Maker* sums up the general feeling towards the band during the period. Reynolds expresses his own bewilderment with *The Cost of Loving*, and uses words such as 'fakeness', 'spineless' and 'naffness' (1987). Dave Rimmer offers a slightly more eloquent but equally scathing review in *Q*, concluding that the album sounds no 'better than a pub band of balding musos who can play slickly enough but haven't got an interesting idea between them. Even after listening through this a half a dozen times I still find myself incapable of singing along with a single song' (1987: 107).

Weller fragmented his audience when The Jam had split, and throughout the Council years the ideological distance between artist and audience increased. For many, he was – purposefully – alienating them both musically and lyrically, his seeming self-importance, stubbornness and continued attempts to advance musically (to sever any ties with his past), was instrumental to The Style Council, and to a lesser extent was a significant factor in his own demise. Weller had, in the eyes of many, regressed. Musically, he had done everything possible to detach himself from driving Rickenbackers, feedback and a powerful uncompromising rhythm section. The music that spoke to so many, had been replaced with angst-free, harmonic, mellow jazz, 'easy listening' numbers which were a world away from the tastes of many fans. DJ and founder of Acid Jazz Records Eddie Piller summarizes their thoughts when he notes 'The Style Council didn't come vaguely close to the emotions captured by The Jam. Musically, I'm sure that they were far superior, but that's no substitute for raw, gutsy passion' (*Highlights and Hang Ups* 1994). There was also confusion lyrically. Insipid love songs and cosmopolitan café ballads sat uneasily alongside his former political vitriol.

The search for identity

If the relationship between Paul Weller and his audience grew ever wider in the 1980s, his emergence as a solo artist in the early 1990s rekindled the kind of devotion not seen since The Jam years. The self-produced release of The Paul Weller Movement's 'Into Tomorrow' (1991) was followed closely by the first solo album, *Paul Weller*. This period in Weller's career was a time of musical and personal rediscovery and he admits that for the first time in years he began to reconnect with his past. The rejection of what had gone before, during the days of The Style Council, had been replaced with a desire to return to his musical and spiritual roots. Speaking with Mojo's Lois Wilson about the period surrounding the recording of 'Into Tomorrow', Weller remembers:

> I went back to Woking for the first time in eight years. It was good to get back in touch with who I used to be, to take stock. I started to feel more comfortable with being me, returning to those places I went to as a kid I'd forgotten about, where I used to live. I'd been living this life, I was so wrapped up in what I'd been doing. I'd forgotten my roots. That fed into my lyrics.
>
> (2012: 72–73)

This reincarnation as a solo artist afforded him a fresh opportunity. Weller himself notes that 'I'd boxed myself into a corner lyrically with what people think you are about and what they expect, or what you think they expect from you … I was "Fuck this, I'll sing and play how I feel"' (2012: 73). The new direction in his writing is nowhere more apparent than in the early solo recordings. These new songs did not possess the same lyrical tones as either those of The Jam or The Style Council. Instead, they revealed, often in confessional tones, the songwriter speaking from a position of weakness, emotionally and spiritually exhausted.

Weller was writing, for the first time, introspectively. Instead of assessing all around him, judging those whom he felt were dishonest and fake, he was talking about himself; his struggles with life, with faith and with his surroundings; these were songs compounded with references to self-doubt, heard in 'Above the Clouds', self-reflection expressed in 'Bull Rush' (1992) and honest self-criticism in 'Bitterness Rising' (1992). He had also reconnected with his musical roots, admitting in an interview with the *NME*'s Paul Moody: 'I started playing a few records that I used to listen to … Stax, R&B, The Small Faces, The Who … everything made sense' (Moody 1995). These influences can be heard across the album, from the sampling of Marsha Hunt's 'Hot Rod Poppa' on 'Uh-Huh-Oh-Yeah' to the climax of 'Bull-Rush', with its 'Everybody's Got Something to Hide Except Me and My Monkey' bell and 'Magic Bus' homage.

Weller's interview on the *Jonathan Ross Show* in April 1991 was markedly different from his appearance in July 1993 on *Later with Jools Holland*. On Ross's show, Weller seemed to be uncomfortable, causing many to think they had seen the last of the ex-Jam and Style Council frontman. Two years on, Weller emerges from the difficult professional and personal time in the 1980s to appear as an individual who is supremely confident. Sporting an open, white shirt and prominent crucifix, Weller strides through the two new numbers 'Sunflower'

(1993) and 'Has My Fire Really Gone Out?' with an attitude not seen since the days of The Jam. It is this appearance on *Later* that captures his rebirth. The uncomfortable, shifting Weller seen on the Ross show has been replaced with an artist who is supremely confident. Was this a straightforward display of faith or something more?

However, without comment from Weller on this, only questions and conjectures can surface. Could he be showing spiritual rebirth, renewed confidence in existing beliefs and a desire to avoid any possible ambiguity or misinterpretation of his lyrics? In a 1994 issue of *Vox*, Max Bell notes that this image is more than 'just' a fashion statement. He observes that Weller 'wears his ... influences like badges of honour, but these are intricately woven and apparently indestructible spiritual totems more than accessories' (1994a: 118). Perhaps then, Weller was also openly displaying more spiritual feelings, alongside the more recognizable choices of fashion, music and lifestyle? What is most striking during this particular performance is the manner in which Weller reclaims his integrity. The mod ethic had returned, the 1960s influence was apparent (heard through The Fleur de Lys inspired riff on 'Sunflower') and, notably, he was playing a guitar again. But, fundamentally, he was reconnecting with his audience. This performance indicated a more mature, more aware and more contemplative songwriter; there was certainly something different about Weller, which could be seen in his image and heard through the music and, of course, his lyrics. In this new material he was writing, for the first time, from a deeply spiritual/reflexive perspective, borne from the uncertain period between 1989–91, which saw the artist creatively bereft, and a time that Weller himself calls 'fucking awful'.

Self-reflection, spiritual discovery, Paul Weller and *Wild Wood*

The resurrection of Paul Weller's career coincided neatly with the reinvention of British guitar bands during the early 1990s. Bands such as Ocean Colour Scene, Blur, Supergrass and Oasis would continually name-check Weller as an influence. Noel Gallagher notes that 'The Jam generation just came through. We were Jam fans' (*Into Tomorrow* 2006). However, despite being lauded by younger artists who were greatly influenced by Weller's back catalogue, his new work was a different proposition. This was an artist on a journey of rediscovery and self-evaluation, and which manifests at emotional, and deeply personal levels. A strong example of this can be heard in Weller's third single from *Paul Weller*, 'Above the Clouds'. Weller acknowledges his insecurities, criticizes his faith and questions his beliefs. Here, Weller is questioning his own axiological characteristics. This early work is extremely spiritual, the title itself connotes heaven and therefore by association, spiritual direction, and Weller is acknowledging this. To secure a foundation from which to exist, to work and create, you must have faith. This in turn encourages belief and arrests indecision. At the same time, however, Weller seems to be struggling with the concept of faith, believing that it must be acquired before he can develop as both an individual and an artist, but at the same time not knowing how to attain it. The song is deeply self-critical and self-evaluative, highlighting recent issues that have haunted and obviously affected him; self-doubt, failure and rejection. The search for something to believe in, singing how, as self-doubt and sadness rises, 'you're scared of living but afraid to die … I must find the faith to beat it'.

These lines open up a new line of discourse about Weller and are arguably some of his most honest and revealing. Ultimately, the only thing able to overcome negativity, and the key to the song, is strength of faith. In theological terms, this idea is one which can be strongly linked to Christianity: 'If you do not stand firm in your faith, you will not stand at all' (Isaiah 7:9). Weller subscribes to this idea, acknowledging that a lack of faith results in failure. With this lack of faith, there is no direction, and the anger he describes results from his 'own self-doubt'. What he once had – fame, success, awards, recognition – is gone, replaced by negativity and uncertainty. Weller elucidates this by referring to it as 'madness'; constantly troubling, 'creeping' into his dreams, perpetuating confusion, constantly reminding him of his failures, and his vulnerabilities. The verse then explores deeper questions and emotions; scared of living (failure as an artist), scared to give (to create new material), afraid to die (fear of rejection).

Along with the display of his crucifix, what is also interesting about this period of his work is the use of the third person in a form of illeism, which can be an indication of a troubled soul. His lyrics, as shown above, have always been deeply personal. In this new phase of his life, it may help him to see himself as he would any other person, which this form of mental separation does. As Andrew Malone writes, 'illeistic reference allows the speaker to present himself from an external perspective. This may be to develop and/or display empathy with another's perspective, and/or even to create distance' (2009: 506–7). Weller discusses this new approach in an interview with Max Bell for *Vox*: Weller notes that 'When I was in the Jam, I wrote about other people's feelings. Now I write about myself, my emotions. I like the way music can get you through dark periods' (1994b: 31). This externalizing could make dealing with his current turmoil less stressful and allow him to think more clearly about the new path he needed to find. He was breaking out of the box he had found himself in. Much like Bowie's decision to kill off his alter ego Ziggy Stardust, Weller was setting aside everything (personal and professional) that had gone before in order to move on. As noted above, he felt that he had boxed himself into a corner.

The answer to these problems is, as can be seen in the final line of the verse, the use of the word 'faith'. Although Weller does not indicate what kind of faith he is ascribing to – religious, personal, faith in others – in this verse of deeply personal and emotional issues, we can think of the word in a spiritual context. Despite this connection, however, Weller is not subscribing to a singular idea, but the confusion and desperate nature of the verse does highlight that he is seeking something which can help to find emotional and spiritual comfort. Ultimately, faith is the assurance of all the things that Weller is hoping for in the future.

In addition to this fear of failure, he also explores his past in the opening verse. Using nature as a metaphor, these lines indicate a poignant self-reflexivity, an exploration of his past. Autumn, threatening winter, indicates his feelings towards the potential end to his creative endeavours or even interpreted as an existential crisis addressing the fear of death itself. Although an artist who has continually stated that he writes for himself, the lyrics show another side; a songwriter who is unsure of himself; self-possession has been eclipsed by self-doubt. Highlighting the criticism of both fans and the media ('Autumn blew its leaves at me'), and the potential of worse to come during his creative rediscovery ('Threatening winter as I walked'), the lyrics explore a resigned reference to 'fleeting fame' ('Summer always goes so quick'), and his state of mind, confused and unsure ('Barely stopping like my thoughts'). The lyrics to 'Above the Clouds' are emotional, intimate and extremely powerful. It is a song which is full of questions, an emotional attempt to find one's personal path, to secure a future.

If 'Above the Clouds' was a question about direction, it is perhaps 'Into Tomorrow' which gives the listener the most poignant indication of Weller's inner thoughts. The song is deeply personal, and throughout contains strong references to a spiritual side of the artist, rarely expressed. It is a dark, foreboding lyric which is in contrast to his uncertainty in 'Above the Clouds'. 'Into Tomorrow' is confidently delivered despite the darker meaning of the song's lyrical content of loss, fear and loneliness. Perhaps he offers a glimpse of hope at the very end, which he is 'praying that it has not passed into tomorrow', fighting to get control over his life before it is too late. Weller is not indicating that it will be good tomorrow or that he is looking forward to tomorrow, rather that he does not want tomorrow, he wants change now. He feels life deeply. When obsession grips, it grips hard, and he has to follow its call, no matter the consequence. He questions all that comes into his life, examines everything from every angle. 'Maybe I take life too seriously', he once told author Paolo Hewitt, 'but I see a depth in things. That's why I feel I have got a heavy soul' (2007: 30).

Confidence, security, fire and skill

Weller's second solo album *Wild Wood* built upon the moderate success of *Paul Weller*, and is written from a more secure perspective, although there are still references to the self-doubt of the first album, indicating that although he is more secure, the element of fear still exists within him. This can be heard in the lyrical content of confident songs such as 'Country', 'Into the Light Out of the Dark', and 'Sunflower' where he affirms his refound confidence: 'I write this now, while I'm in control, I'll choose the words and how the melody goes', which sit alongside 'Kosmos', where he, again, is searching for something. New ideas, salvation or success exists somewhere else, not where he is. *Wild Wood* is also clearer in terms of a greater spiritual influence, with the title track itself a reminder of the song 'The Church in the Wildwood', written by Dr William S. Pitts in 1857, a tale about the building of a church in Iowan woodlands. The idea of a more religious path is also compounded by a more direct lyrical reference, and questions relating to specific religious ideas. Weller had found himself, and, with a newfound confidence, was searching for answers. In his book *Paul Weller: The Changing Man,* Paolo Hewitt notes that Weller was aware of his own spirituality but was unsure about how to express it. Hewitt suggests that Weller had always had an 'intense feeling, that a power is conducting itself through a human vessel' and in his case 'God's wish for him, his purpose on this earth, was to provide music' (2007: 257–8). Hewitt's observations are clarified by Weller in a 2012 interview with Decca Aitkenhead for the *Guardian*. Asked if he believes in God, Weller replies, '"Yeah, definitely. Not in a Christian way, but some kind of force, energy"' (2012). This secular approach, which does not commit to a specific religion, harnesses a spiritual force which is clearly evident across the body of work on his second solo album *Wild Wood*. Reviewing for the *NME*, Paul Moody writes:

> 'Sunflower' and 'Can You Heal Us (Holy Man)' rattle along on the back of distorted guitar and ... gospel-funk respectively, but it's the title track that sets

the tone, suggesting a pastoral take on Nick Drake's 'Chime Of The City Clock', all strummed guitars and world-weary melancholia.

(1994)

Moody's reference to 'gospel-funk' in the song 'Can You Heal Us (Holy Man)?' is interesting. The song is a highly accomplished melding of music and lyrics, gospel driven, highly charged, deeply emotional, and has Weller questioning 'believers'. The search for faith had finally taken Weller into a more specific religious territory. Speaking to the *NME*'s Iestyn George on the issues of religion and spirituality, Weller notes 'I've got no time for organized religion ... But at the same time, I still think that faith is very important. I don't think I have absolute faith yet but I still like the idea that some time I will' (1993). Weller is questioning religious hierarchy and the double standards that those who enforce it take. He is not questioning the existence of God, nor is he attacking religion, or the believers of it, in any form. 'Holy Man' is a quintessential explanation of these comments as primarily it challenges the perception of organized religion, of God's servants on earth, asking if they are any different from us all, and if so, how, and why? The song begins with a statement relating to the Bible, and particularly a sermon. 'Crystal words' are the words of God – clear, concise and pure – however, these will not stop us from falling, but into what, or where?

Considering Weller's experiences prior to the release of *Wild Wood*, as well as his sentiments on the first album, this would almost certainly mean into despair, into a place of uncertainty and self-doubt. Weller is saying that not even the crystal words of the Bible, conveyed through a messenger – in this case a holy man – could help him, they did not stop him falling. This is reminiscent to the opening line in 'Bull-Rush', where he '[tumbled] down into a deep despair, lost and dazed ... until the rain clears the air'. However, this fall into despair was down to Weller himself; a momentary lapse in *his* condition. In 'Holy Man', however, the focus shifts and questions are being asked of others. This is very much in line with Biblical thinking, the notion of the holy man being enlightened, or on a higher plane than others: 'Whoever says he is in the light and hates his brother is still in darkness' (1 John 2:9 [English Standard Version]). Weller then questions this faith in others, asking 'If you feel the hand of God – Can you guide it holy man?' This highlights the notion of those in strong positions of spiritual power, abusing their position. Again, Paolo Hewitt substantiates this argument in his book, *Paul Weller: The Changing Man*, suggesting that Weller wrote consciously about the Church, expressing generally negative thoughts towards its hypocrisy. Hewitt notes that 'Weller instinctively shunned organised religion, its churches and its rituals' (2007: 257). This perspective manifests in the words to 'Holy Man', where his questions regarding dishonesty within religion can be likened to those expressed in the Bible (Matthew 23:1–39 [English Standard Version]):

> ... practice and observe whatever they tell you – but not what they do. For they preach, but do not practice. They tie up heavy burdens, hard to bear, and lay them on people's shoulders, but they themselves are not willing to move them with their finger. They do all their deeds to be seen by others.

Having consciously returned to his roots to find himself, *Wild Wood* is a testament to the fact that Weller was beginning to create music which was, like his Jam days, connecting with his audience, albeit on a more spiritual, mature and deeper level.

'The Changingman', nature and transition

If *Wild Wood* asks questions of religious belief and queries the actions and genuine intentions of those in a position of spiritual power, then *Stanley Road* offers a more profound, personal and self-reflexive view on spirituality. As I have discussed, 'Can You Heal Us (Holy Man)' asks specific questions aimed at specific individuals. There is not one religion questioned; Weller is aiming these thoughts at all who announce that they are able to speak or act upon God's word. In many respects, a number of the songs on *Stanley Road* move beyond this. On this, his third solo album, Weller is more confident, reaccustomed and comfortable with faith and fame, but rejecting any need for external religious guidance. If the roots of Weller's optimism lay in the probing and confused lyrics contained within the albums *Paul Weller* and *Wild Wood*, in *Stanley Road* we finally begin to hear them answered. Love songs such as 'You Do Something to Me', sit alongside the voodoo church inspired, Dr. John cover, 'I Walk on Gilded Splinters'. However, within the eclecticism of *Stanley Road*'s lyrics are some of the most profoundly spiritual of Weller's career.

In 2006, Weller, discussing religion with Ted Kessler, noted how he was 'not interested in any organised religion ... I believe in God, as a spiritual force ... the notion of God being inside you and heaven and hell being here on earth is true' (2006: 62). This quote is one of Weller's most telling and exposes his beliefs and theological ideology, alluding more to Buddhist philosophy than straightforward Christianity and, in a faith context, perhaps notions of 'double belonging' or 'multiple belonging'. In addition, and possibly unaware, he has touched upon arguably the most fundamental difference between Buddhism and other religions in the above quote. Buddhism does not subscribe to the notion of worshipping outside of self, of praying to someone who has overall power, who is beyond human reach. Matsuoka observes that 'Christianity and Islam preach salvation through the grace of an absolute deity' whereas 'Buddhism teaches practitioners to save themselves' (2005: 54). The focus on self-evaluation, expressed within 'The Changingman', focuses upon this belief; the idea that self-change can only be achieved by evaluating and creating harmony within life. This can only come first by self-reflection, and, subsequently, self-change. The ideal goal to create heaven, or worse, hell on earth. This idea is also seen later in Weller's career, heard on 'Brand New Start': 'I'm gonna clear up my earth, and build a heaven on the ground / not something distant and unfound / but something real to me' (Weller 1998). Weller is discussing his planned path, and unlike the 'questioning' lyrics of the previous two solo albums, *Stanley Road*'s mood is one of positivity and single-mindedness. Weller sets out his intentions with the opening track, 'The Changingman', which is an extremely candid exposition of his spiritual journey. Weller talks about taking stock of his life, to re-evaluate everything around him, and attempt to create his own heaven within his own environment, a place where he can find peace and contentment. As Yamamoto notes: 'The effects of an individual living being's past karma manifest themselves in both its subjective life and its objective environment … Both the subject and its environment coexist or are nondual in a situation that is a result of karma' (2003: 243–4). In this context, life is the subjective self that draws upon past experiences and the effects of past actions to create a positive future. Personal environment is the objective realm where the karmic effects of life take shape, and each living being has his or her own unique environment that they are able to shape through their own actions. All of the questions and uncertainties that Weller *had* felt are present in the lyrics of 'The Changingman'.

One of the most poignant sections of the song is during the chorus, where Weller talks of 'shifting sands'. Weller does not necessarily believe in a specific god or religion, but rather feels and knows it to be true. This part of the lyric is very much akin to the Buddhist concept of *shogo-mujo*, meaning all worldly things are transitory. This idea is a fundamental concept in Buddhism, where everything in life is ever-changing, and nothing remains the same. He is describing his own experiences, remembering how he had lost everything and noting how fame, wealth, health, beauty, power – or whatever people aspire to acquire – does not last forever. Such things are built on shifting sands. Buddhism fully acknowledges this fact:

Life is ever-changing, moment to moment. The only constant in life is change. Our minds are constantly in flux, and while one minute we may have the courage to conquer the world, the next minute we can be overwhelmed by even the simplest occurrences.

(*The Winning Life: An Introduction to Buddhist Practice* 2000: 9)

Weller writes as someone who is absolutely aware that constant change is an important element of life. This can be – by his own admission – in a positive or negative way. He is also aware that despite his re-found success, there is always a danger of failure. From a Buddhist perspective, it is fairly clear that Paul Weller understands the connection between an individual's physical environment and their inner reality. Everything is perceived through the self and is dependent on the individual's inner state. Weller is stating that, if he changes, then his circumstances will inevitably change also. This is a liberating concept as it means that there is no need to seek enlightenment outside ourselves or in a particular place. 'Wherever we are, in whatever circumstances, we can bring forth our innate Buddhahood, thus transforming our experience of our environment into 'the Buddha's land' – a joy-filled place where we can create value for ourselves and for others' ('The Oneness of Life and Its Environment' 2017). However, despite Weller's positivism, he does not fully commit to his own ideas. He sings how the 'more I know … the less I understand', a direct indication that he knows his role in life and acknowledges the problems that come with it, but at the same time admits that he does not know how to or believe he can change it. Weller is acknowledging the notion that the wise understand that knowledge is not the end, that there is something more, but what? Weller answers the question how, although time may be 'on loan', he notes that what he 'can't be today, [he] can be tomorrow''. Here he is reflecting on mortality, the circle of life and what is beyond. Knowledge is obtained through life, but also in death. 'Time is on loan' indicates the passing of life, but interestingly, Weller does not allude to a heaven or hell, but more the notion of reincarnation. What is not achieved in this life (today) can be in the next (tomorrow), and that in everyone, there is a chance to make amends, to lead a better, more productive existence.

However, just as Weller feels that he has found the answer, as I mentioned in the analysis of 'Above the Clouds', again his self-doubt begins to manifest. It is also clear that he is an individual who continually seeks change. This is achieved by destroying what he has built, 'lighting a bitter fuse'. This is a deeply personal confession, reflecting his thoughts regarding success and happiness, and his apparent need to destroy both. Earlier, I discussed Weller breaking up with or from The Jam at the pinnacle of their success, which again destroyed something that he, along with bassist Bruce Foxton and drummer Rick Buckler, had worked so hard to achieve. Weller spoke of this split in an interview on *BBC Nationwide* in 1982: 'It was just something I felt inside me, you just gotta go by instinct and I felt it was the right thing to do.' Weller continues, 'I thought about it, it wasn't as if I just made my mind up overnight … it's the first time for years where I haven't had any definite plans … Whatever I do I wanna be successful, or there's no point in doing it' (*BBC Nationwide* 1982). But, this success seems to come at a price, one that not only affects Weller himself, but those around him.

There is little doubt that when Paul Weller took to the Pyramid Stage at Glastonbury in 1994 his reputation was as strong as it had ever been, both personally and professionally. But this was about to change. The idea that I have already suggested, that Weller is uncomfortable with stability and routine, has credence in the events surrounding the gig. For some, Weller was producing some of the greatest music of his career and was husband to soul singer and ex-Style Council member Dee C Lee who he married in 1987. But this was about to change as Weller informed long-time Style Council drummer Steve White that he and Lee were to break up. White remembers that 'they split-up, pretty much, the night we did Glastonbury. He just told me that they had split … and all those horrible things that happen, and I was like "blimey, this is as good as it's been for ages"' (*Into Tomorrow* 2006). Lee also discusses this time and insists there were no serious issues that prompted the break up. Looking back with fondness, she remembers: 'I know that to this day, some people spend their whole lives looking for what I had at that time with Paul and if I never get it again, I actually did have it … that's exactly what we had, it was fantastic' (*Into Tomorrow* 2006). Once again, success had brought instability. Dee C Lee goes on to add that '[h]e [Weller] sabotages his own happiness' (Chalkley 2010: 83), and Steve White concludes that 'there is that element of needy chaos … some people are like that' (*Into Tomorrow* 2006). Weller himself agrees with this observation, recalling that:

> There was a sense that things were going too well, we were too happy, too comfortable, everything seemed too nice. There was a sense that for me as a writer and an artist I might lose my edge. I had to break the shape up, re-arrange things.
>
> (Chalkley 2010: 83)

More than any other song of his early solo career, this destruction of personal, and professional, success is reflected quite clearly in the lyrical content of 'The

Changingman'. First, the image of lighting a fuse, coupled with the use of the word 'bomb', immediately indicates destruction. The fuse is lit, the decision has been made, the bomb explodes and the 'bang!' is the resulting self-destruction. These metaphorical images are rich in personal meaning, and reflects his fear of normality, conformity and, to a lesser extent, success. A desire to destroy what he has built.

This idea of destruction, the fear of normality and the desire to change, is best described in the first verse of the song. Weller's words are those of exasperation, he is questioning himself, his own morals, ideals and faith. Particularly prevalent here is the danger of becoming too self-absorbed, to be wary of those who, at the time, were lauding him as a major influence, a British musical icon, a muse. After a dark period, he has fame and adulation again, he is writing some of the best work of his career, he is lauded by his peers and loved by his fans, but this is not enough, there is an emptiness that must be addressed. Once again, Weller has tapped into another deeply Buddhist concept, and this opening line can be equated to the 'Tarnished Mirror' – 'A mind ... clouded by the illusions of the innate darkness of life is like a tarnished mirror. However, when polished, it is sure to shine reflecting the ... true aspects of reality' (Nichiren 1255: 5). This is not necessarily a negative reflection, but Weller's life has been tainted by certain decisions he has made. There comes a point where the artist, comfortable within himself, has no clear vision and thus needs to clear his thoughts. This idea of a clouded soul being cleansed, and thus going on to shine, are explored deeply throughout the song. It is not clear if Weller achieves his aim, nor if the song allows the writer any closure, but at this stage of his career, Paul Weller is openly questioning the faith he has in himself. However, the ideas posed in 'The Changingman' finally allow Weller to find a semblance of inner peace, albeit temporary, where he finally acknowledges that professional and personal happiness can co-exist and that there is an option other that lighting a bitter fuse.

Conclusion

Throughout his career, Paul Weller has offered lyrics which probe, question, defy and demand answers. His scrutiny focused on complex themes, exploring notions of religion and spirituality and the emotive issues of the social everyday life. Unlike a chameleon reflecting changes in their environment and fitting in, Weller aimed to bring attention to the lives lived by his fans, raising comment in order to help them reflect on their situations. During the early years, these came in the form of more observational lyrics where he would observe his social surroundings and pen words which would encourage change and prevent apathy. Within The Jam days, these would usually be about everyday folk, living everyday lives, but as the 1980s drew on, his ire was directed towards more political themes which, as discussed, alienated those who relied on Weller's lyrics in order to reflect on their own lives. The lyrical tales about the mundane, everyday life and the people that inhabited those spaces served to inspire his fans. However, the change in outlook during The Style Council period could be interpreted as a commercially courageous, albeit risky, enterprise. For many, however, it felt like a self-centred betrayal of those fans who had both supported and relied on his words.

His solo work, however, is a different proposition. As this chapter has argued, the lyrical content of Weller's early solo work is passionate, honest and often uncomfortable. Here, Weller does not look outward, but draws inspiration from his own everyday experiences. His integrity seems to demand that he risks alienating fans. His artistic and interior growth require he takes chances in order to be faithful to his spiritual rebirth, and the candour this requires to connect once again to his evolving fan base. The relationship that this promotes is deep, personal and exists only between the individual and their own beliefs. As mentioned in the introduction, it was never the intention of this work to label Weller as a 'religious' individual, but to seek to establish how much the artist uses elements of spirituality to promote his own thoughts and feelings.

Whether knowingly or not, it is clear that beneath the driving guitars, sharp suits and working-class attitude, Paul Weller is a songwriter who relies heavily on the spiritual domain to convey his thoughts, feelings and beliefs. Sometimes, albeit by accident, his own ideology is one which falls directly in-line with specific religious doctrine and which in turn plays a significant role in determining the lyrical content of his songs.

Notes

1   An individual who recognizes and respects all religions and religious beliefs.
2   A religion or belief system that supports the existence of one true God.

References

Aitkenhead, D. (2012), 'Paul Weller: "People say you make your best work when in despair – but I think happiness is a good place to write from"', *Guardian*, 11 March. Available online: https://www.theguardian.com/music/2012/mar/11/paul-weller-happiness-sonik-kicks (accessed 10 October 2018).

BBC Nationwide (1982), [TV programme] Brighton Centre Final Gig Interview.

Bell, M. (1994a), 'Rising Son', *Vox*, issue 40.

Bell, M. (1994b), 'Paul Weller', *Vox*, issue 46.

Chalkley, D. (2010), 'I'm Still Open to the Magic', *Mojo*, 76–86.

Cook, H. (1984), 'The Style Council: Café Bleu', *New Musical Express*.

Cox, T. (1999), 'Kurt's Gone. So What?', *Guardian Unlimited*. Available online: https://www.rocksbackpages.com/Library/Article/kurts-gone-so-what- (accessed 31 August 2020).

Crowley, G. (2006), 'Paul Weller: A Fan Speaks', *The Independent*. Available online: https://www.independent.co.uk/arts-entertainment/music/features/paul-weller-a-fan-speaks-344378.html (accessed 6 March 2018).

Garbarini, V. (1984), 'The Style Council', *Musician*, 36–40.

George, I. (1993), 'Paul Weller: "It's almost like a curse – music is all I can do in life"', *New Musical Express*.

Gilbert, J. and Pearson, E. (1999), *Discographies: Dance Music, Culture, and the Politics of Sound*, London: Routledge.

Hart, S. L. (1971), 'Axiology–Theory of Values', *Philosophy and Phenomenological Research*, 32 (1): 29–41.

Hewitt, P. (2007), *Paul Weller: The Changing Man*, London: Transworld Publishing.

Highlights and Hang Ups (1994), [Documentary Picture] (UK), P. Romhanyi, Oil Factory.

Into Tomorrow (2006), [Documentary Picture](UK), S. Watts, Double Jab Productions.

Kessler, T. (2006), 'Got my Mojo Working', in *Weller: Modern Classics 1991–2019 – The Collectors Series* (2019), 56–63.

Lester, P. (1998), 'Paul Weller: Last Man Standing', *Uncut*, 1 December.

Malone, A. S. (2009), 'God the Illeist: Third-Person Self References and Trinitarian Hints in the Old Testament', *Journal of the Evangelical Theological Society*, 52 (3): 499–518.

Mathiesen, T. J. (1984), 'Harmonia and Ethos in Ancient Greek Music', *The Journal of Musicology*, 3 (3): 264–79.

Matsuoka, M. (2005), 'The Buddhist Concept of the Human Being: From the Viewpoint of the Philosophy of the Soka Gakkai', *The Journal of Oriental Studies*, 15: 50–65.

Moody, P. (1994), 'Paul Weller: Wild Wood', *New Musical Express*.

Moody, P. (1995), 'Woking Back to Happiness', *New Musical Express*.
Nichiren, (1255), in *The Writings of Nichiren Daishonin, Vol 1*. (1999). Sokka Gakkai International. Available online: https://www.nichirenlibrary.org/en/wnd-1/toc/
Paul Weller INTERVIEW with Clint Boon (2017), [video] YouTube. Available online: https://www.youtube.com/watch?v=5MNU0Q_DfbA (accessed 16 March 2018).
Quantick, D. (1984), 'The Style Council: Cardiff: St. David's Hall', *New Musical Express*. Available online: https://www.rocksbackpages.com/Library/Article/the-style-council-cardiff-st-davids-hall (accessed 16 September 2020).
Reed, J. (1996), *Paul Weller: My Ever Changing Moods*, London: Omnibus.
Reynolds, S. (1987), The Cost of Loving. *Melody Maker*.
Riethmüller, A. (2008), 'Music beyond Ethics', *Archiv für Musikwissenschaft*, 65: 169–76.
Rimmer, D. (1987), 'The Style Council: The Cost of Loving', *Q Magazine* (March).
Snow, M. (1993), 'Paul Weller: We All Make Mistakes', *Q Magazine* (October).
'The Oneness of Life and Its Environment' (2017), Soka Gakkai International. Available online: https://www.sgi.org/about-us/buddhist-concepts/oneness-of-self-and-environment.html (accessed 16 February 2018).
The Winning Life: An Introduction to Buddhist Practice (2000), Santa Monica, CA: World Tribune Press.
Thick as Thieves: Personal Situations with The Jam (2012), [Documentary Picture] (UK), P. Sedazzari, ZANI Media.
Wilson, L. (2012). Remember How We Started. *Mojo*, 72–79.
Yamamoto, S. (2003), 'Environmental Problems and Buddhist Ethics: From the Perspective of the Consciousness-Only Doctrine', in K. H. Dockett, G. R. Dudley-Grant, and C. P. Bankart, *Psychology and Buddhism: From Individual to Global Community*, 239–257. New York: Klewer Academic.

Select discography

Hunt, Marsha (1971), 'Hot Rod Poppa'. [Written by M. Bolan]. On *Woman Child* [Vinyl] [A-3], 2410 101, Track Record.
The Jam (1980), 'Going Underground'. [Written by P. Weller]' [Vinyl 7"] [A]' 2059 216' Polydor Records.
The Jam (1980), 'That's Entertainment. [Written by P. Weller]' [Vinyl 7"] [A]' 0030.364 Metronome Records, Germany.
The Paul Weller Movement (1992), 'Into Tomorrow'. [Written by P. Weller]. On *Paul Weller* [Vinyl] [B-2], 828 343-1, Go! Discs.
Weller, P. (1992c), *Paul Weller*. [Vinyl], 828 343-1, Go! Discs.
Weller, P. (1993a), '(Can You Heal Us) Holy Man'. On *Wild Wood* [Vinyl] [A-2], 828 435-1, Go! Discs.

Weller, P. (1993d), *Wild Wood*. [Vinyl], 828 435-1, Go! Discs.
Weller, P. (1995a), *Stanley Road*. [Vinyl], 828 619-1, Go! Discs.
Paul Weller (1998), 'Brand New Start'. [Written by P. Weller]. [7" Vinyl] [A-1], 572 370-7 Island Records.

Part Two

Christianity

5

'Embracing the Divine Chaos': Transcending the Sacred-Secular Divide in the 1990s British Rave Church Movement

Lucy Robinson and Chris Warne

Introduction

From 1986, St Thomas's Anglican Church, in the Crookes suburb of Sheffield, hosted religious services that took the form of raves. Named after the time that they started on Sunday nights, The Nine O'clock Service (NOS) was welcomed into the Church of England as a way to connect with young people on their own terms, by drawing on their club and dance culture. NOS's Communion and Teaching Services looked and sounded like raves, drawing on its different genres of EDM (electronic dance music) and its visual styles. But they also incorporated elements of various Christian liturgical traditions into the services, for example using Latin chants, candles and incense, or Orthodox iconography, alongside strobe lights and nightclub-style visuals.

The Church of England recognized NOS's potential and its leader, the 'rave vicar' Chris Brain, was accepted for ordination, celebrating his first communion in August 1992. The group became increasingly autonomous from the diocesan structures of the local Anglican church, with apparently increasingly little supervision from 'its parent church' (Spinks 2011). At one point NOS reportedly had more staff and a larger congregation than Sheffield Cathedral (Till 2006: 96). In its status as an experimental form of Christianity, NOS received a fair degree of largely positive media coverage, which often focused on Brain as the central figure; for example, in Radio 4's religious programming in 1990, on the World Service in November 1993 and in a number of accounts of contemporary evangelicalism (BBC Radio 4 1990; Warren 1989). Brain's own account of NOS was included in an overview of evangelism in Britain in 1993, in preparation for then Archbishop of Canterbury's call for a decade of mission (Brain 1993). Brain himself became something of a star and was treated as such by the church. In the subsequently more negative press coverage of the group, there is a much repeated anecdote about Brain wanting the priestly robes worn by De Niro in the 1986 film *The Mission* for his inauguration, and getting them.

The vicar of St Thomas Crookes, Robert Warren, described his experience at NOS services in 1989. He presented Brain as part of a solution for the church: NOS '[was] very well organized, and run much more like a business than a church. In [his] view that [was] a compliment' (Warren 1989: 225). He praised NOS's hard work and justified their high expenditure on equipment – their sound system was no more expensive than a church organ after all. He found preaching at its services the most challenging and rewarding of his various services (1989: 227). Indeed, the NOS services developed in complexity and moved beyond merely presenting an alternative format towards rethinking the entire function of the church. Much of the congregation's broader leadership already lived in community or closely shared environments, and members were frequently engaged with local social justice and environmental concerns. Rather than borrowing space from St Thomas's, NOS moved to their own location at the Pond's Forge Leisure Centre in central Sheffield. The venue had been originally built for the World Student Games in 1991 (Rogerson 2006). The new autonomous space encouraged NOS to hone their own form of worship and explore more maverick theologians beyond the strict confines of the evangelical tradition within which Robert Warren and St Thomas's stood. Their new Planetary Mass was a 'weekly celebration of life' and a 'joint ritual of celebration and repentance on behalf of our culture' (Howard 1996: 96).

In that respect, NOS used their immersion in rave culture and its collective practices to blur the boundaries between the spiritual and the secular, between the sacred and the profane (Spinks 2011). Planning these masses involved about a hundred people working together as artists and designers, technicians, prop-makers, singers, dancers and so on; indeed all the crew one would expect at a large-scale rave. In Brain's words, the team who built NOS 'were at the heart of house music and multimedia experimentation in the early 1980s, and activists in social, political and environmental concern' (1993: 166). They therefore brought this expertise and outlook with them into the church. The Planetary Mass merged DJ with Priest, mixed and sampled together imagery drawn from the world religions, and used contemporary technology to turn spiritual imagery into an immersive sensual experience through sound and light projections.

'On a good day', Warren had written, 'the future of the Nine O'clock Service looks very exciting. On a bad day I wonder what on earth I have got myself into' (1989: 231). In August 1995, NOS ceased to exist as a formal entity in the midst of scandal and recrimination. Brain was accused of bullying, drug and sexual abuse and financial mismanagement. Up to forty women were believed to have been abused by him. He was no longer the face of the church's potential to connect with a new generation in new and exciting ways. Instead, he came to represent everything that could go wrong when power was put in the wrong hands with too few checks and balances in place. Unlike most of the DIY cultures we might associate with rave, NOS had developed a hierarchical and authoritarian structure, with Brain and his inner circle at the heart of it. As the service collapsed, the traditional church structures of pastoral oversight faced criticism. Brain himself was hospitalized and up to 150 members of the church were reported to need counselling.

NOS and the figure of Brain in particular quickly became a cautionary tale and foreshadowed the later exposures of sexual abuse within church structures more generally. However, we see NOS as more than a morality tale. In this chapter, we present a historical analysis of NOS which is broader than a focus on the power of a charismatic personality and which is derived from a focus on subculture as a way of understanding collective actions in a given locality. We believe that by reinserting NOS within its wider context, it is indeed possible to unpick how Brain came to be in such a position of power, but beyond that to more fully grasp what it meant to meld the sacred and the subcultural. While not underplaying the impact of Brain's abuse, we seek to move beyond historical explanations for it based on his character alone. Such a focus has tended to see those who invested their lives into the NOS project, and who were abused in return, as dupes, persuaded by his individual power. This undermines the value of the intellectual and theological labour invested by those that he betrayed. Nor was NOS unique in its merging of rave with church services. Similar experiments emerged around the UK during the same timescale, some still ongoing: in Scotland, the Late Late Service in Glasgow (Cross Rhythms 1997; God in the House 1996); the north, Synergy in Leeds, and Visions in York (Visions n.d.); the midlands, Redemption, initially called The Hap Club, in Birmingham and Joy in Oxford; the south west, Resonance from Bristol ran a spiritual chill-out tent at the Glastonbury Festival for much of the 1990s; and London, Abundant, Grace (Grace n.d.), Thursdays, and Holy Joes, the latter holding 'church in a pub' events in Brixton on Tuesday nights, and running the Harry Music and Arts Festivals from the mid-1980s as a small-scale alternative to the much higher profile

Greenbelt Festival.¹ Indeed, NOS has helped us to think beyond clashes between clerical institutions and commercial popular culture, as seen for example in the rise of the 'trendy vicar' or the backlash against the Beatles (Sullivan 1987), and instead to think about experiences of sanctity and profanity through musical and visual immersion. By focusing on the rave communion as a broader force beyond the NOS scandal itself, we will draw out the historical relationships between religious and subcultural practices, especially the use of music as part of those practices, and test their wider relevance for an understanding of the mutual connections between the sacred and the profane.²

It is instructive in that respect to place our understanding of NOS in relation to existing academic work on youth and subcultures, the social and cultural history of the Christian churches and theological practice. Academic and popular responses to NOS at the time and since act as markers in the history of how popular culture and religion, and indeed culture and identity, have been understood. From NOS's early days, through its demise and into the subsequent theological literature, it has been repeatedly used as a moral lesson. NOS sometimes features in theological training literature, largely as a warning against cultism, or chasing youth cultures, or as an example of how not to deal with predatory abuse within the church (Kennedy 2002; Puttick 1997; Villiers 1996). A 'Chris Brain-style cult' quickly became shorthand in guidance literature (Angier 1997). In contrast, Rupert Till's article on NOS from 2006 used it as an access point into the role of popular culture within wider debates on the advance of secularization (2006). Here, NOS acts as shorthand for the appropriation of contemporary cultural styles by the church. These styles were more akin to the daily performances of Hebdige's subcultures than the rites and rituals of the Church (Hebdige 1979). In that respect, Till usefully demonstrated, perhaps unwittingly, how work on NOS service has tended to re-enact the history of work on subcultures more generally. It has thus been understood either in terms of delinquency and degeneracy affecting even the Church of England ('the moral panic'), or as illustrating the incorporation of once autonomous ('authentic') subcultures into traditional structures of power ('the sell-out'), whether that be rave selling out to the church, or more commonly the church selling out to the world in pursuit of power and popularity.³

Subcultural histories

However, there are limits to analyses of NOS through moral panics and the sell-out alone, be they based on naughty vicars, celebrity cults or secularization. They both tend to downplay the agency of those involved in subcultures and paint them as subject to forces they can't control. We might recognize the value of the models, while also thinking historically about the role of context. For example, critics of the 'moral panic' concept, and especially the central role accorded to the mass media in the generation of a panic, have emphasized the agency of the public, who don't necessarily believe what they read in the press after all. The originators of the model, Stanley Cohen and Jock Young, who had developed it to understand social representations of youth crime in the 1960s (Cohen 1972; Young 1971), have both subsequently revisited their model in this light (Cohen 1999; Young 2009). Cohen himself has also noted that the proliferation of moral panics has simultaneously led to an increasingly self-conscious use of the term within the press, presumably creating a similar space for them to be consumed ironically by the reader. Angela McRobbie and Sarah Thornton further questioned the assumed subjugation of the reader by mass media within a moral panic, arguing that both inhabit much more complex mediated worlds, an analysis they developed especially in the light of the forms of micro-media produced by subcultures themselves, and by rave especially (1995). There is also the possibility that the moral panic reflects actual social concerns. In the case of NOS, we might point to the genuine concerns in the public about sexual abuse in and outside the church, that were still largely unrecognized, and that the moral panic at least created a space for airing.

In the same way, we can look beyond the often top-down structures of the 'sell-out' narrative, where popular experience is corralled into safe, institutional frameworks. Some theological scholars have recently explored a more complex understanding of the relationship between popular culture and religious practice. Victor Turner, for example, argued that leisure, including popular culture, filled the secularization gap though 'the function of the ritual frame'; a concept picked up nearly twenty years later by Graham St. John (St. John 2004; Turner 1987). In the American context, works like R. Laurence Moore's *Selling God* (1994), Colleen McDannell's *Material Christianity* (1996), David Morgan's *Visual Piety* (1997) and Leigh Eric Schmidt's *Consumer Rites* (1995) are all recognized as a new genre of work that moved away from the grand narratives of historical materialism within Cultural Studies (Schofield Clark 2007: 20; Morgan 2007: 24). Both Christopher Partridge and Graham St. John, for example, argue that the transmission of alternative spiritual ideologies is founded in the practices, technologies and experiences of popular culture (Partridge 2006; St. John 2004; 2009). It is significant that both writers place rave at the heart of their analyses. We will go a step further by seeing how the rave church movement can be used to understand how young Christians in the British context of the late 1980s and 1990s worked through the issues and concerns of their era from their lived immersion in popular culture, and through their engagement with the musical styles of rave in particular.

As historians we therefore want to add the experiences of the subculturalists themselves to the story, mediated and culturally reproduced through institutions as they may be. As academic research in the 2000s started engaging more and more explicitly with concepts of experience and participation, work around subcultures and religious practices (and their overlap) became increasingly produced through the ethnographic lens, with subcultural work developed by the participant observer, merging his or her experience with analysis (Beck and Lynch 2009; Gregory 2009; Kavanaugh and Anderson 2008; Lynch and Badger 2006; Marsh 2006; Rill 2010). Although not subcultural historians themselves, the perspectives on NOS developed by William John Lyons and Rupert Till would both fit into this category (Till 2006). For example, Lyons analysed a sermon given by John Rogerson, then Professor of Biblical Studies at Sheffield University, at NOS in August 1992, which the latter published with a short reflective introduction in 2002. Lyons traced the relationship between the text and the 'cultural setting of the Church of England' both before and after the news of the abuse within NOS was made public (Lyons 2014: 232). We must think, therefore, not just in terms of the press and media representations of NOS, not just in terms of the powerplay at work as an institution adjusts to new challenges, but also of the ideas, the active analysis and the experiences that lay behind the headlines.[4] Thus, in this chapter we integrate the different elements of both subcultural practices and religious identities: sound, visual, affective networks, intellectual communities, structural processes and cultural representation. NOS services were, after all, both the noisiest and the quietest that many people had ever attended (Warren 1989: 227). Working within this domain, we explore the ways in which rave and religion can be seen as part of a shared agenda and context, rather than using one to illustrate the other (Till 2006).

Subcultural agency and secularization

By the time that NOS came to St Thomas's, the changing role of the inner-city church was at the front of concerns facing the Church of England. As part of a longer trend of post-war secularization, there had been a decline in religious practice according to traditional measures such as opinion polls and church attendance numbers, with a corresponding growth of new religious movements and what has been described by historian Callum Brown as 'discursive

Christianity' (2001). Whether rooted in the early 1950s or in the 1960s, secularization became an umbrella term not just for changing belief and weekly practices, but also for a decline in deference, shifting national identity and legal liberalization (Black 2004: 109; Gilbert 1994: 520; Gill 2017; Green 2010). It is clear that the churches of the 1980s were divided over the role of female leadership, and facing new ecumenical challenges from a broadening of faith practices such as the growth of new age spiritualities, the spread of charismatic experiences more usually located within the non-establishment Pentecostal traditions and the more visible presence of heterodox off-shoots of Christianity such as the Jehovah's Witnesses and Mormons (Black 2004: 111–12). However, while there were campaigns to maintain the traditions of religious worship, such as Campaigns to Keep Sunday Special and the Prayer Book Society (founded in 1972), some of the countermeasures developed by various Christian groups were nonetheless based on an increasing value of social purpose and relevance. These tensions around purpose and relevance gave rise to some important political forces in Thatcher's Britain.

Quakers were central to the peace movement at Greenham Common. The Campaign for Nuclear Disarmament (CND) was by the 1980s led by 'the most famous Catholic Priest in the country', Bruce Kent (Turner 2010: 309). The Archbishop of Canterbury, Robert Runcie, became 'a thorn in the Conservative side', speaking out over the Falklands War and the Miners' Strike. He called for a compassionate response to unemployment, supported women priests and made moves to conciliate with Rome. Runcie commissioned a report on the impact of social deprivation in cities, and the Church of England's possible responses. *Faith in the City* was released in autumn 1985 and promoted by David Shepherd, the Bishop of Liverpool, himself more associated with the evangelical tradition in the church, in contrast to Runcie's liberalism (Archbishop of Canterbury's Commission on Urban Priority Areas 1985). Runcie himself published a set of lectures on 'authority in crisis', in which he set out an alternative to the pulls of authoritarianism and permissiveness (1988). In 1990, he wrote about the importance of prison reform and the possibility of ecologically responsible scientific knowledge (1990a; 1990b). Under Runcie, the response to secularization was to build a more social gospel, delivered in a more contemporary manner (Black 2004: 108). The role of evangelism in this rejuvenation was nonetheless problematic. Was there room within Runcie's social gospel for the type of conversion experience that he himself had had as an adolescent? Would caring for the social welfare of the populace also care for their spiritual welfare? Such questions were also inseparable from anxieties around the direction of popular culture under Thatcher, and the apparent drift from the collective social obligations of the post-war consensus towards the individualisms of market capitalism, a development often connected with the wider story of secularization. In his book *The Death of Christian Britain*, which traces these trends, Callum Brown nonetheless points out that evangelicalism and its relative numerical and cultural retrenchment is one of the key elements that has been largely omitted from historical work on secularization (2009: 118–26). He also points out that it has developed in the UK context in an intensely gendered form, mediated as it has been by a succession of prominent male, charismatic leaders and teachers, from William Wilberforce and the Wesleys, through to David Watson and John Stott. We might take Brown further and argue that evangelicalism's resilience was in part down to its ability to function as a coherent subculture, built around its own networks, forms of identification, styles, codes and languages (Robinson and Warne forthcoming). Indeed, it was evangelicalism in its gendered form which was key to NOS's development, with Brain another potential addition to the line of successful, male, evangelical leaders. And yet, for all its resilience, evangelicalism in the UK in the 1970s and 1980s was increasingly marked by internal debates about its incapacity to materially influence the central forces driving British society. The term 'subculture' was readily deployed within such debates, but purely as a negative marker of the extent to which Evangelicals were trapped within a bubble of their own creation.[5] For all the emphasis on NOS by the wider church as a solution to the problem of outreach, it is notable, however, that most of NOS's successes came from recruiting from within the church, rather than bringing in people who were previously unconnected with it. According to Lyons and Till, it was the switched off, Christian young rather than the sinners in need of saving who were attracted by NOS. This suggests that they saw in it the potential for solutions to a number of problems that they had experienced within and without the church. If we consider the broader rave church movement in this way, that is as a subcultural solution to a series of specific, contextual issues faced by a generationally and socially aligned cohort, then we can begin to understand its wider significance for the relationship between the sacred and the profane.

The rave church movement as practice transcending the sacred and the profane

Our point, then, is that rave culture presents itself as a subcultural solution for a number of dilemmas faced by young evangelicals in late 1980s and early

1990s Britain. Rave had a number of advantages: it was young and dynamic, understood as the first genuinely revolutionary subculture since punk; it was precisely of its moment. It simultaneously articulated the reach of Thatcherism and also provided the grounds for its rejection. Rave was part of their world too and offered every opportunity to escape the parallel evangelical subculture. Finally, the respective practices of each subculture were closely aligned, and gave credence to the rave church as a space in which to overcome a series of binaries and contradictions which had served to marginalize earlier forms of evangelical practice: religious versus secular, mind versus body, sacred versus profane. In this section, we will therefore look at three ways in which this more general alignment of subcultural practices resulted in specific forms of sacred song expression within the broader evangelical rave church movement.

'In the world but not of it': redemption and creation

One of the key threads that runs through evangelical subcultures is an ambivalence about the believer's presence in the world, and especially her or his relationship to contemporary culture. The foundational commitment to the authority of the bible within evangelicalism usually means there is a straightforward biblical trope to represent the way that any dilemma or faith problem is understood. In this case it revolves around condensing a prayer of Jesus for his disciples (John 17:14–15), with Paul's injunction to the early Christians at Rome (Romans 12:1–2) into the phrase 'be in the world but not of it'.[6] Before their engagement with rave, evangelical Christians therefore did so from within a long tradition of debate and discussion about the extent to which it was helpful to engage with contemporary phenomena, especially in the realm of music, leisure and popular entertainment. For those specifically involved in the rave church movement, this often came in the form of discussions about rock and pop music, whether at church youth groups, University Christian Unions, one-off youth gatherings and festivals, or through engaging with the burgeoning Christian media devoted to the question.[7]

Alongside a strong defensive position that saw all engagement with contemporary secular pop culture as problematic and likely injurious to spiritual health, two strands moulded those who resisted such isolationism, which we identify as Redemption on the one hand, and Creation on the other. It is important to underline that these are not necessarily formally held positions – although they were certainly formally articulated by certain Christian writers and theologians[8] – but rather informal or even subconscious ways of structuring the frameworks of faith and belief. In some ways, it is possible to understand the story of NOS as a collective in the process of moving from one perspective to the other – the more they embraced creation theology, the more they emphasized their autonomy as a group from the rest of the evangelical movement, which was more comfortable with a theology of redemption. In that respect, it was perfectly possible for groups or individuals to move across these two frameworks according to need, or to remain ambivalently committed to neither or both.

Adhering more classically to the broad evangelical perspective is the Redemption framework: this starts with the premise that the world is fallen, and that the consequences of that fall run through all human activity and creativity. Thus, all contemporary culture bears its trace to a greater or lesser degree. However, the fallen nature of humanity provides the context for its redemption. The incarnation and redemptive sacrifice of Christ is therefore understood not just as a means to rescue individual sinners, but as a way of bringing all of creation back in line with its original purpose. It was then a simple step to develop a position whereby the concept of creation extended beyond the original divine creation in order to encompass all human acts of creativity that stem from that original inspired act. Therefore, all products of human creativity, providing they bear the sign of the divine spark, are potentially redeemable for the believer.

The Creation perspective on the other hand, more loosely connected with Catholic and liberal traditions, may perhaps be seen as the more radical in relation to evangelical orthodoxy. This approach took issue with the notion of a fallen creation, and argued that traditional Christianity's emphasis on sacrifice, sin and worldly corruption are historically derived from patriarchal structures that have sought to eliminate both the natural, and its embodiment in the feminine, from patterns of spiritual thought and action. Contemporary Christians were consequently seen as both alienated from their own bodies (the origins of the contemporary crisis of sexual identities) and from the natural world (the origins of the contemporary environmental crisis). The Creation perspective therefore presented itself as a break with modern forms of evangelical Christianity and emphasized the need for a thorough reworking of worship practice, pastoral care and church organization.

It is important to underline that each respective emphasis on Redemption or Creation produced very specific forms of practice that sought to reshape the relationship between the worldly and the divine. Through their interest in the potentially divine nature of culture, Redemption-ers were free to use any contemporary form and redeem it through incorporation into worship: a club night became a worship night. Songs that celebrated love were reinterpreted as picturing the relationship between God and the believer.⁹ Sampled vocal phrases – a feature especially of American garage house, Italo house, happy house and early hardcore rave – and themselves taken out of their original context, were recontextualized in a set list, or harmonized with chosen visuals to emphasize their new spiritual meaning. The origins of disco and house in the African-American church traditions of singing, yearning for freedom, call and response, and full body engagement were also welcomed as a form of historical recovery, and a means of connecting to historic civil rights movements where religious activism had brought about meaningful social change.

In contrast, Creation-ers emphasized the need to counter male hierarchies of stardom and performance, hence the initial attraction of anti-hierarchical rave. This highlighted the need to recover the physicality of worship, with a focus on styles that appealed to the whole body and all the senses, and its reinsertion into the horizontal, social relationship of the collective. By the mid-1980s, much of evangelical charismatic Christianity's worship styles had become oriented towards the individual ecstatic experience within the crowd, replicating the format of a pop/rock concert where everyone faces the front and venerates the performer. NOS themselves adopted this format in their initial services but were clearly exercised by its limitations, and played with it in sometimes provocative ways. When they presented their Planetary Mass at the Greenbelt festival in 1992, parts of the audience were shocked by the 'bikini-clad dancers' who took part in the production. Brain explained to his detractors that he was invoking a universal eroticism, and reclaiming it from the pornographers. Of course, in retrospect, revelations about Brain's sexual abuse gave a subsequently more sinister tone to this justification, but if we accept that such production decisions were not taken by Brain alone, then we can also place it in the context of the wider endeavour to challenge ideas of what constitutes worship, of what constitutes a performance, and how both might align as part of an effort to overcome mind-and-body or sacred-and-profane dualisms. This notion of 'worship in the round' had pushed NOS to move outside of the traditional ecclesiastical architectural space of St Thomas's, initially in the form of the Sunday nightclub 'Fruit' in a centrally located night club in Sheffield, and subsequently to the Ponds Forge leisure centre. NOS's designated DJ, Winnie Brain (Chris Brain's wife and the mother of their child), used the Fruit club nights to build the mood to a climax using group favourite floorfillers selected from the repertoire of tunes generally doing the rounds on the contemporary post-rave scene, interspersed with periodic short bursts of NOS-produced ambient music also used in their more formal worship services, to enable individual meditation and reflection within a context of shared euphoria. In the same way, Oxford's Joy and Birmingham's Redemption deliberately hid the DJ behind a projection screen or placed her or him at the back of the room with the sound desk, in order to let the visuals take centre stage. The underlying point here is that the physical arrangement of the liturgical space mattered, whether events were held in a church, festival tent, nightclub, pub function room or leisure centre. Both Redemption-ers and Creation-ers sought the total occupation and reclaiming of those spaces through elaborate, carefully planned architectural combinations of sound and vision.

Eclecticism and sampling

The second way in which rave could find common ground with evangelical Christianity was in its global eclecticism. For all its origins in the Western heartlands of central Europe, the UK, and of course the US, evangelical Christianity was accustomed to adopting a global perspective on its historical development. Whether that be in its formal origins in the nineteenth-century abolitionist movement or its long-standing commitment to the project of world evangelization through the various missionary movements, evangelical Christians were comfortable with being locally situated, but connected to a global web of knowledge interchange, cultural exchange, geographical mobility and supranational organization. Any evangelical church would provide access to pamphlets, books and devotional literature from a global network of otherwise cottage-industry scale publishers. It would be typical to find some form of DIY display highlighting the missionary work of members of the congregation spread across the globe. Periodic visits from globetrotting celebrity speakers or worship leaders accompanied the growth of developing world and charity action in the 1970s and 1980s.[10] Organizations such as Tear Fund and World Vision sat alongside more traditional charitable enterprises of evangelization and Bible translation (for example, the Wycliffe Bible Translators). The theology of incarnation is also important here: from this perspective, Christianity belonged to all, and could embed itself in any local language or culture, while retaining a universal dimension that transcended local difference.

Rave made similar claims to eclectic universality, and its myriad genres and sub-genres, its cross subcultural appeal – bringing together ex-punks, ex-indie kids, ex-hip hoppers, ex-hippies, even serving military personnel[11] – while potentially competitive and fragmentary, could also be celebrated under a multicultural umbrella. This emphasis on the federative force of rave and post-rave was exemplified in the self-consciously unitary ethos of the mid-1990s UK dance music festival Tribal Gathering. The practice of electronic music composition using specific forms of technology encouraged an approach to creating tracks by the process of assembling layers, loops and blocks, structured around a dynamic of crescendo and the breakdown. In turn, digital sampling potentially opened up the whole history of recorded music as a source from which these compositional elements could be drawn.

In the rave church context, this started with the reuse of existing records: 'spiritual' tracks such as The Source Feat. Candi Staton 'You've Got the Love', itself a hybrid of disco, gospel and the Ibiza Balearic scene (1991); Inner City's social-spiritual positive 'Hallelujah '92' (1992); or the more traditionally gospel-styled Voices of 6th Avenue's 'Call Him Up' (1992). Alternatively, DJs created their own club-oriented sacred songs: Perotin's 'Viderunt Omnes' (1989) mixed perfectly with Dub Poets 'Black and White' (1992) even to the point of the seemingly preordained breakdown at 3:53 into the mix;[12] Thomas Tallis's 'Spem in Alium' (1985) blended with a track from DJ Pierre's *Love Trax* (1992);[13] the 'Introitus "Resurrexi"' from the Gregorian Easter Mass (Chor Der Mönche Der Benediktiner-Erzabtei, Beuron and Pfaff n.d.) sounded like it was deliberately composed to align with Darkman's 'Annihilating Rhythm' (1992), and so on.[14]

Existing Christian worship forms were equally transformed by adding an expedient backbeat. Musical practices of folk and everyday culture were especially attractive idioms when they were drawn from other ecumenical groups experimenting with the sense of embodied worship; for example, chants from the Taizé Community in France or songs from Scotland's Iona Community written by John Bell and Graham Maule (Bell and Maule 1987; Taizé Community 1991). This apparent historical eclecticism, often characterized by contemporaries as postmodern, held a specific purpose in the context of the rave church. The eclecticism reached back to early modern, medieval and classical forms of religious practice and organization, which pre-dated the hard divide between the religious and the secular established by the modern liberal political settlement and which these groups sought to transcend. It is no coincidence that the republished texts of various medieval and early modern religious mystics also circulated widely within the movement. These writings were seen to embody forms of spiritual practice that reflected a more integrated vision of the relationship between sacred and profane, and provided a ready source of inspirational texts for use in the visual environment of a rave service.[15]

In fact, this eclectic approach extended right through the creation of that visual environment. The process of sampling audio could be easily mapped onto that of sampling video, and the notion of the loop was also widely used to present images replete with symbolism, for example NOS's use of black-and-white images of a high diver plunging into a pool to reinforce the lyrical content of embracing the divine. Here contemporary filmic practices such as those time-lapse sequences seen in films such as Godfrey Reggio's *Koyaanisqatsi* (1982), or BBC nature documentaries slipped in alongside images plundered from music video and overlaid with aspects of Christian iconography. Rave itself was used to play around with religious imagery, especially traditions of Catholic Sacred Heart imagery often celebrated for their kitchiness, but this was extended into borrowing from the icon traditions of Eastern Orthodox Christianity, or the visual language of banners and murals developed in the contexts of liberation theology in Latin America. This created an initially much less-familiar visual palette for evangelical Christians habituated to the more generally austere emphasis of their worship traditions, and perhaps explains why some critics from the more conservative evangelical wing seized on this visual range as a sign that the movement had lost its anchor in biblical orthodoxy (Cummings 1995).

Mapping the structures of rave organization onto the structures of the Christian church: the DJ as prophet

The final way in which rave culture was aligned with evangelical Christianity came through an understanding of how leadership and authority could be exercised. One of the challenges for the Western Christian churches of all denominations in the latter part of the twentieth century was how to adapt its essentially hierarchical and ecclesiastical patterns of authority and management onto an era that demanded less deference and more collective participation in order to achieve organizational goals. Here evangelicals drew on long Free Church traditions that were sceptical of centralized religious authority and combined them with patterns of organization found rather frequently on the free party rave scene, with its emphasis on collective organization and shared contribution. Rave worship nights were similarly collective enterprises, involving creative contributions from DJs, musicians, visual artists, technicians, sculptors and set builders, as well as promoters, graphic designers and production managers. Here the overlap with the para-student worlds of the recently graduated in college and university towns, such as NOS's connection to the theology departments at Sheffield University and Ridley Hall, Cambridge, became an important sociological dimension of the rave church movement, with individuals frequently able to develop roles within the group that mirrored or tracked their early moves into their post-tertiary education professional and work careers. Here, the rave church provided an arena for sustaining the often intensive experiences of shared living in the proto-familial relationships characteristic of shared student accommodation.

While this seems an entirely secular model for understanding the dynamics of collective organization, rave culture also offered the possibility of giving this a spiritual twist, specifically through the idea of the DJ as tribal shaman, who channelled the spiritual collective subconscious through her or his timely choice of tracks to express the group's emotional self-understanding. Put in simple terms, for the evangelical rave church movement, the DJ became a prophet. This perspective gained anecdotal resonance in the story of when Winnie Brain met with the Kansas City Prophets on a visit to the Toronto Airport Vineyard Christian church at the height of the so-called Toronto blessing movement. Reporting on the meeting to the NOS congregation in late 1991, the Brains presented what they saw as the ultimate endorsement for their experiments in rave Christianity. One of the Kansas prophets, Bob Jones, was given to bestowing 'spiritual mantles' onto those whom he identified as having a special role to play in the forthcoming prophesied revival. In Winnie's case, Jones suggested her role had something to do with an unusual gift, which he represented by making a gesture akin to a DJ mixing. The general astonishment and appreciation of the NOS congregation for this story was confirmed when it was underlined that Bob Jones had never met the Brains prior to this encounter, neither had he heard of NOS, nor rave culture.

Conclusion

This anecdote underlines the extent to which NOS itself came to resemble something of a hybrid between traditional forms of church authority, new collective forms of organization, and as the group came to wider national prominence within Christian circles, a form of subcultural celebrity. Brain's ordination only further emphasized the connection between NOS, St Thomas's and the wider historic context of evangelical subcultural traditions in the UK, especially with regards to the prominence of conservative forms of masculine authority. In particular, NOS simply replicated the broader tendency to celebrate especially charismatic, often male leaders, whose teaching and ministry seemed to offer the solutions to a number of problems faced by the church in its time. Evangelical history is marked by a succession of these celebrity leaders, perhaps less frequently by their subsequent fall from grace as in Brain's case. This peculiar leadership dynamic can be used to explain the success of NOS, but also provides a clear structural explanation for the abuse of power, and particularly the abuse of sexual power that lay at the heart of its ultimate collapse.

However, those very same subcultural traditions also created a space for a creative encounter between the sacred and the profane in 1990s Britain, in which relatively small groups of evangelical Christians conducted experiments that sought to connect their everyday cultures with a yearning for social transformation and spiritual transcendence. In their critical and conscious engagement with the contemporary, in their deployment of sampling as a means to root eclecticism in time and place and in their striving for forms of collective, communicative organization, they underlined how the meeting between the sacred and the profane could produce more than just the cautionary tale of excess and abuse represented by NOS. Their example pushes us to re-examine the dynamics of contemporaneous experiments in popular culture completely unconnected with religion.

The relationship between contemporary religion and popular culture in the UK has certainly developed since the 1990s in general, and NOS in particular. Understanding this relationship invites interdisciplinary approaches. Hitherto, the focus has more predominantly been on how ideas about popular culture can illuminate research in theology (Lynch 2007: 1), often by using popular culture as a cipher through which to then interpret events 'that transcend popular culture itself' (Schofield Clark 2007: 6). We hope that through our own focus on the British rave church movement as an intertwined subcultural history, we have shown how a focus on popular culture can do more than just service the understanding of religion, but that the reverse can also be true.

Notes

1 At the time of the NOS scandal in 1995, Tim Riches of Synergy in Leeds is quoted as estimating that 200 rave-style services existed in the UK, although this figure seems rather high to the authors (Brown and McKie 1995). Although last updated in 2012, the 'Alternative Worship' website gives a decent overview of the range of groups that can be historically connected to the original rave church movement (Collins 2012).
2 Theologian Rachel Atkinson connects NOS and the rave church movement to an ongoing thread of experimentation broadly grouped under the term 'alt.worship' (2006). While acknowledging these broader currents, we are strictly concerned in this chapter with understanding its expression in the context of early 1990s Britain.

3 For a more detailed analysis of how NOS can be seen as both moral panic and sell-out, see our companion piece Robinson and Warne (forthcoming).
4 It should be noted that one of the authors writes as a former participant in a rave church in Birmingham, and that much of the analysis of the subcultural practice of the movement featured below is derived from that experience.
5 We might put the contemporary emergence of the evangelical right in the US as emerging from a similar apprehension of failure to shape the secular world. The overtly political solution adopted there, such that the terms 'evangelical' and 'right Republican' are now more or less synonymous, was not mirrored to nearly the same extent in the UK, despite the potential appeal of Thatcherism, doubtless in part because of the historic links between evangelicalism, Methodism and the labour movement.
6 A good example of the often folksy advice that can be attached to this trope can be found on one of the numerous American evangelical websites, GotQuestions.org, a 'Christian, Protestant, evangelical, theologically conservative, and non-denominational ... para-church ministry, coming alongside the church to help people find answers to their spiritually related questions' (GotQuestions.org n.d.).
7 The Greenbelt Festival has been mentioned above, but it was one of several on the Christian circuit, with each representing a broad strand within evangelicalism. These included the 'Spring Harvest' gatherings at various Butlins holiday camps over the Easter vacation, the 'Crossfire Festival' on the Aintree racecourse and the 'Soul Survivor' family festival at Minehead. Specific media targeted at young Christians included *Buzz*, *Strait* and *Cross Rhythms* magazines. Books tackling the question of Christianity and rock music: Lawhead (1981); Blanchard with Anderson and Cleave (1983); Ward (1992). The debate is neatly summarized by Hughes (2005).
8 In the UK during the 1980s and 1990s, the Redemption focus was prominently represented by *Third Way* magazine and its attempts to work through theologian Os Guinness's appeal for evangelical Christians to find a middle way between outright rejection and uncritical acceptance of contemporary culture. Creation theology was most associated in the 1990s with the writings of ex-Dominican Matthew Fox (especially 1983).
9 The Biblical precedent here is the 'Song of Solomon' (or 'Song of Songs'), an Old Testament love poem interpreted by Christian theologians as picturing the relationship between Christ and the church.
10 The origins of NOS itself were frequently traced to the visit by the American evangelical charismatic pastor John Wimber, leader of the Vineyard churches, to St Thomas's in 1985. The group that became its leaders reportedly experienced various overwhelming manifestations attributed to a new presence of the Holy

Spirit. The same year saw a UK speaking tour by American evangelical and social justice activist Jim Wallis, of the Washington-based Sojourners movement.

11   For the range of possible 'ex-es' who found their way into rave, see, for example, Griffiths (2013); Stone (1999); Courtney (2000); Boy George (1995).
12   Mix uploaded to: https://soundcloud.com/user-138192158/perotin-in-black-and-white.
13   Mix uploaded to: https://soundcloud.com/user-138192158/spem-in-acidium.
14   Mix uploaded to: https://soundcloud.com/user-138192158/acid-gregorian.
15   In the wake of the success of evangelical mystic and theologian Richard J. Foster's writings on everyday spiritual practice (1978 and 1981), for which he drew on a diverse range of mystics from a number of Christian traditions, his UK publisher Hodder & Stoughton reissued the writers referred to by Foster in a standalone series called 'Christian Classics'. UK evangelicals in the 1990s were not the first to explore the capacity of youth subcultures or popular music to reinvigorate Christian expression: Larry Eskridge (1998) explores how the Billy Graham Crusades sought to re-engage with youth in the 1970s via the creation of an evangelical youth culture. In a similar vein, Lillian Taiz (1997) explores how late-nineteenth century Salvationists sought to deploy 'the devil's works' (notably elements of contemporary popular culture) in their efforts to take their message beyond those already familiar with church.

References

Angier, P. (1997), *Changing Youth Worship*, London: Church House Publishing.
Archbishop of Canterbury's Commission on Urban Priority Areas (1985), *Faith in the City – A Call for Action by Church and Nation: Report of the Archbishop of Canterbury's Commission on Urban Priority Areas*, London: Church House Publishing.
Atkinson, R. (2006), 'Alternative Worship: Post-Modern or Post-Mission Church?', *Anvil*, 23 (4): 259–73.
BBC Radio 4 (1990), 'Changing Churches'. The segment on NOS is available online: '"The Nine O'Clock Service" – Radio 4 – 1990', https://www.youtube.com/watch?v=IYOunsaMZSU (accessed 12 August 2018).
Beck, G. and G. Lynch (2009), '"We Are All One, We Are All Gods": Negotiating Spirituality in the Conscious Partying Movement', *Journal of Contemporary Religion*, 24 (3): 339–55.
Bell, J. and G. Maule (1987), *Wild Goose Songs. Volume 1, Songs of Creation, the Incarnation, and the Life of Jesus*, Glasgow: The Iona Community.
Black, J. (2004), *Britain Since the Seventies: Politics and Society in the Consumer Age*, London: Reaktion.

Blanchard, J., with P. Anderson and D. Cleave (1983), *Pop Goes the Gospel*, Darlington: Evangelical Press.

Brain, C. (1993), 'Untitled', in D. Gillett and M. Scott-Joynt (eds), *Treasure in the Field: The Archbishop's Companion for the Decade of Evangelism*, 164–75, London: Fount.

Brown, A. and J. McKie (1995), '"Cult" priest in hospital and barred as minister', *Independent*, 26 August. Available online: https://www.independent.co.uk/news/cult-priest-in-hospital-and-barred-as-minister-1597924.html (accessed 14 August 2018).

Brown, C. G. (2009), *The Death of Christian Britain: Understanding Secularisation, 1800–2000*, London and New York: Routledge.

Chor Der Mönche Der Benediktiner-Erzabtei, Beuron and Pater M. Pfaff (n.d.), 'Introitus "Resurrexi"', *Gregorianischer Choral: Ostermesse (Missa In Dominica Resurrectionis)*, Archiv Produktion. Available online: https://www.discogs.com/Chor-Der-M%C3%B6nche-Der-Benediktiner-Erzabtei-Beuron-Pater-Maurus-Pfaff-Gregorianischer-Choral-Ostermes/release/1024398 (accessed 16 September 2020).

Cohen, S. (1972), *Moral Panics and Folk Devils*, London: MacGibbon & Kee.

Cohen, S. (1999), 'Moral Panics and Folk Concepts', *Paedagogica Historica*, 35 (3): 585–91.

Collins, S. (2012), 'Alternative Worship Website'. Available via Internet Archive: https://web.archive.org/web/20130723103105/https://www.alternativeworship.org/index.html (accessed 11 September 2020).

Courtney, D. (2000), *Raving Lunacy: Clubbed to Death: Adventures on the Rave Scene*, London: Virgin.

Cross Rhythms (1997), 'The Late Late Service: The Glasgow Dance Worship Pioneers', 39, 1 June. Available online: http://www.crossrhythms.co.uk/articles/music/The_Late_Late_Service_The_Glasgow_dance_worship_pioneers_/40758/p1/ (accessed 14 August 2018).

Cummings, T. (1995), 'The Media Scandal Behind Sheffield's Nine O'clock Service', *Cross Rhythms*, 29, 1 October. Available online: http://www.crossrhythms.co.uk/articles/music/The_Media_Scandal_Behind_Sheffields_Nine_OClock_Service_/40388/p1/ (accessed 12 August 2018).

Darkman (1992), 'Annihilating Rhythm (Tha Original London Monster Mix)', *Annihilating Rhythm/Seduction*, Strictly Rhythm. Available online: https://www.discogs.com/Darkman-Annihilating-Rhythm-Seduction/release/70823 (accessed 16 September 2020).

DJ Pierre (1992), 'Love Izz …', *Love Trax*, Strictly Rhythm. Available online: https://www.discogs.com/DJ-Pierre-Love-Trax/release/68947 (accessed 16 September 2020).

Dub Poets (1992), 'Black and White', Massive B. Available online: https://www.discogs.com/Dub-Poets-Black-White/release/39939 (accessed 16 September 2020).

Eskridge, L. (1998), '"One Way": Billy Graham, the Jesus Generation, and the Idea of an Evangelical Youth Culture', *Church History: Studies in Christianity and Culture*, 67 (1): 83–106.

Foster, R. J. (1978), *Celebration of Discipline*, San Francisco, CA: Harper & Row.
Foster, R. J. (1981), *Freedom of Simplicity*, San Francisco, CA: Harper & Row.
Fox, M. (1983), *Original Blessing*, Santa Fe, NM: Bear.
George, Boy (1995), *Take It Like a Man: The Autobiography of Boy George*, London: Sidgwick & Jackson.
Gilbert, A. D. (1994), 'Secularization and the Future', in S. Gilley (ed.), *A History of Religion in Britain Practice and Belief from Pre-Roman Times to the Present*, 503–21, Oxford: Blackwell.
Gill, R. (2017), *The 'Empty' Church Revisited*, London and New York: Routledge.
God in the House (1996), Part 3, 'World of Wonder' on Glasgow's Late Late Service, Channel 4 (UK). Available online: 'Late Late Service', https://www.youtube.com/watch?v=QQQbcb5YPBA (accessed 12 August 2018).
Grace (n.d.), 'Grace: Fresh Vital Worship since 1993'. Available online: http://www.freshworship.org/ (accessed 14 August 2018).
Green, S. J. D. (2010), *The Passing of Protestant England: Secularisation and Social Change, c.1920–1960*, Cambridge: Cambridge University Press.
Gregory, J. (2009), 'Too Young to Drink, Too Old to Dance: The Influences of Age and Gender on (Non) Rave Participation', *Dancecult: Journal of Electronic Dance Music Culture*, 1 (1): 65–80.
GotQuestions.org (n.d.), 'How can believers be in the world, but not of the world?', Available online: https://www.gotquestions.org/in-but-not-of-world.html (accessed 10 August 2018).
Griffiths, S. (2013), *Pig's Disco*, London: Ditto Press.
Guest, M. (2006), 'Nine O'clock Service', in P. Clarke (ed.), *Encyclopedia of New Religious Movements*, 461–3, London and New York: Routledge.
Hebdige, D. (1979), *Subculture: The Meaning of Style*, London: Routledge.
Howard, R. (1996), *The Rise and Fall of the Nine O'Clock Service*, London: A&C Black.
Hughes, T. O. (2005), 'Pop Music and the Church's Mission', *Anvil*, 22 (1): 41–53.
Inner City (1992), 'Hallelujah '92', 10 records. Available online: https://www.discogs.com/Inner-City-Hallelujah-92/release/44781 (accessed 16 September 2020).
Kavanaugh, P. R. and T. L. Anderson (2008), 'Solidarity and Drug Use in the Electronic Dance Music Scene', *Sociological Quarterly*, 49 (1): 181–208.
Kennedy, M. (2002), 'White Collar Crime: Vulnerable Women, Predatory Clergymen', *The Journal of Adult Protection*, 4 (4): 23–33.
Lawhead, S. R. (1981), *Rock Reconsidered: A Christian Looks at Contemporary Music*, Leicester: Inter-Varsity Press.
Lynch, G. (2006), 'The Role of Popular Music in the Construction of Alternative Spiritualities and Ideologies', *Journal for the Scientific Study of Religion*, 45 (4): 481–8.
Lynch, G. (2007), 'Introduction', in G. Lynch (ed.), *Between Sacred and Profane: Researching Religion and Popular Culture*, 1–4, London and New York: I.B. Tauris.
Lynch, G. and E. Badger (2006), 'The Mainstream Post-Rave Club Scene as a Secondary Institution: A British Perspective', *Culture and Religion*, 7 (1): 27–40.

Lyons, W. J. (2014), 'Preaching at the Nine O'clock Service: A Study of Shifting Meaning in a Published Sermon', in W. J. Lyons and I. Sandwell (eds), *Delivering the Word: Preaching and Exegesis in the Western Christian Tradition*, 231–45, London and New York: Routledge.

Marsh, C. (2006), 'Understand Us Before You End Us: Regulation, Governmentality, and the Confessional Practices of Raving Bodies', *Popular Music*, 25 (3): 415–30.

McRobbie, A. and S. L. Thornton (1995), 'Rethinking "Moral Panic" for Multi-Mediated Social Worlds', *British Journal of Sociology*, 46 (4): 559–74.

Morgan, D. (2007), 'Studying Religion and Popular Culture: Prospects, Presuppositions, Procedures', in G. Lynch (ed.), *Between Sacred and Profane: Researching Religion and Popular Culture*, 21–33, London and New York: I.B. Tauris.

Partridge, C. (2006), 'The Spiritual and the Revolutionary: Alternative Spirituality, British Free Festivals, and the Emergence of Rave Culture', *Culture and Religion*, 7 (1): 41–60.

Perotin (1989), 'Viderunt Omnes', *The Hilliard Ensemble – Perotin*, ECM Records. Available online: https://www.discogs.com/Perotin-The-Hilliard-Ensemble-Perotin/release/1557025 (accessed 16 September 2020).

Puttick, E. (1997), *Women in New Religions: In Search of Community, Sexuality, and Spiritual Power*, New York: St. Martins Press, 1997.

Rill, B. (2010), 'Identity Discourses on the Dancefloor', *Anthropology of Consciousness*, 21 (2): 139–62.

Robinson, L. and C. Warne (forthcoming), 'Moral Panic, Sell-out or Subcultural Solution? the 1990s British Rave Church Movement Caught Between the Local and the Global'.

Rogerson, J. (2006), 'The Lord is Here: The Nine O'Clock Service', in I. S. Markham and M. Percy (eds), *Why Liberal Churches Are Growing*, 45–52, London: T&T Clark.

Runcie, R. A. K. (1988), *Authority in Crisis? An Anglican Response*, London: SCM Press.

Runcie, R. A. K. (1990a), *Reform, Renewal and Rehabilitation*, London: Prison Reform Trust.

Runcie, R. A. K. et al. (1990b), 'God is Green, So is Science. (Ecology)', *New Perspectives Quarterly*, 7 (2): 68.

Schofield Clark, L. (2007), 'Why Study Popular Culture?', in G. Lynch (ed.), *Between Sacred and Profane: Researching Religion and Popular Culture*, 5–20, London and New York: I.B. Tauris.

Spinks, B. D. (2011), *The Worship Mall: Contemporary Responses to Contemporary Culture*, New York: Church Publishing.

St. John, G. (2004), *Rave Culture and Religion*, London: Routledge.

St. John, G. (2009), *Technomad*, Oxford: Berghahn.

Stone, C. J. (1999), *The Last of the Hippies*, London: Faber & Faber.

Sullivan, M. (1987), '"More Popular Than Jesus": The Beatles and the Religious Far Right', *Popular Music*, 6 (3): 313–26.

Taiz, L. (1997), 'Applying the Devil's Works in a Holy Cause: Working-Class Popular Culture and the Salvation Army in the United States, 1879-1900', *Religion and American Culture: A Journal of Interpretation*, 7 (2): 195–223.

Taizé Community (1991), *Songs and Prayers from Taizé*, London: Geoffrey Chapman.

Tallis, T. (1985), 'Spem in Alium', *The Tallis Scholars, Peter Phillips*, Gimell. Available online: https://www.discogs.com/Thomas-Tallis-The-Tallis-Scholars-Peter-Phillips-Spem-In-Alium/release/1248813 (accessed 16 September 2020).

The Source featuring Candi Staton (1991), 'You Got the Love', Truelove Communications. Available online https://www.discogs.com/The-Source-Featuring-Candi-Staton-You-Got-The-Love-Erens-Bootleg-Mix/release/6272800 (accessed 19 November 2020).

Till, R. (2006), 'The Nine O'clock Service: Mixing Club Culture and Postmodern Christianity', *Culture and Religion*, 7 (1): 93–110.

Truelove Presents …; The Source Featuring Candi Staton (1991), 'You Got the Love (Erens Bootleg Mix)', Truelove Electronic Communications. Available online: https://www.discogs.com/release/66632 (accessed 16 September 2020).

Turner, A. W. (2010), *Rejoice! Rejoice! Britain in the 1980s*, London: Aurum.

Turner, V. (1987), 'Carnival, Ritual, and Play in Rio de Janeiro', in A. Falassi (ed.), *Time Out of Time: Essays on the Festival*, 74–90, Albuquerque: University of New Mexico Press.

Villiers, J. D. (1996), 'Clergy Malpractice Revisited: Liability for Sexual Misconduct in the Counseling Relationship', *Denver University Law Review*, 74 (1–2): 22–9.

Visions (n.d.), 'Visions: Feet on the Ground, Living on the Edge'. Available online: http://www.visions-york.org/ (accessed 14 August 2018).

Voices of 6th Ave. (1992), 'Call Him Up', Ace Beat Records. Available online: https://www.discogs.com/Voices-Of-6th-Ave-Call-Him-Up/release/95411 (accessed 16 September 2020).

Ward, P. (1992), *Youth Culture and the Gospel*, London: Marshall Pickering.

Warren, R. (1989), *In the Crucible: The Testing and Growth of a Local Church*, Crowborough: Highland Books.

Young, J. (1971), *The Drugtakers: The Social Meaning of Drug Use*, London: Paladin.

Young, J. (2009), 'Moral Panic: Its Origins in Resistance, Ressentiment and the Translation of Fantasy into Reality', *British Journal of Criminology*, 49 (1): 4–16.

6

Pop Goes to Church: Pentacostal Evangelism and 'Chav' Christianity

Georgina Gregory

At the average British church, hymns continue to play a central role in a tried and trusted repertoire of sacred music, yet in an increasingly secular society, adhering to traditional music potentially alienates some members of the community who might benefit from taking part, especially those unfamiliar with hymns and the practice of public choral singing. Nowadays, hymn singing is no longer the shared cultural practice it once was when established favourites were a regular feature at school assemblies, weddings and funerals. As a result, the words and melodies of former classics may appear obscure and archaic, making participation problematic. At the same time, church attendance in the UK is steadily declining, and while there may be multiple reasons for diminishing congregations and waning commitment, is it possible that secular chart music might help to reverse the trend and attract the disaffected and under-represented? There is evidence the genre has already infiltrated into important rituals formerly dominated by sacred music – so much so, it is no longer unusual to hear pop songs played at church weddings and funerals. Indeed, a 2019 survey of data collected from British funeral directors revealed there were no hymns in the top ten songs used in funeral services, and the results point to a similar drift towards pop music at weddings, religious or civil.[1] This suggests that people are actively choosing to relate popular music to important life events and are likely to continue to do so.

This chapter explores declining churchgoing and how music is used to articulate sacred religious experience in Britain, looking at the role played by social class in determining which music dominates. Early attempts to harness popular music to Christian evangelism provide a context for a case study of Ignite Elim Pentacostal church in Lincoln, where a pastor uses drum and bass and mainstream pop songs to attract socially excluded parishioners. In doing this, he has helped them to access practical and spiritual support from their local church. By analysing specific songs enjoyed by the congregation, I demonstrate how, in an era where the state is relinquishing its duties to protect disadvantaged families, popular music is proving to be a powerful medium of social inclusivity. The chapter's aim is not to promote Christian religious observance or the idea that the church should be a substitute for state support, rather, in an increasingly secular era, it seeks to illustrate utility of popular music as an egalitarian evangelical tool.

Christianity in decline

Throughout the twentieth century the number of self-professed, practising Christians in the global north has diminished (Bellofatto and Johnson 2013; Gushee 2016), noticeably so in the UK where historian Callum Brow notes how '[i]n unprecedented numbers, the British people since the 1960s have stopped going to church, have allowed their church membership to lapse, have stopped marrying in church and have neglected to baptise their children' (Brown 2009: i). By way of evidence, he observes that in some parts of Britain only 3 per cent of the population attend church on a regular basis, a paltry figure compared with the surges in active church membership during the 1940s and 1950s (Brown 2009: 3). A report on religion commissioned by the Christian charity Tearfund (2007: 6) states around two-thirds of the British public claim no religious belief whatsoever; moreover, if current trends continue, Steven Bruce predicts Christianity's potential demise by 2025 (Bruce 2000). In light of the above information, it is easy to assume that Christianity lacks relevance in modern British life and with the advent of more secular thinking, negative perception of overt declarations of Christian faith is leading to a scenario where according to one believer:

> [Calling] yourself a Christian in contemporary Britain is to invite pity, condescension or cool dismissal. In a culture that prizes sophistication, non-judgmentalism, irony and detachment, it is to declare yourself intolerant, naive, superstitious and backward.
>
> (Gove 2015)

Rather than espousing a recognized religion, the UK public are much more likely nowadays to refer to themselves as 'spiritual but not religious' (Hughes 2012; Mercadante 2014).[2] The proliferation of Mind, Body, Spirit festivals since the late 1970s is symptomatic of this shift towards personalized 'spiritual' practices which are replacing regular church attendance.[3] Various scholars offer explanations for the popularity of these bespoke practices, notably Matthew Guest (2007), who suggests the term 'spirituality' is invoked to express dissatisfaction with traditional religious observance and a desire to break with convention. Others link the newer forms of spirituality to a wider subjective turn, where sensitivity to inner life is viewed to be more important than outward displays of conformity to religious convention (Heelas et al. 2004). Similarly, in the case of Christianity, Andrew Yip (2002) identifies a preference for personalized interpretations of the Bible, based more upon lived experience than religious authority.

Nevertheless, it is interesting to note that more than 26 million of the UK population still claim some affiliation with Christianity, even if they rarely go to church (Tearfund 2007: 6). Reasons cited for infrequent attendance by the loosely affiliated followers include a complaint that 'the Church is an out of date, out of touch institution that doesn't reflect their values' (McKay 2014). The point is elaborated by Rupert Till who contends,

> in a literate culture with widespread education, where religions have become heavily influenced by accumulated cultural practices rather than their original teachings, if those cultural practices and preferences become out of pace with public opinion, then the religion concerned is in danger of no longer being culturally relevant.
>
> (Till 2010: 4)

Public campaigns to preserve the tradition of churchgoing do not appear to have been particularly successful and the need to address post-war secularization remains a challenge for many churches.[4] By following their example and using social media platforms such as Facebook, Twitter or YouTube to communicate (Webb 2012: 246), some ministers are responding to demands for greater relevance by drawing on the success of fast-growing, media-savvy megachurches described by Susan Codone (2014). Despite worthy intentions, these efforts have not been entirely successful in reaching the socially disadvantaged, many of whom remain stubbornly disengaged.[5]

Disturbingly, in areas of socio-economic deprivation, the waning of religious observance is four times faster than in more prosperous communities (Sherwood 2016) and church attendance among those living in social housing now stands at less than half the national figure (Tearfund 2007: 6). Even if they do choose to engage, the less well-off are likely to find themselves marginalized at an institutional level and under-represented in church leadership roles where there are few peers or role models (Beckford 2012: 20). This suggests churches will need to employ some radical solutions if they are to reach socially excluded communities.

Sacred and secular solutions to poverty

If we look at the present dilemma within a historical context, Christians have consistently tried to fulfil the biblical remit to look after those with limited resources, whether by promoting religious observance as a source of psychological support, giving alms or providing much-needed practical help. During the nineteenth century, for example, distressed families could look to their local church for a combination of support and spiritual guidance. The Salvation Army was set up in 1865 by William Booth with the expressed aim of reaching out to the poor, offering practical help while introducing notions of Christian spirituality (Woodall 2017: 43–68). Rather than relying on conventional church attendance, Booth and his followers took religion to the streets, preaching and singing in public places alongside the homeless and hopeless, conducting evangelistic meetings in makeshift tents.

In a similar spirit, altruist John Pounds drew on his faith to establish the Ragged Schools movement in 1818, giving free education to needy working-class children (Schupf 1972). These initiatives show that nineteenth-century Christians attacked poverty head on, whereas in the twentieth century, a post-war consensus assumed the state would embrace many practical aspects in addressing economic and social inequality (Lowe 1998). However, with the resurgence of laissez-faire capitalism, post-1970s government intervention has diminished significantly. Successive austerity regimes are creating major hardship as the number of people experiencing poverty has risen concomitantly since the 1980s:

> During the 1960s, just over 10% of the population lived in a low-income household ... In 1979, when Margaret Thatcher was elected Prime Minister, changes in economic and social policy resulted in a trebling of the proportion of people living in low-income households.
>
> (Pantazis, Gordon and Levitas 2006: 4)

Increasingly, it seems, the state is jettisoning its obligations, offering instead vague notions of social solidarity centred around voluntarism as a free-market solution to deprivation. The point is elaborated by Stuart Hall who makes the following observations:

> According to the neoliberal narrative, the welfare state mistakenly saw its task as intervening in the economy, redistributing wealth, universalising life-chances, attacking unemployment, protecting the socially vulnerable, ameliorating the condition of oppressed or marginalized groups and addressing social injustice.
>
> (Hall 2011)

Quite recently, under the rhetoric of moving 'from state power to people power' (Cameron 2010), programmes of structural change like 'The Big Society' were designed to divest the state of a responsibility to look after those who cannot cope (Coote 2011: 82). An Oxfam case study describes the detrimental impact of this neoliberal approach to social problems:

> When all austerity measures are taken into account, including cuts to public services and changes to taxes and welfare, the poorest tenth of the population are by far the hardest hit, seeing a 38 per cent decrease in their net income over the period 2010–15. By comparison, the richest tenth will have lost the least, comparatively, seeing a 5 per cent fall in their income.
>
> (Oxfam 2013)

Amplifying these findings, a report compiled by The Trussell Trust, a charity dedicated to addressing food poverty, notes that UK housing costs are among the highest in Europe; moreover, 'low and stagnant wages, insecure and zero-hours contracts mean that for many low-income households, the money they are bringing home is less every month than their essential outgoings' (Cooper et al. 2014: 4). There may be a lack of state sympathy regarding the dilemma of those least well-off but Christian faith-based organizations are fully aware of a need for intervention. Over thirty years ago, the realities of social injustice were outlined in a *Faith in the City* report (Archbishop of Canterbury's Commission 1985). Subsequent reports including *Faithful Cities* (Commission on Urban Life and Faith 2006) and *Faith in Urban Regeneration* (Farnell et al. 2003) highlight the importance of ameliorating the impact of poverty, whether by means of state welfare programmes, church-based initiatives or a combination of both.

Social class and Christianity

Although Christian organizations are committed to offering help, as Michael Argyle (2000: 189) notes, regular religious observance is much more optional today than it once was. As a result, the local church may only be visited for occasional weddings, funerals or christenings.[6] Yet during the nineteenth century when Christianity flourished, so did regular churchgoing in areas of deprivation, mainly due to fervent efforts of the middle classes whose concerns were heightened when a census revealed only 50 per cent of the population attended church on Sundays (Robinson 2011). Influenced by contemporary cultural critic Matthew Arnold, wealthier members of society believed that policing the culture of an irreligious underclass and promoting respectable behaviour would help protect society from the threat of anarchy (Midgley 2012: 2). Poverty was perceived as threatening due to its potential to instigate revolutionary impulses, therefore churchgoing and notions of respectability, although 'potentially a great social leveller' were 'more often employed as an instrument of middle-class ideology' (McLeod 2016: 14).

As a poet and advocate of classical literature, Arnold's vision of civilizing the masses did not encompass drawing on popular culture to promote enlightenment. Instead, it involved making acquaintance with the classics, a strategy linked to middle-class notions of self-improvement and spiritual advancement. To this end he suggested cultural interventions reflective of 'the best that has been thought and known in the world current everywhere; to make all men live in an atmosphere of sweetness'. This definition would almost certainly have excluded the popular pastime of attending music halls because as Derek Scott (2008: 68) points out, as 'Culture for Arnold is not a broad term: he spares no time on the music hall'. No doubt the institution's lowbrow associations rendered it unsuitable as a medium for serious contemplation, but this labelling illustrates the extent to which critiques of popular culture are as much political as they are aesthetic or moral.[7] Popular songs heard in music halls were designated unacceptable and in churches, too, distinctions were enforced as different styles and sounds competed for acceptance, more so if they had any associations with the secular sphere.

Like some today, early Christians were particularly suspicious of expressions of devotion by means of bespoke song, which they believed, in the wrong hands, could introduce and transmit faulty doctrine. As a result, worshippers were encouraged to sing psalms or other passages from the Bible verbatim. Subsequently, hymns based around Christian themes were deemed acceptable, but religious leaders continued to police when and where they could be heard. Their efforts were not entirely successful, however, because people continued to sing hymns beyond the confines of church, 'often in the streets as well as the churches. Sometimes [singing] them in the streets because they could not sing them in the churches' (Castle 2012). Following the Reformation, hymns grew in popularity, with notable songwriters such as Isaac Watts helping to reform the character of congregational singing (Gant 2017: 223). Starting from the premise that songs should go beyond a literal interpretation of the Bible, he aimed to express everyday religious experience in classic texts such as 'O God Our Help in Ages Past' and 'Joy to the World'. Other prolific contributors like John and Charles Wesley also influenced the spread of choral hymn singing which soon became a central aspect of communal worship in Methodist churches.[8]

These developments illustrate that the preferences of those in power largely predominated over popular taste, yet some Victorian religious reformers, presumably mindful of music hall's capacity to engage the poor, attempted to draw on popular melodies enjoyed by the masses. A study of the work of British evangelist Smith Wigglesworth describes how one night in 1877 a large crowd gathered in Bradford's marketplace, their curiosity aroused by members of the Christian Mission, 'who were singing what appeared to be jaunty music-hall songs with great gusto, accompanied by a brass ensemble and the resonating thud of a big bass drum'. It transpired that the song was 'Bless His Name: He Sets Me Free', set to the tune of the popular music hall number 'Champagne Charlie is My Name'. By adhering closely to Christian lyrics, reformers were careful to avoid charges of sacrilegiousness and the venture's success undoubtedly helped to secure converts, including 'former prostitutes, convicts, thieves and drunkards' (Wilson 2011: 14), most of whom would not have enjoyed a welcome at staid, middle-class Christian church gatherings.

Contemporary sacred and secular intersections

If we extend the concept of harnessing popular music's power to promote Christianity in the present day, commercial pop is often viewed with suspicion. For instance, the medium was labelled a mindless form of entertainment by the sociologist Theodor Adorno, who famously claimed it 'does not involve the effort of concentration at all' (Adorno 1941: 17). In a similar vein, social theorist Jacques Attali complained how 'in a world now devoid of meaning' pop is little more than musical wallpaper, providing 'a background noise' (Attali 1985: 3). Others condemn the popular music's 'barbaric appeal to sexual desire' (Bloom 1987: 73) and its 'crude, loud, and tasteless' character (Pattison 1987: 4). Notwithstanding any potential utility it may offer, associating pop, rock and folk with liturgical practice is not universally accepted in sacred circles. Indeed, the 'use of popular styles of music in the Church has often proved contentious [and] a great deal of literature has appeared elaborating on the inappropriateness of such music' (Jones and Webster 2006: 429). Among others, 'middle-class people, aspiring socially upward, [perceive] working class and African American music as beneath them' (Wren 2000: 139), and yet 'the Church struggles to know how to engage with the working class, and the difficulties and issues they face, that perhaps the middle class don't face themselves' (Ferguson 2015). Furthermore, those who already lack agency have no say in establishing the repertoire since '[i]n the realm of religious music, ministers, worship leaders, and deacons' typically decide 'which music gets heard and in what circumstances'.

Taking onboard any moral and aesthetic objections, the assumption that secular and sacred music should operate in isolation from one another, fails to account for pop music's resonance with those born since World War II. Some scholars (Kelton 2005; Kommers 2011) suggest that for baby boomers, popular music has taken on various characteristics formerly attributed to mainstream religion; moreover, Virinder Kalra (2015: 8) argues that since what constitutes sacred is ultimately subjective, secular songs can become imbued with important spiritual meaning. Finally, we are reminded that '[t]heologians and religious scholars are not the only ones who pursue what people call divine' (Beaudoin 2013: ix–x). Certainly, there are some compelling examples of biblical themes overlapping with the popular music mainstream. Moreover, there are instances where pop styles and sounds are deliberately integrated within praise and worship songs, notably in contemporary Christian music, or 'Jesus Music', a genre synthesizing Bible-based lyrics with rock which began during the 1960s. Acknowledged pioneers, Children of the Day, recorded the album *Come to the Waters* in 1971 followed by *With All Our Love* in 1973 (Powell 2002: 164). In a similar manner, The Fisherfolk's album *Songs from Sounds of Living Waters* (1974) exemplified the charismatic Christian movement's efforts to fuse countercultural sentiments into the medium of contemporary folk music.

Many celebrated popular music auteurs, drawing on a lifelong personal commitment to Christianity, have traversed the boundaries of secular and sacred throughout their careers, appealing to believers and non-Christians alike via a mixture of religious and secular songs. For instance, Stevie Wonder's pensive album track 'Visions' (1973) alludes indirectly to passages from the book of Exodus, and in 'People Get Ready' (1965) Curtis Mayfield creates a deep sense of Christian spirituality through a vivid picture of an imagined return to the holy land, harnessing the song's universal appeal by transcending its biblical allusions to resonate with the civil rights movement.[9] In both cases, the artists were able to integrate African American gospel heritage within Christian-inflected themes to reach a mainstream audience. Others have used the medium to express newfound religious leanings following a mid-career conversion.[10] During the 1970s, following his conversion from Judaism, Bob Dylan recorded *Slow Train Coming*, an album expressing a strong Christian faith. Fellow singer-songwriter Van Morrison renewed his own 'non-denominational Christianity' in the 1989 album *Avalon Sunset* on tracks such as 'Whenever God Shines His Light' and

'When Will I Ever Learn to Live in God' (Mills 1994: 99). Some musicians have made a move from recording and performing for a predominantly Christian audience to gain acceptance in the secular mainstream: in the case of the metal band Stryper, their album *To Hell with The Devil* (1986) sold over a million copies and was recognized as a landmark in the glam metal movement (Christe 2004: 154). It is not uncommon, either, for musicians to reference matters biblical within a fundamentally secular repertoire. The song 'Turn, Turn, Turn' (1965) by The Byrds quotes directly lines from the book of Ecclesiastes; in 'Blessed' (1966) Simon and Garfunkel allude to The Sermon on the Mount; and in a more recent example, the artist Coolio speaks of Psalm 23 ('The Lord is my Shepherd') in the song 'Gangster's Paradise' (1994).[11]

A case study of Elim Pentacostal church, Lincoln

Most UK schools no longer include hymns in morning assembly and when it comes to singing them, a growing unfamiliarity is compounded by the public's lack of expertise in choral hymn singing. While choirs are acknowledged as a popular leisure pursuit (a recent survey indicated that over two million in the UK sing regularly), the majority do not focus on Christian music (Voices Now 2017: 2). Thus, although Simon Frith argues that 'most of us have sung hymns and carols at some stage of our lives [and] have come to associate church music with rituals of grief and celebration' (Frith 2001: 106–7), this is not necessarily so today. It is not surprising, then, to see why mainstream secular pop is making major inroads at church weddings and funerals, where it is by no means unusual to hear rock, pop, rap, soul, jazz or blues. At funerals, instead of hymns, 'bereaved families are inclined towards choosing contemporary songs which they closely identify with and reflect the life of their loved one' (Co-operative Funeral Care 2016).

Rather than traditional Christian songs like 'Abide with Me' or 'The Day Thou Gavest', families report a preference for modern pop classics such as Frank Sinatra's 'My Way' and 'Always Look on the Bright Side of Life' taken from the Monty Python film *The Life of Brian* (1979). The popularity of popular music in churches demonstrates changing perceptions of a medium once viewed as wholly incompatible with Christian values. Not only is it central to everyday experience, the regular repetition of rock and pop on radio, television and public places makes the songs easy to master. These are important considerations for anyone new to liturgy who may lack confidence with unfamiliar language and feel uncomfortable singing in front of others.

If we look now at the innovative template provided by pastor Darren Edwards in Lincoln, where according to a recent report (City of Lincoln Council 2011), around 10,000 people live in areas ranked as the most deprived in the UK. Pastor Edwards draws on personal experience of social deprivation (he was raised by a single mother and later by his grandparents, before embarking on a life of crime and drug addiction). For these reasons, he rejects religious robes in favour of tracksuits, shorts, hoodies, beanie hats, baseball caps and trainers.[12] In doing so, he signifies a powerful demonstration of allegiance to the dress code of his local community, many of whom are stigmatized as 'chavs' due to their espousal of similar clothing.[13] Edwards recognizes that poor parishioners may be put off attending church if they are expected to wear expensive 'Sunday Best', arguing he wants 'the average person to be given the opportunity to meet with God in their own way, and to feel comfortable' (Darren Edwards, interview with author, 8 June 2015).[14] Here he addresses head on, the difficulties local people face when trying to conform to middle-class conventions, a dilemma acknowledged over a century earlier by Victorian social reformer Henry Mayhew, who described the sartorial deficiencies of poor costermongers:

> They see people come out of church and chapel, and as they're mostly well dressed, and there's very few of their own sort among the church-goers, the costers somehow mix up being religious with being respectable, and so they have a queer sort of feeling about it. It's a mystery to them.
>
> (Mayhew 2010: 21)

By endorsing the espousal of mass-produced casual wear, Pastor Edwards allows parishioners to feel at home in church, helping to reject the negative stereotype of a social group who are '[r]outinely demonized within news media, television comedy programmes, and internet sites (such as thechavscum)', with levels of disgust 'suggestive of a heightened class antagonism that marks a new episode of class struggle in Britain' (Tyler 2006).

His radical approach also extends to the use of so called 'chav' pop songs in praise and worship services expressly designed to 'encourage unchurched people to come to church' – again giving his parishioners permission to take part on their own terms rather than insisting they identify with prescribed texts. (Darren Edwards, interview with author, 8 June 2015). Official sources outlining 'chav' music tastes are hard to find. According to one (Wallace and Spanner 2004: 94), drum and bass, while originally an underground genre, on reaching the mainstream, was adopted by 'the chav'. This comment implies that drum and bass was colonized by chavs and as a result, it automatically lost its social cachet as an esoteric music form for discerning insiders.

In addition to drum and bass, a genre semantically linked to chav culture, mainstream pop songs are enjoyed by many in the congregation. At the time of researching, the favourites included 'Burn' (2012) by Ellie Goulding, Jason Mraz's 'I Won't Give Up' (2012) and 'Crying For No Reason' by Katy B (2014). Other popular songs are 'Lifted' (Naughty Boy ft. Emeli Sande) (2013); Wiz Khalifa's 'See You Again' (2015); 'Rather Be' by Clean Bandit (2014); James Bay's 'Running' (2015) and the Emeli Sande song 'Wonder' (2013).

From an evangelical perspective, Edwards shows he recognizes the barriers presented by archaic language and unfamiliar melodies, using mainstream music to connect with those lacking middle-class Christian cultural capital, who might otherwise struggle. His aim is to help people overcome any resistance they may have to joining the congregation. In his words:

> Half of the problem is that people are scared to invite their friends to church because church is weird. If we try to make church less weird and more fun, people will automatically start inviting their friends to their 'awesome new church'. With this in mind, our church has seen lots of new people through the doors, maybe equal to churches that are a lot bigger and better funded than our own.
>
> (Darren Edwards, interview with author, 8 June 2015)

As part of his strategy, pop is interspersed with regular hymns and contemporary Christian music because Edwards avoids maintaining a strict binary between secular and sacred music on grounds that 'some of our guys don't know which songs are secular and which are Christian because the lyrics are so good' (Darren Edwards, interview with author, 8 June 2015). Elaborating on the function of his music choices, he says, 'We see our Sunday morning service as less of a church service, and as more of an outreach event that we do every week. We choose these songs in particular because they have suitable lyrics, and because they are known by anyone that listens to Radio 1' (Darren Edwards, email to author, 28 June 2015).

BBC Radio 1 is a flagship radio station in the UK specializing in mainstream popular music, playing chart favourites throughout the day. By deliberately choosing songs played on this platform, he effaces rigid distinctions between worldly and religious music. The strategy is not unique and it aligns his approach to the long-standing synergy between Pentecostalism and the secular music sphere. At different points, Elvis Presley, Jerry Lee Lewis, Johnny Cash,

B. B. King, James Brown, Tina Turner, Marvin Gaye, Sly Stone and Al Green all drew on personal experience of the church as they shaped the style, content and delivery of their music (Mosher 2008: 95). His choice of music also capitalizes on the extraordinary reach of popular culture since he knows that if a song fails to resonate on a personal level with a singer, it is unlikely to achieve the desired effect. These views are endorsed by music theorist Tia DeNora who suggests people generally prefer music which resonates with their lived experience because it provides 'a template of self'. Further she contends, we tend to choose 'music that produces self-images that are tenable, that seem doable, habitable. Respondents access the music of "who they are" through an elective affinity, through a feeling for what seems comfortable and what is exemplary' (De Nora 2000: 73). Just as stories in the Bible express Christian truths in vivid, easily grasped language, a simple, everyday pop song can be imbued with existential significance, addressing themes such as doubt, fear and social justice. Pastor Edwards capitalizes on pop music's universal appeal, seeing in it the potential to capture the popular imagination. In his words: 'I felt playing secular music in church would be a good idea to reach the lost', pointing out how '[f]or years, people have been trying to reach the "common man" with music, different dress codes, fast cars, and colloquial language' (Darren Edwards, interview with author, 19 March 2018). Also, he finds mainstream popular music facilitates participation in surprising ways, allowing people to feel comfortable enough to access emotions and locate personal spirituality:

> If someone has come to church for the first time ever, and they don't know any traditional hymns they can often feel like they don't belong. Playing songs that they know already allows them to feel more comfortable and able to connect with God in their own way. Where they might not have been able to connect to God at all, suddenly they may feel certain emotions and be more open to him.
> (Edwards, interview with author, 8 June 2015)

Mainstream pop's secular spirituality

If we analyse some of the song lyrics heard at Elim in more detail, it is easy to see that far from being incongruous with Christian spirituality, the congregation's preferred texts articulate a wide range of existential themes including grief, loss or fear. For example, Wiz Khalifa's song 'See You Again' draws on the experience of despair experienced on losing a loved one. The song's message of loss and longing for reunion with the departed taps into Christian views on post-death resurrection. Similarly, while containing oblique references to the occult, Emeli Sande's uplifting vocals on the gospel inflected 'Lifted' (2013) speak of the joy and elation felt by those who overcome fear, regardless of its source. The message can also be interpreted as a more literal escape from Satanic forces, making its use in a Christian context doubly meaningful. The congregation's song preferences highlight the inner pluralism which is so characteristic of postmodern spirituality, where meaning is drawn from a diverse range of sources and where the boundaries religion and popular culture are effaced permitting individuals to occupy secular and sacred spheres simultaneously.

Music's utility as an expressive tool cannot be underestimated, notably when trying to process complex emotions: as one observer contends: 'It captures feelings, emotion, and mood, thereby giving expression to what cannot be said through words alone' (Grenz 1994: 64). Hymns are not the only vehicle for spiritual advancement, a point emphasized by Brian Castle who reminds us that 'the primary purpose of the hymn is the praise of God' (Castle 2012). Likewise, Christian commentator and hymn writer Brian Wren suggests 'congregational song' should refer to 'anything that a worshipping congregation sings, not as presentation or performance to someone else, but as a vehicle for its encounter with God' (Wren 2000: 2). Research shows that aesthetic and spiritual experience are directly linked to the same neurological pathways hence any music may effectively heighten sensations within a religious context (Alma 2008: 28).

Although the charismatic church movement has a reputation for endorsing success and prosperity as manifestations of divine approval (Attanasi and Yong 2012: 3), in the UK, Pentecostalism has a tradition of reaching out to the poor. By cultivating a lively and growing congregation, Edwards helps economically disadvantaged parishioners to benefit from the social support Christian fellowship can offer. His approach may appear unconventional, but in the Pentacostal denomination, religious experience takes precedence over formal liturgy and abstract theorizing.[15] At a typical service, music is likely to have 'a contemporary beat to it … modulated to reflect various moods of worship, from praise to interest reflection'; similarly, rather than adopting religious garments, 'worship leaders as well as the audience wear street clothing' (Miller et al. 2013: 2). The movement's success, as one of the fastest growing religious denominations worldwide, lies in its ability to engage new followers, and in this respect, the use of music is crucial because research indicates that congregants' satisfaction with music heard at church is a strong predictor of continued attendance (Wuthnow 2003: 181). This imaginative use of pop not only illustrates music's universality as a medium of expression, it demonstrates that there are numerous symbolic musical languages, and each is best interpreted by those who use and understand it. Moreover, in a largely secular society, parishioners are perfectly capable of drawing upon their interpretation of mainstream pop songs as a point of personal spiritual departure. Churches struggling to engage those who are difficult to reach, might reflect upon the success of the approach used by Darren Edwards and others under the rubric of 'council house' or 'chav' churches. Finally, addressing anyone who refutes the use of the unholy medium of pop in church, Edwards justifies the practice from a faith-based perspective:

> In the same way that we believe Jesus can redeem our souls and the word chav, we also believe he can redeem songs that are written for a secular audience. When we treat something as sacred it becomes sacred.
>
> (Edwards, interview with author, 8 June 2015)

Notes

1 A Spotify survey indicates that pop songs predominate at weddings (Spotify 2018).
2 The term 'spiritual but not religious' can be linked to the writings of Sven Erlandson whose book *Spiritual But Not Religious: A Call to Religious Revolution in America* outlines the reasons for the exodus away from Christianity towards more esoteric and individualized belief systems.
3 The Mind, Body, Spirit Festival was founded by Colin Wilson in 1977 with the aim of bringing together foremost authorities and key organisations associated with matters relating to eco-living, natural health and medicine, alternative technology, personal growth and spirituality.
4 The campaign group Keep Sunday Special was set up in the 1980s to oppose the plan to introduce Sunday trading in England and Wales. Like the earlier Lord's Day Observance Society, the group acknowledged the need to preserve Sundays as a day of rest and worship.
5 The Church of England claims to be reaching around 1 million people each month using social media (https://www.churchofengland.org/more/media-centre/news/church-england-reaches-more-million-social-media-every-month).
6 Although the middle classes still gain social benefits from regular observance, as capitalism has evolved, education and the media are far more influential in communicating hegemonic discourse.
7 Hence, Gilbert and Sullivan's *HMS Pinafore* was castigated on the grounds that while it pleased audiences, it was decidedly low brow.
8 In contrast, the Church of England was less accommodating, and until 1819 members of the clergy could face a church court for permitting the practice. As

doctrine is clearly established within the Bible, The Historic Creeds and the Book of Common Prayer, The Church of England never had an official hymn book.

9   In Mayfield's own words: 'That was taken from my church or from the upbringing of messages from the church. Like there's no hiding place and get on board, and images of that sort. I must have been in a very deep mood of that type of religious inspiration when I wrote that song' (Hombach 2012: 89).

10 In a *Goldmine* interview (1997) he said, 'It doesn't matter what color or faith you have … I'm pleased the lyrics can be of value to anybody.'

11 'Turn, Turn, Turn' was written originally in the 1950s by Pete Seeger. Its lyrics are taken directly from the first eight verses of the third chapter of the Book of Ecclesiastes.

12 The term 'hoodie' is used to describe sweatshirts with hooded tops. It has also been used as a signifier of social exclusion by the establishment, notably in the 2011 riots where the mainstream media depicted rioters as a hooded topped mob.

13 According to Owen Jones when the word 'chav' first appeared in the *Collins English Dictionary* it was used to describe 'a young working-class person who dresses in casual sports clothing' but the connotations connected to the label imply a degree of cultural inferiority (Jones 2012: 8).

14 See Arnesen et al. (1998).

15 According to The English Church Census of 2005, two-fifths of the UK's churchgoing population attend an evangelical church.

References

Adorno, T. (1941), *Studies in Philosophy and Social Science*, New York: Institute of Social Research.

Alma, H. A. (2008), 'Religious and Aesthetic Experiences: A Psychological Approach', in T. H. Zock (ed.), *At the Cross-roads of Art and Religion: Imagination, Commitment, Transcendence*, 22–38, Leuven: Peeters.

Archbishop of Canterbury's Commission on Urban Priority Areas (1985), *Faith in the City: A Call for Action by Church and Nation*, London: Church House Publishing.

Argyle, M. (2000), *Psychology and Religion: An Introduction*, London: Routledge.

Arnold, M. (1910), *Sweetness and Light (Reprinted from 'Culture and Anarchy') and an Essay on Style*, London: The Macmillan Company.

Arnesen, E., J. Greene and B. Laurie (1998), *Labor Histories: Class, Politics, and the Working Class Experience*, Chicago, IL: University of Illinois Press.

Attali, J. (1985), *Noise: The Political Economy of Music*, Mancester: Manchester University Press.

Attanasi, K. and A. Yong, eds (2012), *Pentecostalism and Prosperity: The Socio-economics of the Global Charismatic Movement*, New York: Palgrave Macmillan.

Beaudoin, T. (ed.) (2013), *Secular Music and Sacred Theology*, Collegeville, MN: Liturgical Press.

Beckford, M. (2012), 'Dr John Sentamu: Church must avoid being "too middle class"', *The Telegraph*. Available online: http://www.telegraph.co.uk/news/religion/9045765/Dr-John-Sentamu-Church-must-avoid-being-too-middle-class.html (accessed 10 February 2017).

Bellofatto, G. A. and T. M. Johnson (2013), 'Key Findings of Christianity in its Global Context, 1970–2020', *International Bulletin of Missionary Research*, 37 (3): 157–64.

Bloom, A. (1987), *The Closing of the American Mind: How Higher Education Has Failed Democracy and Impoverished the Souls of Today's Students*, New York: Simon and Schuster.

Brown, C. G. (2009), *The Death of Christian Britain: Understanding Secularisation, 1800–2000*, London: Routledge.

Bruce, S. (2000), 'Mainstream Churches RIP', in British Sociological Association Sociology of Religion Study Group Conference, Exeter, England (April).

Cameron, D. (2010), Big Society Speech, 19 July 2010. Full transcript available online: http://www.number10.gov.uk/news/big-society-speech (accessed 11 August 2020).

Castle, B. (2012), 'Developments in the Near Future: Hymnals in England', *The Hymn Society of Great Britain and Ireland: Treasures*, Bulletin 271, Spring. Available online: https://hymnsocietygbi.org.uk/2012/04/13/treasure-no78-developments-in-the-near-future-hymnals-in-england/ (accessed 10 July 2018).

Christe, I. (2004), *Sound of the Beast: The Complete Headbanging History of Heavy Metal*, The University of California: Allison & Busby.

City of Lincoln Council (2011), *Lincoln in 2011*. Available online: http://thelincolnite.co.uk/wp-content/uploads/2011/11/Lincoln-Drivers-Report-2011.pdf (accessed 10 February 2017).

Cobb, K. (2008), *The Blackwell Guide to Theology and Popular Culture*, Toronto: John Wiley & Sons.

Codone, S. (2014), 'Megachurch Pastor Twitter Activity: An Analysis of Rick Warren and Andy Stanley, Two of America's Social Pastors', *Journal of Religion, Media and Digital Culture*, 3 (2): 1–32.

Commission on Urban Life and Faith (2006), *Faithful Cities: A Call for Celebration, Vision and Justice*, Peterborough: Methodist Publishing House.

Co-operative Funeral Care (2016), 'Funeral Music Chart'. Available online: http://www.co-operativefuneralcare.co.uk/funeral-music-chart/ (accessed 10 February 2017).

Cooper, N., S. Purcell, R. Jackson, C. Niall, P. Sarah and J. Ruth (2014), 'Below the Breadline: The Relentless Rise of Food Poverty in Britain', Oxfam GB. Available online: http://policy-practice.oxfam.org.uk/publications/below-the-breadline-the-relentless-rise-of-food-poverty-in-britain-317730 (accessed 10 February 2017).

Coote A. (2011), 'Neoliberalism, Big Society, and Progressive Localism', in M. Stott (ed.), *The Big Society Challenge*, Cardiff: Keystone Development Trust Publications,

82-9. Available online: https://www.researchgate.net/publication/277663391_Neoliberalism_Big_Society_and_progressive_localism (accessed 10 September 2018).

DeNora, T. (2000), *Music in Everyday Life*, Cambridge: Cambridge University Press.

Farnell, R., R. Furbey and S. S. A. H. Hills (2003), *'Faith' in Urban Regeneration?: Engaging Faith Communities in Urban Regeneration*, Bristol: Policy Press.

Ferguson, M. (2015), 'Is the Church Too Middle Class?', *Idea: the Magazine of the Evangelical Alliance*, May/June, 13. Available online: https://www.eauk.org/news-and-views/idea (accessed 31 August 2020).

Frith, S. (2001), 'Pop Music', in S. Frith, W. Straw and J. Street (eds), *The Cambridge Companion to Pop and Rock*, 93–108, Cambridge: Cambridge University Press.

Forbes, B. D. and J. H. Mahan, eds (2017), *Religion and Popular Culture in America*, Oakland: University of California Press.

Gant, A. (2017), *O Sing Unto the Lord: A History of English Church Music*, Chicago, IL: University of Chicago Press.

Gove, M. (2015), 'In Defence of Christianity', *Spectactor*, April. Available online: http://www.spectator.co.uk/2015/04/in-defence-of-christianity/ (accessed 7 February 2017).

Grenz, S. (1994), *Theology for the Community of God*, Nashville, TN: Broadman & Holman Publishers.

Guest, M. (2007), 'In Search of Spiritual Capital: The Spiritual as a Cultural Resource', in K. Flanagan and P. Jupp, *A Sociology of Spirituality*, 181–200, Aldershot: Ashgate.

Gushee, D. (2016), 'Why is Christianity declining?' Available online: http://religionnews.com/2016/09/06/why-is-christianity-declining/ (accessed 4 March 2017).

Hall, S. (2011), 'The March of the Neoliberals', *Guardian*, 12 September. Available online: https://www.theguardian.com/politics/2011/sep/12/march-of-the-neoliberals (accessed 7 February 2017).

Heelas, P., L. Woodhead, B. Seel, K. Tusting and B. Szerszynski (2004), *The Spiritual Revolution: Why Religion is Giving Way to Spirituality*, Malden, MA: Blackwell Publishing.

Hombach, J. (2012), *Bob Marley: The Father Of Music*, Charleston: CreateSpace Independent Publishing Platform.

Hughes, P. (2012), 'Spiritual but Not Religious', *Pointers: Bulletin of the Christian Research Association*, 22 (4): 13.

Jones, I. and P. Webster (2006), 'Anglican "Establishment" Reactions to "Pop" Church Music in England, c.1956–c.1990', *Studies in Church History*, 42: 429–41.

Jones, O. (2012), *Chavs: The Demonization of the Working Class*, London: Verso books.

Kalra, V. S. (2015), *Sacred and Secular Musics: A Postcolonial Approach*, London: Bloomsbury Publishing.

Kelton, C. (2005), *The Blackwell Guide to Theology and Popular Culture*, Hoboken, NJ: Wiley.

Kommers, H. (2011), 'Hidden in Music: Religious Experience and Pop Festivals', *Journal of Religion and Popular Culture*, 23 (1): 14–26.

Lowe, R. (1998), *The Welfare State in Britain Since 1945*, London: Macmillan International Higher Education.

McKay, C. (2014), 'A Church Out of Touch?' Available online: http://www.christianweek.org/church-touch/ (accessed 10 February 2017).

McLeod, H. (2016), *Class and Religion in the Late Victorian City*, London: Routledge.

Mayhew, H. (2010), *London Labour and the London Poor*, Oxford: Oxford University Press.

Mercadante, L. (2014), *Belief without Borders: Inside the Minds of the Spiritual But Not Religious*, Oxford: Oxford University Press.

Midgley, P. (2012), *The Churches and the Working Classes: Leeds, 1870–1920*, Newcastle: Cambridge Scholars.

Miller, D. E., K. H. Sargeant and R. Flory, eds (2013), *Spirit and Power: The Growth and Global Impact of Pentecostalism*, Oxford: Oxford University Press.

Mills, P. (1994), 'Into the Mystic: The Aural Poetry of Van Morrison', *Popular Music*, 13 (1): 91–103.

Mosher, C. (2008), 'Ecstatic Sounds: The Influence of Pentecostalism on Rock and Roll', *Popular Music and Society*, 31 (1): 95–112.

Oxfam (2013), *The True Cost of Austerity and Inequality UK: Case Study*. Available online: https://www-cdn.oxfam.org/s3fs-public/file_attachments/cs-true-cost-austerity-inequality-uk-120913-en_0.pdf (accessed 17 February 2017).

Pantazis, C., D. Gordon and R. Levitas (eds) (2006), *Poverty and Social Exclusion in Britain: The Millennium Survey*, Bristol: Policy Press.

Pattison, R. (1987), *The Triumph of Vulgarity: Rock Music in the Mirror of Romanticism*, New York: Oxford University Press.

Powell, M. A. (2002), *Encyclopedia of Contemporary Christian Music* (vol. 1), Peabody, MA: Hendrickson Publisher.

Robinson, B. (2011), 'All Change in the Victorian Age', BBC. Available online: http://www.bbc.co.uk/history/british/victorians/speed_01.shtml (accessed 4 July 2018).

Schupf, H. W. (1972), 'Education for the Neglected: Ragged Schools in Nineteenth-Century England', *History of Education Quarterly*, 12 (2): 162–83.

Scott, D. B. (2008), *Sounds of the Metropolis: The 19th-Century Popular Music Revolution in London, New York, Paris and Vienna*, New York: Oxford University Press.

Sherwood, H. (2016), 'Church Life is Fading Fast in Poorer Communities, Synod Warned', *Guardian*, 16 February. Available online: https://www.theguardian.com/world/2016/feb/16/church-life-is-fading-fast-in-poorer-communities-synod-warned (accessed 7 February 2017).

Spotify Playlist Top 20 Wedding Songs 2018 Available online: https://open.spotify.com/playlist/06Xmo0ptj2H9hYr8w6ESQf (Accessed: 16 November 2020).

Tearfund (2007), 'Churchgoing in the UK: A Research Report from Tearfund on Church Attendance in the UK'. Available online: http://news.bbc.co.uk/1/shared/bsp/hi/pdfs/03_04_07_tearfundchurch.pdf (accessed 7 February 2017).

Till, R. (2010) Pop Cult: Religion and Popular Music, London: Continuum.

Tyler, I. (2006), 'Chav Scum: The Filthy Politics of Social Class', *M/C Journal*, 9 (5). Available online: http://www.journal.media-culture.org.au/0610/09-tyler.php (accessed 11 August 2020).

Voices Now: the Big Choral Census (2017). Available online: https://www.prsformusic.com/m-magazine/news/number-uk-choirs-time-high/ (accessed 17 September 2020).

Wallace, M. and C. Spanner (2004), *Chav! A User's Guide to Britain's New Ruling Class*, London: Bantam Book.

Webb, M. S. (2012), 'Diversified Marketing Media and Service Offerings Prove Successful for Nondenominational Churches', *Services Marketing Quarterly*, 33 (3): 246–60.

Wilson, J. (2011), *Wigglesworth: The Complete Story: A New Biography of the Apostle of Faith*, Milton Keynes: Authentic Media.

Woodall, A. M. (2017), *What Price the Poor? William Booth, Karl Marx and the London Residuum*, London: Routledge.

Wren, B. A. (2000), *Praying Twice: The Music and Words of Congregational Song*, Louisville, KY: John Knox Press.

Wuthnow, R. (2003), *All in Sync: How Music and Art are Revitalizing American Religion*, Berkeley, CA: University of California Press.

Yip, A. K. (2002), 'The Persistence of Faith among Nonheterosexual Christians: Evidence for the Neosecularization Thesis of Religious Transformation', *Journal for the Scientific Study of Religion*, 41 (2): 199–212.

7

'The Time Has Come, Exodus!': Congo Natty and the Jungle (R)evolution

Shara Rambarran

Introduction

'We're living in a time that's hard', notes Congo Natty in conversation with the journalist Joe Clay. 'And it's been like this for a long time now. And music is the one medium where we can be free … And that's what jungle is – it's that escape' (2013). Formed in the 1990s from the remnants of rave (and in particular the breakbeat hardcore scene), jungle soon evolved into a style influenced by a plethora of musical styles and culture, including hip hop, ragga and jazz. The UK scene, in particular, continues to have a strong following, with the likes of Goldie, Ray Keith and, key to this chapter, Congo Natty: all of whom still perform and write to this day. Although much has been written on the musical and cultural background of jungle,[1] which is not normally observed as 'spiritual' music but more of a dystopian musical genre, this chapter will question how Natty's approach to jungle should be considered as a form of movement that expresses spirituality through music. It begins with a brief overview of Natty's life and music career, followed by a contextualization of Natty's influence and work within jungle as a musical genre and its transition to a movement, not least in Natty's influences of Rastafari in his work. To place these ideas into perspective, a musicological reading of the track 'London Dungeons' will demonstrate how Natty offers the listeners spiritual 'escapism' through lyrics, sounds and sentiment. Overall, this chapter aims to bring further understanding to the reader on Natty's passion in illuminating his own turbulent socio-cultural experiences and spiritual beliefs in jungle, and how he shares and educates the movement to his fans and listeners.

'People Get Ready' for Congo Natty

Congy Natty is perhaps better known as the Rebel MC, a successful music artist who scored a number of UK chart hits in the late 1990s. Born as Michael West, Natty was raised in Tottenham, north London. While growing up, Natty faced a lack of social acceptance for his mixed-race background (he is of Jamaican and Welsh heritage) (see in-lay sleeve Natty 2013; Beaumont-Thomas 2013), making him question his identity and the worthiness of his human presence in British society. Thankfully, his father educated him on his Jamaican cultural heritage and introduced him to reggae music, providing a creative outlet for his frustrations and, during the 1980s, he performed with his sound system crew, the Beat Freak. Here, he used this musical set-up and space to freely express his emotions and critiques on life in Britain, especially with the 1988 track the 'Rich Getting Richer'. From here, Natty collaborated with the music production team Karl 'Tuff Enuff' Brown and the late Michael Menson (better known as Double Trouble). Together, they created hip-hop- and hip-house-inspired music and scored the chart-topping hits 'Just Keep Rockin'' and 'Street Tuff' in the late 1980s.

As Natty began to experiment further with his music, he became increasingly frustrated with the music industry and media for not showing interest in the meaning behind the lyrical content, breakbeats and reggae samples presented in his work. Highlighting his experience of working in the music industry, Natty notes how 'at first it's all good ... It's a bit like Hansel and Gretel when they get to the house and they're hungry and there's all sweets and so on. But then you start to feel a little bit sick and then we all know what happens next. The machine that loved you decides it hates you' (www.congonatty.com). Natty's disillusionment with the music industry encouraged him to return to his independent roots by setting up his own record label called 'Tribal Bass' (Wood 2002), and propelled him towards developing jungle music as an expressive medium.

Natty also visited Jamaica, where he began to learn about the musical and cultural origins of jungle, eventually performing the genre in its capital city, Kingston. It was also here that he made contact with Rastafarian communities, which inspired him to create *Tribute to Emperor Haile Salassie I: King of Kings* (2000) and thus furthering his understanding of his Jamaican heritage. He subsequently converted to Rastafarianism, changing his name to Mikail Tafari, and staying (with his family) in a Rastafarian community in Shashamane, Ethiopia for seven months in 2007. During his stay, Natty envisioned Jah

(Selassie) telling him to return to Britain and educate the suffering (especially the youth) through music (Clay 2013). When Natty and his family returned to Britain, he focused upon referencing Rastafari in jungle as well as maintaining the strong musical links with roots reggae and dub. For Natty, therefore, jungle became both a form of healing and escapism, noting how 'it's cleansing. After the session it's always the same, it's like [a heavy sigh of relief] – jungle music sets you free' (as told to Clay 2013).

Jungle

Before we dwell too deeply on Natty's work, a discussion on the origins of the genre will be explored in two parts: first, the socio-cultural setting, and secondly, its musical characteristics. In terms of the socio-cultural setting of the style, jungle is observed as an offshoot of the rave scene in the early 1990s. After rave's demise, jungle began to gain particular popularity in London, and, after its peak in 1994 (Congo Natty 2018), splintered into various sub-styles and forms (e.g. drum 'n' bass, jump-up, darkcore, ragga, jungle, intelligent, etc.). The term 'jungle' itself carries various definitions, with its most common meaning referring to a 'junglist', a resident of Trench Town, West Kingston (and other areas alike), which is perhaps more known for socio-economic hardships.[2] Also known as 'concrete jungle', it has been referenced in reggae music, with Bob Marley and the Wailers serving as an example, with their 1973 track 'Concrete Jungle', describing the harsh realities of living in Kingston at that time (a topic revisited below in relation to Natty's 'London Dungeons'[3]).

Musically, jungle is digitally/electronically driven, and is supported with a blend of roots reggae, dub, hip hop, and electronica – which sometimes provide a vehicle for social commentary.[4] The music is mostly created on machines and electronic instruments (computers, samplers, synthesizers, etc.). The tempo of the drums are very fast, typically set at least 150 bpm, while the bass runs at half the speed (Christodoulou 2011: 59). Jungle is also well known for its low-frequency *tenuto* (a held/sustained note) rolling bass line, and is supported either by breakbeats (borrowed from African American soul and funk music, notably the 'Amen Break', for example) or programmed drum patterns. Natty explains that fast-driven drums are vital in jungle because 'the tempo of how we bill a tune is the tempo of what we're feeling in the environment' (as told to Beaumont-Thomas 2013). To elaborate, the speed of the drums represents a 'picture of social disintegration and instability ... a nonverbal response to troubled times' (Reynolds 1999: 251–2). This frustration is also represented by the half-speed deep bass line that signifies the heartbeat of the suffering; that is, the oppressed (Hebdige 1987: 82; *Dub Echoes* 2008), such as, for example, the migrant settlers who came from the Caribbean to work in Britain and struggled to integrate in society (Gilroy 1993: 81).[5] Arguably, the bass is used as a musical weapon against notions of authority, institution, etc.[6] As Steven Quinn argues: 'Within the history of reggae's opposition to institutional and colonial authority, the bass sound evolved into the signifier of that opposition' (2002: 4). Therefore, the use of bass is a highly significant musical characteristic that is occasionally referred to as the 'dread'[7] or 'rebel' bass (Gilroy 1993: 81).[8]

Although jungle appeals to the second to fourth generations of the British Caribbeans, it has also been a voice of a wider audience. That being said, listeners are mainly from socially deprived backgrounds – Reynolds argues that the 'music [is] for desperate times … and so junglist has become the soundtrack of Britain's underclass' (2007: 145–6). The musical presence of jungle in Britain was mainly underground and was often accessed via pirate radio such as the notable Kool FM and Rinse FM. Jungle musicians created music with inexpensive music technology, which resulted in 'an opportunity for a lot of urban youngsters, black and white, to actually inform music of their own, with their own sampling, with their own experiences, and to make the music a bit more relevant to what they wanted to hear and what they were feeling' (2007: 145–6).

The jungle revolution

After the acclaimed 1991 album, *Black Meaning Good* (under the name of Rebel MC), where Natty exposed the grim reality and challenges he faced (most of which centred around the racism that he and his associates had to confront in British society), he began to incorporate elements of Rastafari in his music. As heard in the track 'Jungle is I and I', 1994 was a crucial year for Natty: first, he became a Rastafarian and, second, jungle became more popular in the UK. It could be argued that the combination of these two factors was the point at which Natty took jungle to another level by expressing his stories and catharsis through his spiritual beliefs and music. As told to the journalist Joe Clay, Natty confirms that Rastafari and jungle 'are at one. If I think about when I was a yout [*sic*] and I was in a dance and they'd be playing Rastafari music, with heavy bassline, echo, distortion, filters – everything. And it was a holy vibe. You felt the Holy Spirit. I couldn't move from the speaker. Jungle for me, it's revisiting everything that was before it' (2013). This is demonstrated in 'Lion of Judah – Exodus' (1998) where Natty incorporates themes of Rastafari and Jamaican music into his music. For instance, the track is over layered with samples of two Bob Marley songs, 'Exodus' and 'Iron Lion Zion'. Here, these biblical and spiritual references represent Natty's inclusion of spirituality in jungle, supported with a piercing sub bass, disjointed and accelerated drums and distorted electronic sonics that are blended with roots reggae horn samples. Interestingly, the listeners are reminded that this is jungle when Natty shouts the word 'massive' throughout the track. This term simply means 'crew' (or collective) and is directed at the junglist followers. In addition, what also makes Natty's musical features stand out from other styles of jungle is that the music typically begins at a moderate pace (usually represented with a hip hop breakbeat, vocal melody, percussion or samples) before gradually breaking into a full track as heard on 'Emperor Selassi I' (1997), 'Rastafari Rebel' (2002), and 'Jungle is I and I' (2013).

Rastafari developed in Jamaica during the mid-twentieth century – although its origins are evident much earlier on. The beliefs and teachings of the Rastafarian movement are centred around the concept of Zion (the promised land of Africa), and the religion has a deep connection with Ethiopia (particularly a place called Shashamane). The formation of the movement cannot be separated from the distressing cultural history of the Jamaicans who were enslaved and removed from their families of origin. Understandably, the slave trade history in Jamaica (and in general the Caribbean) casts a lengthy shadow over the lives of Jamaican/Caribbean people (e.g. ancestors, generations, future generations, etc.), and continues to influence the lives of those who migrated to the UK.

The oppression imposed on Jamaicans has also motivated many to learn, share and appreciate their cultural roots, including Afrocentric values, some of which are reflected in Rastafarian ideology. As Mike Alleyne argues, 'it's not surprising to see the emergence of an Afrocentric doctrine focused on anti-imperialist ideas. By affirming belief in a black – rather than white – God, Rastafari posed a major threat to colonialism's brand of Christianity, which was based on racial hierarchy' (2012: 89). Advocacy and political thoughts on the racial hierarchy were preached and validated in the works of prominent thinkers, with Marcus Mosiah Garvey (1887–1940) being a well-known example.

Although Natty is a Rastafarian and indeed endorses those beliefs in his work, he does not fully live by its tenets, especially where it is expected that believers should live in purity and isolation (Clay 2013). That being said, Natty has dedicated his life to Rastafari by not only changing his name to Mikail Tafari, but also by having dreadlocks which shows dedication to Jah (God) (based on the Old Testament);[9] smoking the 'holy herb' otherwise known as ganja (marijuana) as a form of spiritual practice (BBC Religions 2009); wearing or displaying the colours green (vegetation and hope to end oppression), black (race) and gold (representing gold of Africa and natural riches);[10] making lyrical references to the symbol of the lion (Jah), Haile Selassie (Jah and King of Ethiopia) and the Jamaican political thinker Mosiah Marcus Garvey (who was not a Rastafarian but his black advocacy was considered to have shaped the teachings of Rastafari and influenced reggae music) (Alleyne 2012: 92); and showing his admiration for the acclaimed roots reggae musician Bob Marley who (famously) converted to the movement (S.J. 2017). These connotations of Rastafari are presented in Natty's music, particularly roots reggae, a musical characteristic that is often featured in jungle.[11] Although roots reggae has always been part of jungle, over time, along with his spiritual beliefs, Natty has established the style as a prominent feature in today's jungle. He states that he now sees jungle as a 'reboot of roots reggae for a new century' (as told to Clay 2013), and alongside his spiritual beliefs, this supports the transition and transformation, or to be precise, the evolution and revolution, of jungle.

Natty's approach in modernizing jungle as both a spiritual and musical movement is demonstrated on the album *Jungle Revolution* (2013). In this magnum opus, the artist collaborated with the likes of Adrian Sherwood (British dub producer), Soundsystem MCs (the late Tenor Fly, Tippa Irie, General Levy), and musicians (Audioweb's Robin File and Alabama 3's Steve Finnerty). The musical themes on *Jungle Revolution* present a fusion of past and present sounds of jungle, reggae and other forms of electronica, with lyrics centred around contemporary socio-cultural experiences, love, unity, revolution and faith in Rastafari. To investigate further into how Natty combines spirituality and music in jungle, a track from *Jungle Revolution*, 'London Dungeons', will now be explored.

The *Jungle Revolution*: 'London Dungeons'

Displaying signs of suffering, hope and Rastafari, 'London Dungeons' can be heard and observed as a fresh interpretation of Bob Marley and the Wailers song 'Concrete Jungle' (1973) which was based on living in Trenchtown. To support this concept in a musical manner, the song presents a history of reggae, as it visits styles such as roots and dub. In a socio-cultural context, 'London Dungeons' serves as a reflection on the inner-city parts of London. On the one hand, one may refer to 'London Dungeons' as a famous tourist attraction in the city where spectators are entertained and educated on the historical dark side of metropolis.[12] In British history, criminals were rejected in society and locked away in the dungeon (or prison), and subjected to torture and execution. Metaphorically speaking, Natty is applying similar notions of rejection by society but in a different context: that is, the oppressed people who are not criminals but are treated as such due to being outcasts in society while simultaneously suffering in the 'dungeon' (i.e. London, but obviously this could also apply to any oppressive society, country, life situation, etc.). Another aspect of the metaphor is that the dungeon represents 'hell' where one is ostracized and suffering in society. The concept was elaborated in a sample used in the opening introduction of *Babylon* (a film set in 1980s Brixton which highlights the tense relationship between British Caribbeans and the UK establishment),[13] where the listener hears racist remarks being directed at a group of British Caribbean friends as highlighted in the following excerpt:

> Mature English Lady (played by Maggie Steed):
> look at you good for nothing, noisy ... [Natty interrupts/overdubs by shouting
>   'yeah'] stinking filth, lazy you're everywhere, jungle bunnies, this was
>   a lovely area before you come here, lovely. And you [looks at the white
>   English character Ronnie] you should be ashamed of yourself ain'tcha, you
>   know what you are don't you? You're traitor to your kin and King, traitor
> Ronnie (Karl Howman): you're no relation of mine lady
> Mature English Lady: Fuck off back to your own countries you jungle bunny,
>   and you ...
> Beefy (Trevor Laird): This is my fucking country lady ...

This sample sets the song's theme, especially in the line 'this is my fucking country lady' where the protagonist challenges the notion that he should be considered an outsider. The sample is delicately supported with spaced sub bass drops and offbeat echo/reverb synth chords reminiscent of dub and reggae and creates an environment where the listener can begin to connect with the song. Natty then toasts the line 'London, London city of darkness, I'm down in the dungeons ...' and is responded to by Martha Kean ('Marf' of La La & Boo Ya) who channels the words 'light up the darkness' to the listener. The subtle drum and bass along with the squelching and hypnotic sonics (evaporating from the bass) along with the internal gated synth sounds and the offbeat piano chords all carry the introduction and almost creating a trance like state until Natty brings the listener back to consciousness and shouts out 'Rastafari'.

In this first verse, Natty confirms that 'London Dungeons' is showing allegiance to Bob Marley and the Wailers 'Concrete Jungle' when he interpolates 'darkness has covered my light and has changed my day into night' to 'darkness has covered my day and has turned it into night ... '. The binaries of dark and light could arguably reflect a biblical perspective; for example, in St John's Gospel, it states: 'God is light, and in Him is no darkness at all' (1 John 1:5). This statement is suggesting that one of the key words in this song, 'light', is a metaphor for God. While dub, reggae and moderately paced jungle are still musically present and supported with a deep and gentle rolling bass line, Natty anxiously stresses the grim reality of life in the (concrete) jungle by referring to the youths who lost their lives to 'chedder' (drugs) and 'redder' (murder). At the end of the first verse, the sample 'this is my fucking country lady' re-enters and paves the way for the chorus. In this section, Martha Kean preaches to the listeners that 'we are all different but same ..., recover your soul, discover what you need, we gain control through unity ...'. This concept of people being united or, indeed, being 'I' is musically supported with a roots-reggae-based style with the bass maintaining its significant presence, serving as a counter melody to the vocals, accompanied by an electric guitar with a clean effect that gently decorates over the vocals. Towards the end of the chorus, Keen stresses the word 'unity' while Natty cites 'London, the city of darkness, I'm dying in the dungeons, Jah, Rastafari'. The reminder of being trapped in the dark and in the depths of the dungeon (or indeed hell) sets the theme of the second verse where Natty reflects on spirituality and his faith as a Rastafari by referring to the people as 'angels of the light' (remember light signifies God), 'inside the Israel Nazarite',[14] 'out of the darkness must come to light, people of the world you better unite', and then he chants these words again in a dynamic tone.

The second chorus becomes musically significant because it is enhanced with the frequent bass drops blending with the sounds of roots reggae. The guitar becomes more apparent and sonically interferes with the detuned gated synth sounds resulting in a dark and haunting noise. These dark and haunting sonics remind us of dub where sound effects and manipulated sounds signifies the frustration of the suffering as well as representing the absence of light in the 'dungeon'. This section then leads on to the first bridge, where the dark timbre momentarily subsides and paves the way for Nancy Correia, who soulfully sings the uplifting words 'light up the darkness, time for a new day …'. This signals the initiation of the song where the jungle transforms into the revolutionized sound and movement. Musically, the jungle epiphany is represented by a pulsating polyrhythmic fusion of bass drops and retro synth-orchestral hit stabs, that are blended with both live and programmed drums. This whirlwind of sounds results in a spiritual ecstasy for Congo Natty, his crew and listeners (fans), where they can free themselves from troubles and congregate together and experience liberation, soulfulness and unity. 'London Dungeons' articulates the troubles and problems that still exist in the concrete jungles (or indeed 'dungeons' or 'hell'), with the hope that these issues could be challenged by people uniting together, and practising some teachings of Rastafari – as demonstrated in the video.

At the start of the video, there are passing shots of Natty's music set-up: recording studio, effects unit, mixing desk, microphone and a drum set. Then a disused and neglected area in London is shown which, as a metaphor, could represent a concrete jungle or, indeed, the 'London Dungeons'. An excerpt from the film *Babylon* (the sample heard at the start of 'London Dungeons' – see above) is shown at the start, setting the tone of the video, with a particular focus on London and the experience of racism. Interestingly, the famous Transport for London's Underground logo is shown to serve as a reminder of the song's theme but also inferring that jungle (music) and concrete jungle (dungeon) are 'underground'. Furthermore, the logo used here is not in the traditional (Union Jack flag) colours of red, blue and white. Instead, it is two-tone: black and white – a symbol that represents racial unity and an intertextual reference to the British ska/two-tone music scene of the 1970s.[15] This adapted logo could represent what would be regarded as inner cities or less popular places in London. Historically, the Transport for London's map of the Underground would only display tube stations associated with places of interest (such as tourist attractions).[16] The touristy spots gave a false impression that these were the only towns in London and that other towns (mainly consisting a majority of inner-city places) were not included on the map (e.g. Hackney, Peckham, Lewisham, etc.). These 'invisible' towns, however, were visible on separate Network Rail maps. The maps offered a full picture of the places/stations in London and made the unfamiliar tourists aware that there are in fact many towns in the city. Thankfully, the London rail transport has evolved over the last century, and there is a more accessible map displaying all the stations (known as the 'London Rail and Tube' map). With this in mind, the quick passing shot of the Underground sign is a binary play on the tourist's expectations regarding the significance of the logo (supported with pretty images of the main tourist attractions such as Piccadilly Circus, River

Thames, historical monuments, etc.) versus the *real* underground (disused and neglected/deprived areas) in London.

The washed-out and grimy sunset montage display the dark setting of the performance. The only bright and colourful images that are present in the video are made of quick passing shots of colours representing Rastafari (red, gold, green and black), the Lion of Judah and Congo Natty's logo (a lion and his name). Other signs include Natty's tam (also known as a Rastacap), his children representing the 'angels of light', musicians smoking ganja and, more importantly, the bright visible flame on Natty's lighter that symbolizes the light, i.e. Jah. As well as the visual signs of Rastafari, Natty stands out by wearing a military outfit, confirming his dedication to those around him.

Conclusion

Congo Natty is on a mission: a mission to educate the youth and his fans of peace, love and unity through jungle music. Natty began his journey in 1991 and he has transformed jungle by expanding it into a spiritual and musical movement. As his Jamaican heritage has encouraged him to learn about his cultural identity, he has become more drawn to the teachings of Rastafari and Jamaican culture. While it could be considered that he is not a traditional Rastafarian (such as the lifestyle and removing himself from the public eye or even Babylon), he respects and applies certain teachings where he can. This is evident in his music, lyrics, promotional material and social media posts. We can perhaps think that this is Natty's way in adding a fresh stance on Rastafari. As Rastafari can be a complex study, a good and approachable starting point in understanding this movement would be to start with Natty's work.

This coincides with Natty taking jungle to another level by transitioning from representing a dystopian and frustrating environment to focusing more on finding hope, love and unity. For example, as heard in 'London Dungeons', the revolutionized jungle music blended with roots reggae and dub offers haunting yet sanctified sounds that aides the listeners to journey through the music and, yet, to be still in their moment of escapism and spirituality by experiencing despair, love, hope, Rastafari and Jah. This is displayed visually in the video with Natty being joined by his family and friends. The idea of representing unity is very important for Natty, and his videos and live shows include his family, friends (who are also his crew) and fans. Natty's life, spirituality and music have motivated him to embark on a revolution, a jungle revolution, where the disaffected are not judged for who they are, and can unite and absorb the music and savour the spiritual messages. Natty confirms that he is indeed, on a mission: '… I see jungle as our soul in the 21st century [and] it's got no colour … it's our story … I got my army greens on for a reason—I'm running a revolution' (Natty, 2013).

Notes

1. See, for example, Borthwick and Moy (2004), Melville (2019), James (1997) and Reynolds (1999).
2. For further information, see Reynolds (2007).
3. It should also be mentioned that the term 'junglist' was 'slang for people who operated outside of the law, or according to the "law of the jungle" such as rudeboys and gangsters'. In a British context, Matt Grimes applies the term 'junglist' to underground (unlicensed and illegal) UK soundsystem events that conflicted with authorities (Grimes 2018: 36).
4. See Bennett (2001); Borthwick and Moy (2004).
5. For further reading on British Caribbean history, see Gilroy (2002 [1987]); Grant (2019); Monrose (2019); British Library (https://www.bl.uk/).
6. See Gilroy (2002 [1987]).
7. The term 'dread' is a Jamaican term for 'rebel' – see Barrett Sr. (1997: 138).
8. To support Gilroy's argument musically, listen to Black British Poet, Linton Kwesi Johnson's 'Reggae Sounds' (1980). His describes the bass as '[the] bass his'try is a-hurtin' black story', and the reggae sound as 'Ridim of a tropical, electrical storm, Cool doun to de base of the struggle … '.
9. Leviticus 21:5 states: 'Thou shall not make baldness upon their head, neither shall they shave off the corner of their beard, nor make any cuttings in the flesh.' Numbers 6:5 states: 'All the days of the [Nazarite] vow of his separation there shall no razor come upon his head: until the days be fulfilled, in which he separateth himself unto the LORD, he shall be holy, and shall let the locks of the hair of his head grow.'
10. See Barrett Sr. (1997: 143) for more information on the colours.
11. Roots reggae is an early sub-style of reggae where its lyrics includes cultural and Rastafarian contents. The music is led by the bass, and is rhythmically supported with drums and meditative chords (usually played by guitar and keyboards/piano).
12. See www.thedungeons.com for more information.
13. *Babylon* featured British Guyanese actor and founding member of the reggae band Aswad, Brinsley Forde.
14. An ascetic of ancient Israel (dictionary.com), with a strict religious lifestyle based on the readings on the Book of Numbers in the Old Testament. For further information, see Reiss (2014).

15 For further reading on the Union Jack and race in British popular music, see Rambarran (2015); Hopkins (2017); Lloyd and Rambarran (2017); Whiteley (2010).
16 See Quinn (2002).

References

All Black – Jungle Fever (1994), [Documentary] UK: BBC.
Alleyne, M. (2002), 'White Reggae: Cultural Dilution in the Record Industry', *Popular Music and Society* 24 (1): 15–30.
Alleyne, M. (2012), *The Encyclopedia of Reggae: The Golden Age of Roots Reggae*, New York: Sterling.
Babylon (1980), [Film] Dir. Franco Rosso, UK: National Film Finance Corporation.
Barrett Sr., L. E. (1997), *The Rastafarians*, Boston, MA: Beacon Press.
BBC Religions (2009), 'Rastafari', BBC. Available online: https://www.bbc.co.uk/religion/religions/rastafari/customs/customs_1.shtml (accessed 8 June 2016).
BBC History (2014), 'Marcus Garvey', BBC. Available online: http://www.bbc.co.uk/history/historic_figures/garvey_marcus.shtml (accessed 8 June 2016).
Beaumont-Thomas, B. (2013), 'Congo Natty and the Jungle Revolution', *Guardian* 4 July. Available online: https://www.theguardian.com/music/2013/jul/04/congo-natty-Jungle-revolution-rebel-mc (accessed 1 July 2015).
Bennett, A. (2001), *Cultures of Popular Music*, Berkshire: Open University Press.
Borthwick, S. and R. Moy (2004), *Popular Music Genres*, Edinburgh: Edinburgh University Press.
Bradley, L. (2000), *This is Reggae Music: The Story of Jamaican Music*, New York: Grove Press.
Cashmore, E., ed. (2004), *Encyclopedia of Race and Ethnic Studies*, London and New York: Routledge.
Clay, J. (2013), 'I've Got Souls To Save: An Interview With Congo Natty', *The Quietus*, 11 July. Available online: http://thequietus.com/articles/12795-congo-natty-interview (accessed 1 July 2015).
Christodoulou, C. (2011), 'Rumble in the Jungle: City, Place, and Uncanny Bass', *Dancecult: Journal of Electronic Dance Music Culture*, 3 (1): 44–63.
Clifton, J. (2015), 'Jungle, Raves, and the Pirate Radio: The History and Future of Kool FM', *The Vice*. Available online: https://www.vice.com/en_uk/article/4wba59/kool-fm-Jungle-pirate-london-945 (accessed 9 November 2018).
Discovery Society (2014), 'Focus: When Britain Loved Rastafari'. Available online: https://discoversociety.org/2014/07/01/focus-when-britain-loved-rastafari/(accessed 4 April 2017).
Dub Echoes: Sonic Excursions in Dub and Beyond (2008), [Documentary] dir. Bruno Natal, UK: Soul Jazz Records.

Dunkley, D. A. (2012), 'Leonard P. Howell's Leadership of the Rastafari Movement and his "Missing Years"', *Caribbean Quarterly*, 58 (4): 1–24.
Gilroy, P. (1993), *The Black Atlantic: Modernity and Double Consciousness*, London and New York: Verso.
Gilroy, P. (2002 [1987]), *There Ain't No Black in the Union Jack*, London: Routledge.
Grant, C. (2019), *Homecoming: Voices of the Windrush Genration*, London: Vintage.
Grimes, M. (2018), 'Dis one is for alla Junglists: From Rebel MC to Conquering Lion and Beyond', *Riffs Journal*, 2 (2): 34–31.
Grish, N. (1999), 'Jungle', in L. Henderson and L. Stacey, *Encyclopedia of Music in the 20th Century*, 335, London and New York: Routledge, 2014.
Hall, T. (2017), 'Rastafarianism: Origins and Beliefs', *The Telegraph* [online], 12 April. Available online: https://www.telegraph.co.uk/news/uknews/1548384/Rastafarianism-Origins-and-beliefs.html (accessed 1 July 2015).
Hebdige, D. (1987), *Cut 'n' Mix: Culture, Identity and Caribbean Music*, Oxon and New York: Routledge.
Hopkins, J. (2017), 'Flag of Convenience? The Union Jack as a Contested Symbol of Englishness in Popular Music or a Convenient Marketing Device?', in L. Brooks, M. Donnelly and R. Mills (eds), *Mad Dogs and Englishness Popular Music and English Identities*, 125–42, London: Bloomsbury.
James, M. (1997), *State of Bass: Jungle: The Story so Far*, London: Boxtree.
Jones, K. (2003), *The Adventures of Marcus Garvey*, Kingston, Jamaica: Jones.
Johnson, L. (1980), 'Reggae Sounds', in *Bass Culture* [album], Island Records, London.
Lloyd, C. and S. Rambarran (2017), '"Brand New You're Retro": Tricky as Engpop Dissident', in L. Brooks, M. Donnelly and R. Mills (eds), *Mad Dogs and Englishness Popular Music and English Identities*, 162–73, London: Bloomsbury.
Mandara, A. (2014), *Up You Mighty Race: An Introduction to Marcus Garvey*, Kingston, Jamaica: LMH Publishing.
Melville, C. (2019), *It's a London Thing: How Rare Groove, Acid House and Jungle Remapped the City*, Manchester: Manchester University Press.
Monrose, K. (2019), *Black Men in Britain: An Ethnographic Portrait of the Post-Windrush Generation*, London and New York: Routledge.
Moskowitz, D. V. (2007), *Bob Marley: A Biography*, Westport, CT: Greenwood Press.
Natty, Congo (2013), *Jungle Revolution*, [CD] London: Big Dada.
Natty, Congo (2014), 'London Dungeons', [video]. Available online: https://www.youtube.com/watch?v=jbYsqeRydaI (accessed 1 July 2015).
Natty, Congo (2018), Jungle. [Instagram] 5 August. Available online: https://www.instagram.com/congonatty_official (accessed 5 August 2018).
Partridge, C. (2010), *Dub in Babylon*, London and Oakville: Equinox.
Quinn, S. (2002), 'Rumble in the Jungle: The Invisible History of Drum 'n' Bass', *Transformations*, 3: 1–12. Available online: http://www.cqu.edu.au/transformations (accessed 1 July 2015).

Rambarran, S. (2015), '"You've got no time for me": Martin "Sugar" Merchant, British Caribbean Musical Identity and the Media', in D. P. Hope (ed.), *Reggae from Yaad: Traditional and Emerging Themes in Jamaican Popular Music*, 64–82, Kingston, Jamaica: Ian Randle Publishers.

Reiss, M. (2014), 'Samson: The Only Nazarite Hebrew Bible and his Women!', *Scandinavian Journal of the Old Testament*, 28 (1): 133–46.

'Reggae Sounds' (1980), [Sound Recording] performed by Linton Kwesi Johnson, Island Records: London.

Reynolds, S. (1999), *Generation Ecstasy: Into the World of Techno and Rave Culture*, New York: Routledge.

Reynolds, S. (2007), *Bring the Noise: 20 Years of Writing About Hip Rock and Hip Hop*, London: Faber and Faber.

Reynolds, S. (2013), *Energy Flash: A Journey through Rave Music and Dance Culture*, London: Faber and Faber.

Ryman, C. (2014),' Kumina', in D. Horn, J. Shepherd, H. Feldman, M. Courteau, P. Jerez and H. Malcomson (eds), *Bloomsbury Encyclopedia of Popular Music of the World, Volume IX Genres: Caribbean and Latin America*, 422, London and New York: Bloomsbury.

S.J. (2017), 'Simply Spliffing: Bob Marley, Before He Was an Icon', *The Econonmist*, [Online]. Available online: https://www.economist.com/prospero/2017/01/03/bob-marley-before-he-was-an-icon (accessed 9 November 2018).

Stratton, J. and N. Zuberi, eds (2015), *Black Popular Music in Britian Since 1945*, Oxon: Ashgate.

Thornton, S. (2015), *Club Cultures: Music, Media, and Subcultural Capital*, Oxford: Polity.

Whiteley, S. (2010), 'Trainspotting: The Gendered History of Britpop', in A. Bennett and J. Stratton (eds), *Britpop and the English Music Tradition*, 55–70, Oxon: Ashgate.

William, P. H. (2007), 'Black History: Leonard P. Howell The First Rasta', *Jamaica Gleaner*, 2 February. Available online: http://jamaica-gleaner.com/gleaner/20140202/news/news41.html (accessed 1 July 2015).

Wood, A. (2002), 'Rebel MC', in Alison Donnell (ed.), *Companion Contemporary Black British Culture*, 261, Oxford: Routledge.

8

'Between Hipsters and God There is Sufjan Stevens': Sufjan Stevens and His Fans

Katelyn Medic

Introduction

It's Friday night at the Chicago Theater in downtown Chicago, IL. The bright white lights move and flash in unison, creating a rhythmic design around the building's kiosk, stating 'Chicago Theatre'. I shuffle in following a line of ticket holders wrapped around the building. As I enter the theatre, I bump shoulders with other attendees as we all try to find our assigned seats. Once settled, the lights dim and the crowd begins to cheer and applaud. Fans are ready to see, sing, dance and cheer with Sufjan Stevens, the main musical act for the night. Like a celestial being, Stevens emerges from the back of the stage. He is dressed in all black with multicoloured fluorescent tape clinging to his clothes. The tape strands are patterned lines outlining his arms, legs and torso. They glow fluorescent green, yellow, pink under the stage lighting. Accompanying his dress are large multicoloured feathered wings that extend out and up towards the ceiling. His winged feathers also carry streaks of hot pink, neon green and bright yellows patterns. They flutter and flicker as he moves across the stage as though Stevens is about to take flight. Here, Stevens wraps his electric guitar around his winged, fluorescent body and begins to play and sing to his listening fans. The crowd cheers in response to Stevens's holy sounds. Indeed, Stevens looks like an eccentric angel coming down from heaven to deliver a sacred message to his readied fans.

Sufjan Stevens (b. 1975) is a Brooklyn-based singer, songwriter and multi-instrumentalist who has been actively producing solo records since the early 2000s.[1] Before settling in Brooklyn, Stevens spent his formative years in Michigan, studying piano and oboe as an undergraduate student at Hope College, a Christian liberal arts college in Holland Michigan. There, Stevens joined the folk-rock band Marzuki. Stevens's stepfather, Lowell Brans, later joined him to create the record label Asthmatic Kitty Records (est. 1999) where

Stevens produced the majority of his musical projects.[2] Stevens mixes themes of personal narrative, spirituality and mysticism for lyrical content. Commentators often describe Stevens's musical style as Americana, indie and folk. Reviews of Stevens's albums regularly appear in numerous media platforms including *The Washington Post*, *The New Yorker*, *Rolling Stone* magazine and National Public Radio (NPR). For almost twenty years, Stevens has produced many records, received numerous accolades including an Oscar nomination for his song 'Mystery Love' for the film *Call Me By Your Name* (2018) and cultivated a strong fan following. While Stevens maintains his status in pop culture, he has also developed a strong fan base of evangelical Christians. Although Stevens does not produce music from an explicitly Christian music label, his public acknowledgment of practicing Christianity, attending a private Christian college and employing theologically themed lyrics in some of his songs have caught the attention of openly Christian fans. Indeed, there are a plethora of discussion boards on websites including Reddit where fans collaborate, speculate and theorize regarding the relationship between Stevens's private biographical history and his music.

In this essay I explore this relationship between Sufjan Stevens and his fans. Specifically, I examine how fans draw from his music and limited biographical information to construct Stevens as an ideal 'hipster Christian' through what ethnomusicologist Tom Wagner calls the practice of anointing, where fans overlay biblical themes onto Stevens's music and biography (Wagner 2014: 324). To show this, I examine public discussion boards including reddit, YouTube and Tumblr where fans anoint Stevens as an 'ideal' hipster Christian by posting the artist's select musical contributions that contain Christian undertones. This case study illuminates a relationship between popular Christian music industries and its consumers.

Christian versus secular music

Sufjan Stevens's public life and music represent a strain of secular popular music and culture in the United States often described as 'Americana', 'folk' and 'indie'. While Stevens cultivates a strong pop culture fan following, he also draws Christian fans and is regularly covered by Christian publications including *Christianity Today* and *Relevant*. Stevens's regular use of Christian themes found in his lyrics and personal interviews draw the attention of Christian listeners and organizations. Referring to this musical genre where lyrics and music are considered 'Christian' and 'Christian popular music (CPM)' is what ethnomusicologist Tom Wagner defines as a genre mirroring aesthetics of popular music (e.g. pop, metal, rap, rock, etc.) with Christian overtones during the later twentieth century into the twenty-first century (Wagner 2014: 325). To be labelled as CPM, music contains religious-based lyrics and is often produced and marketed by distinctly Christian record labels.

Musicologists (Busman 2015; Haynes 2014; Ingalls 2008; Justice 2014; Mall 2012; Porter 2017) have covered contemporary popular music in church services and music festivals. Music genres including 'Christian worship music', 'praise and worship', 'Christian popular music' and 'contemporary Christian music' – types that are defined by explicitly Christian lyrics, music produced on explicitly Christian record labels and musicians who openly confess to being practicing Christians – are well documented by scholars.[3] The CPM industry sonically, visually, instrumentally and thematically mirrors the aesthetics of popular music. Generally, CPM combines instrumentation rooted in the traditional rock band (a drum set, electric guitars and a keyboard) with texts directly referencing and/or quoting the Christian Gospel. Practically, CPM is music created for commercial use, usually geared toward youths by incorporating Christian-themed imagery into popular music instrumentation. Although distinctions are made between these Christian genres, for this essay I will not focus on these nuances. Rather, CPM, in its broadest sense, is a mediated consumer culture designed to attract youth-based Christians (Hendershot 2004; Miller 2004).[4]

While there are Christian popular industries and platforms designed to parallel similar developments in secular popular culture, musicologists are interested in how these media intersect and influence one another. For example, ethnomusicologist Mark Porter's close look at CPM's influence in church services shows how worship band members consume and produce elements of popular music in services (Porter 2017). Here, Porter investigates how congregants, especially worship band members, programme, rehearse and perform musical worship in services based on secular musical tastes. As Porter studies how mainstream secular popular music is consumed and performed by practicing Christians within religious services, Tom Wagner focuses on how church organizations create, brand and disseminate distinctively Christian products to Christian consumers. Hillsong is a sizeable multipronged organization founded by the Pentecostal megachurch of the same name in Sydney, Australia.[5] In his close study of this organization, specifically the Hillsong worship band, Wagner studies the relationship between Hillsong celebrities and their fans. Music journalists have also assessed the growing influence of Christian popular music practices since the early 1960s. Similar to Wagner's work, *Spin* writer Andrew Beaujon focuses on the relationship between the evangelical youth culture and mainstream Christian rock bands (Beaujon 2006), examining how self-professed Christian musicians attract both Christian and non-Christian audiences.

Considering this body of scholarship over CPM's relationship to secular popular music, it could be argued that Sufjan Stevens and his work bring these two industries closer together. For example, while Stevens produces his own musical works on his religiously unaffiliated record label, Asthmatic Kitty, he mixes autobiography and religious fantasy in his lyrics. *Silver & Gold: Songs for Christmas* (2012) is the artist's second compilation album, and the album's liner notes describe Christmas as a 'true horror-show catharsis of Christmas: The existential emptiness that perseveres in the heart of modern man as he recklessly pursues his search for happiness and comes up empty-handed.'[6] The writer of the album's liner notes reflects on excess and the desacralization of Christmas.

This compilation is a continuation of Stevens's first Christmas collection and directly illustrates the tension between the sacred and the secular through the commodification of Christmas. One example of ensuring tension is heard in the lyrics for 'Christmas Unicorn':

> …. Oh I'm a Christian holiday
> I'm a symbol of original sin
> I've a pagan tree and magical wreath
> And a bowtie on my chin …

The first two lines of the text allude to Christianity's meaning of Christmas: 'I'm a symbol of original sin' refers to the story of Adam and Eve in the Garden of Eden. The last two lines of this text immediately pivot to a pagan and commercial meaning of Christmas: 'I'm a pagan tree and magical wreath and a bowtie on my chin'. Objects such as 'pagan tree' and 'magical wreath' refer to traditional commercial objects consumed during the Christmas season. These commercial Christmas objects of clutter also extend to Stevens's critique of the mainstream's holiday season of excess buying, such as commercial ads pushing for consumer consumption and holiday discounts including annual 'Black Friday' sales promotions.

Stevens's cover art also illustrates the commercialism of Christmas: designed by Stevens and drawn by Jessica Dessner, it represents his notion of Christmas as a clutter of commodity and distortion of sacredness. The words 'Sufjan Stevens' and 'Silver & Gold' hug around a distorted, rotted-looking Christmas ornament. The curling font of the text 'Sufjan Stevens' is written to look like a ribbon tied on top of a present. Inside the ornament looks like a lump of coal or a rotting cavity. The background is outer space, and the Christmas ornament resembles a star within its nebula birthplace. Could this be interpreted as the Star of Bethlehem? This illustration could be viewed as a distant depiction of such ambiguity.

As Stevens continues to meld Christian themes within his role as a marketed independent musician, both Christian and non-Christian media chronicle his work. Despite his musical contributions coming out of secular industries, the artist maintains a strong fan base from both secular popular culture and openly Christian groups. His public acknowledgment of Christianity, attending a private Christian college and employing theologically themed lyrics in songs may have gathered fans from both sides of the aisle.

Hipster Christian fans

As Stevens establishes his career within mainstream media in the US, he also develops a following from Christian publications. For example, *Christianity Today* (est. 1956), a popular evangelical Christian periodical founded by Billy Graham, chronicles Stevens's career over the past several years (Beaty 2010; Breimeier 2005; Farias 2004; 2006; Heng Hartse 2015; Saunders 2015; Spinks 2017; Whitman 2012). By way of example, writer Joel Heng Hartse describes Sufjan Stevens as an 'artist [who] has been making fold, rock, electronic, and neoclassical music for 15 years, music that's always informed by his Christian faith, even if not always explicitly so' (Heng Hartse 2015).

With such a consistent following of Christian fans and publications, how do acolytes or those who endorse his message identify and draw out Stevens's Christian tendencies? Indeed, listeners closely examine his religiously themed lyrics, as briefly described above. Moreover, fans regularly draw meaning from his biographical accounts via overlaying his song lyrics. For example, fans posted a thread on reddit asking about Stevens's autobiographical relationship to his song writing:

> u/juliankoster: Sorry if this has been asked/discussed before, but does anyone know when the events of the song took place in Sufjan's life? …
>
> signandwonders: The story is mostly fictional so it's really not worth trying to figure out when it supposedly happened. The holiday is just a framework for Sufjan to tell the story around. I read a post by someone recently who had first

hand(?) knowledge of the real life story. The girl actually recovered from her illness. I think Sufjan's only childhood experience with death that we've heard about is Opie of Opie's Funeral Son.[7]

Since Stevens remains private about his personal life, fans are tempted to fill in the gaps. They regularly post speculations and theories of the artist's biography and interests, especially how Stevens 'performs' Christianity.

One example of a publication overlaying Christian-themes onto Stevens's music is in *Christianity Today*'s album review of *Planetarium* by Sufjan Stevens, Nico Muhly, Bryce Dessner and James McAlister (Spinks 2017). In an interview with *NPR*, he explains his mix of astrology and 'horoscope-like concepts' for inspiration in creating this electronic symphony album (Boilen 2017). Interestingly, Christian connections are absent from many artists' interviews and reflections. However, *Christianity Today* published a more God-centric review to this album titled, 'Sufjan Stevens' "Planetarium" Charts a God-Sustained Cosmos' (2017). Indeed, Casey Spinks unpacks Stevens's *Planetarium*, citing theological writings of Dietrich Bonhoeffer and Karl Barth to illustrate connections between biblical themes of Creation and Genesis in Stevens's *Planetarium*. He writes:

> Of all the themes Stevens has emphasized, the most current muse is Creation. … Those familiar with Stevens's earliest work know that Creation has been one of his concerns since the beginning. Throughout his music, Stevens does not merely consider the beauty of nature and then mix it with a few scriptural references, nor does he sing a contemporary environmentalism sprinkled with Christian blessing. Instead, he has something deeper – and more evangelical – in mind.
>
> (2017)

After setting up these religious or evangelistic themes in *Planetarium*, Spinks goes on to situate the album's theme of a Christian Genesis within a twentieth-century evangelical debate over Earth's creation citing Bonhoeffer and Barth as sources of inspiration.

Like his fans, Stevens personally contributes to his Christian branding. In the album *Carrie & Lowell* (2015), for example, he mixes autobiography and Christianity for lyrical themes. In his song 'Should've Known Better', lyrics including 'When I was three, three maybe four / She left us at that video store' and 'My brother had a daughter / The beauty that she brings, illumination' are inspired by autobiographical accounts throughout the artist's life. The song 'No Shade in the Shadow of the Cross' includes the lines 'There's blood on that blade, fuck me, I'm falling apart / My assassin like Casper the ghost / There's no shade in the shadow of the cross' detailing themes of Christianity within Stevens's autobiographical narratives.

Stevens admits his active involvement with Christianity while growing up in Michigan in an interview with *Pitchfork*:

> We [Stevens and his immediate family] would go to Methodist church, because that's what my great grandmother attended. I was the acolyte in charge of lighting the candles, which was really exciting to me. I had this childhood fantasy of becoming a priest or a preacher, so I would read and study the bible and then make my family listen to me read a passage from the New Testament before meals – and they very begrudgingly accommodated that for a while. I was just fascinated; some of my most profound spiritual and sexual experiences were at a Methodist summer camp.
>
> (Dombal 2015)

Indeed, Stevens admits to practicing Christianity and highlights these personal accounts in his album *Carrie & Lowell* (2015).[8]

To understand how Christian fans of Sufjan Stevens treat him as *their* celebrity, I find scholars' focus on celebrity construction useful (Cashmore 2006; Dyer 1986; Holmes and Redmond 2006; Wagner 2014). As Holmes and Redmond argue, there are two categories when discussing celebrities: those who are famous and those who help make those famous – the fans (2006). Indeed, Stevens's fans do the work of constructing and interpreting his celebrity by piecing together public elements of views expressed in his interviews, performances and media publications. Specifically, Stevens's incorporation of Christian elements, especially expressed in his lyrics, attract fans with similar taste who in turn highlight, or repost, those elements on fan pages. Likewise, Stevens cultivates his public individuality, weaving together Christianity and autobiography in his music, that fans can then confine him to those aspects of his image (Dyer 1986: 3–4). I will discuss this in more detail in the 'Stevens and his wings' section.

To understand how Christian fans form Stevens into a Christian celebrity, I find Tom Wagner's notion of 'anointing' useful. Wagner argues that individual, institutional and spiritual authorities are necessary authorizers in condoning performers, including Stevens, as an anointing example (2014: 325). Further, Wagner points out, the anointed Christian celebrity's public performances are examples of ideal Christian behaviour to fans (2014: 324). Rather than focus on the artist's anointing power over his Christian fans, I see Stevens's power as constructed by fans and Christian publications including *Christianity Today* and *Relevant*. Indeed, one article published by *Christianity Today* reviewing

Stevens's *Carrie & Lowell* (2015) album is titled 'How Not to Listen to the New Sufjan Stevens Album: Can we avoid turning the Brooklyn-based artist and Christian into a poster boy?' (Heng Hartse 2015). Essentially, these participants do the anointing work of reconstructing Stevens's biographical past and present musical performances to fit a biblical framework of an ideal Christian celebrity.

Hipster Christianity and fandom

Stevens's fan base is a mix of secular and openly Christian participants. Specifically, he draws a particular white Christian fan, a 'hipster' Christian. To be a 'hipster' is to be part of a subculture whose alienation is expressed by resisting classification by the larger culture. Hipster Christians prioritize notions of authenticity, sincerity and realness. Defining 'hipster Christians', journalist Brett McCracken writes:

> Today's Christian hipsters retain their faith, but they want it to be compatible with, not contrary to, secular hipster counterculture. Their mission is to rebrand Christianity to be, if not completely void of its own brand altogether, at least cobranded and allied with the things that it had previously set itself in opposition to: art, academics, liberal politics, fashion, and so on.
>
> (2010: 26–7)

For McCracken, Christians' rebellion against past generations of the contemporary evangelical movement marks them as hip. Broadly considering past notions of 'evangelicalism' associated with 'The Religious Right' (starting in the 1980s Ronald Regan presidential campaign and presidency), contemporary Christian industries (paralleling popular culture expressed in clothes, books and music, etc.) and mega churches as epicentres for regulated community activities for emerging suburban towns in the US. Additionally, what makes hipster Christians hip is by way of doing; a verbal denial of the label 'hipster' while maintaining its aesthetic conditions regarding dress and tastes in music, food, etc. According to McCracken, some elements to being a hip Christian include cursing, dressing in clothes from American Apparel, using social media technologies including Instagram and Twitter and listening to indie and folk rock music made by artists such as Sufjan Stevens (2010: 26).[9] Churches are indeed following in this trend. For example, in my dissertation research I focused on church communities in the Twin Cities who market to specifically hip Christian millennials. Elements incorporated in services are similar to McCracken's checklists including meeting in microbreweries for bible studies, renting out comedy clubs for Sunday morning services and church leaders advertising their social media details for further connections.

There are countless internet articles, blog posts and social media pages highlighting the relationship between Sufjan Stevens and (self-identified) 'hipster' Christians. For example, Dave Dunham, a writer for *Christ and Popular Culture*, writes:

> Currently, as I type this article, I am sitting in a dimly lit coffee shop with books next to me sipping on my mocha, listening to Sufjan Stevens play over the house stereo. I am wearing a slightly tight fitting retro 80s tee, Dickies shorts, and black chucks. Tomorrow night I will be going out with friends to drink imported beer and talk about the plausibility of theistic evolution. The church I preached at on Sunday morning was full of people with tattoos (including the guy behind the pulpit ... i.e. me), and my wife is dressed like a 1950s movie star (she looks good). Next Tuesday I will visit our local Farmers' Market because I believe it's important to buy local and to avoid all the wasteful packaging of commercial products. Apparently this makes me a Christian hipster, or at least that's what Brett McCracken, author of *Hipster Christianity: When Church and Cool Collide*, says.
>
> (Dunham 2010)

For Dunham, the marriage of being openly Christian with elements of popular culture (in this case including drinking beer and socializing with people who have tattoos all while listening to the music of Sufjan Stevens) is what makes a 'hipster Christian'. Further, Stevens's music contributes to an identity espoused by Christian hipsters.

As discussed above, Christian fans often note correlating Christian themes alongside biographical narratives within Stevens's music. For example, *Dappled Things*, a quarterly Catholic literary magazine, posted an essay centred on the relationship between Sufjan Stevens's music and Christian listeners titled 'Sufjan Stevens and the Plight of the Christian Hipster' (Grimes 2017). In this essay, the author writes a self-reflective response about Stevens's work over the years. In Grimes's words:

> For me, the 2005 release of *Come on Feel the Illinoise* by Sufjan Stevens lit the path to being, at last, a genuinely cool Christian of the kind I hoped was possible – deep, quirky, and poetic. ... Two popular songs on the album, the gentle 'Casimir Pulaski Day' and the dark 'John Wayne Gacy, Jr', deal with

particularly relatable topics for Christian college students – respectively, the complexity of a God who allows very bad things to happen to young believers and the depth of our individual sins.

(Grimes 2017)

In this excerpt, Grimes situates the artist as a successful example of a hipster Christian for his 'deep, quirky, and poetic' songs. In 'Casimir Pulaski Day' lyrics include 'All the glory when he took our place / But he took my shoulders and he shook my face / And he takes and he takes and he takes' suggests Stevens recognizing the 'complexity of a God who allows very bad things to happen to young believers'. And lyrics in 'John Wayne Gacy Jr' include 'And in my best behavior / I am really just like him / Look beneath the floor boards / For the secrets I have hid', which Grimes links to 'the depth of our individual sins'.

It may be that Stevens's directness of doubt and evil expressed in his lyrics in 'Casimir Pulaski Day' and 'John Wayne Gracy Jr' provide a renewed sense of Christianity that was once absent in past generations. By exploring notions of God and humanity within the unfathomable circumstances of death to 'good' people ('Casimir Pulaski Day') and the existence of 'bad' people, simplistic and unverifiable pronouncements of Christian doctrine as expressed by extreme evangelists are challenged. These discussions rebel against more simplistic and unverifiable pronouncements of Christianity and the afterlife as traditionally linked to Billy Graham's evangelism style of the twentieth century.

While Christian fans perceive Stevens as a bridge between secular and non-secular fans, I see their use of Stevens, notably within the context of the Tumblr web page fuckyeahsufjanstevens.com, as a form of anointing, thereby verifying him as an approved role model. Although hipster Christians could be viewed as breaking new ground by adopting a secular artist as 'one of them', their portrayal of Stevens, I argue, is even more evangelistic. Fuckyeahsufjanstevens.com is a crowd-sourcing centre for anything related to the artist. In addition to the web address, the page's only title is located on the top left-hand corner of the website, 'Between Hipster and God There is Sufjan Stevens'. Indeed, this web page drives home the relationship between hipster Christians and Sufjan Stevens.[10] Using the word 'fuck' as part of the web address and using profanity in everyday language is a rebellious act against an evangelical social norm where swearing is socially distasteful or commonly viewed as 'not Christian'. This defiant act is a form of performing 'hipness'.

The website is simple. At the top of the left-hand column, there is a picture of Stevens: dressed in a ball cap, jeans jacket and a graphic T-shirt, holding an acoustic guitar over his lap in one hand while adjusting a synthesizer in front of him with the other. Against a dark backdrop and what may be streaks of spotlights in the back, a microphone points towards him. This action shot perhaps captures a live stage performance. A figure appears on the left side of the website partway down the page. It is a photo of Stevens playing the piano. His back is to the viewer, and rock gear and an electric guitar surround him. A single spotlight shines down on him as he plays. Down the left column, there are links to specific Stevens paraphernalia. These links read: 'Upcoming Events', 'Photos', 'Audio', 'Quotes', 'Chats', 'Videos', 'Writing', 'Bootlegs', 'Downloads: Unreleased, Rarities, etc.', 'Michigan Stories', 'Setlists', 'Sufjan's Tumblr', 'Sufjan's Website' and 'Archive'. To the right of this column of links is the main content of the web page. Sorted chronologically (latest to less recent), this section of the web page is dedicated to posting the latest content related to Stevens. Participants post news publications featuring Stevens, upcoming tour schedules, art and poetry made by fans inspired by Stevens's previous works, videos, song links, the list goes on.

Commentators' and fans' efforts to identify and promote Christian themes in Stevens's music are what ethnomusicologist Tom Wagner calls 'anointing', or God-given blessings identified and promoted by Christian fans, to rationalize or to make real how Stevens has become a celebrity for Christian audiences (2014: 336). In his article, 'No Other Name? Authenticity, Authority and Anointing in Christian Popular Music', Wagner studies the relationship between Darlene Zschech, a high-profile worship pastor of Hillsong, a multipronged evangelical church based in Australia, and her fans. Wagner writes:

> For more than twenty years, Zschech and Hillsong have shaped an image of 'Darlene' through her biography, which while always evolving, has consistently emphasized the Christian values of humility and deference to God ... Zschech's story does not deny her rise to fame, but present it as unsought and, to some degree, inevitable – the confluence of God-given talent and personal devotion.
>
> (2014: 331)

Indeed, Darlene's public actions alongside fans identifying and promoting biblical themes in Darlene's biography present here as a Christian leader personally selected by God (Wagner 2014: 338). For Stevens, his Christian overtones (expressed in his lyrics, dress and autobiographical interviews) and performances are woven together, making his public presence an exemplar Christian artist for his Christian fans.

Stevens and his wings

The Tumblr fan page's statement arguably draws out characteristics of Stevens as a Christ-like figure, where, similarly, the conferment of divinity is overlaid onto his body. In concerts, he often appears wearing a set of large white-feathered angel or colourfully drawn butterfly wings. In these moments, with the stage lighting shining through the wings, he appears as a divine celestial being, singing to fans from the stage, like an angel proclaiming God's good news to his people.

The consistent use of adorning wings in concerts clearly captures the attention of fans too, as witnessed in a reddit post entitled 'Why does Sufjan wear wings in concert?' (u/Headstreams 2016). This question results in a small stream of conversation between participants centred around citations made by Stevens. A small excerpt:

> He says the wings basically represent him overcoming his fear of flying things (mibuger)
>
> I know in 'no Shade in the Shadow of the Cross' he said his mother could give wings to a stone but I knew the wings long predated that (Headstreams).
>
> I've always hypothesized that Sufjan has entertained the idea of doing a concept/themed album on birds. There are a couple of unreleased songs about birds (Lord God Bird is another example and until 2010, The Owl and Tanager would have been another). There's also lots of bird stuff that overflows into other albums (timmeh_green).
>
> (u/Headstreams 2016)

As these participants exchange reasons as to why Stevens consistently wears wings in concerts they reference lyrics from past albums and previous interviews, even offering up their theories like 'doing a concept/themed album on birds'.

The consistent use of wings in live performances may also serve as part of his celebrity making in what Richard Dyer describes as the 'individual', where the celebrity contains both a separate and coherent entity (1986: 7). For Stevens, the regular wearing of wings during concerts immediately distinguishes him from other celebrities who do not wear wings in public. This difference is noted by fans, 'Why does Sufjan wear wings in concert?' (u/Headstreams 2016), and Stevens's regular use of wings gradually becomes part of his identity for fans (Dyer 1986: 7).

Another fan writer of Sufjan Stevens reflects on the wings in a BuzzFeed article titled 'The sexy sadness of Sufjan Stevens': 'There's a security in his sadness, because it also comes with wearable butterfly wings and impressive but approachable muscles' (Koul 2018). To Koul, Stevens's use of colourful 'butterfly wings' in concerts may appear as a separation from a kind of masculinity but is actually expanding the boundaries of permissive masculinity by accompanying 'butterfly wings' with 'impressive but approachable muscles'. In the article, Koul hyperlinks each phrase, 'butterfly wings' and 'impressive but approachable muscles' with images of Stevens in these corresponding descriptions. These images serve as specific examples to the author's definition of 'the sexy sadness of Sufjan Stevens': Stevens wearing both wings and exposed muscular arms.

Furthermore, the 'sexiness' of Stevens and his wings is furthered by how his wings were conceptualized. Designer Adam Selman created one version: with white feathers extending feet up and out behind Stevens. Apparently, models wearing wings – especially white, feathered, angel-like wings – in runway fashion shows by the lingerie company Victoria's Secret inspired Stevens's wings (Welk 2018).[11] These associations with an iconic lingerie brand heightens Koul's observation of his 'sexy sadness' in that Stevens and his wings blur together elements of cultural feminine sexuality (as advertised by Victoria's Secret Angels) and masculine sexuality (visible exposure of arm muscles).

Alongside his use of wings to cultivate his individual celebrity, I argue that fans attach their own narratives to Stevens's song lyrics. One writer confesses her personal connections to growing up listening to Stevens's 'Casimir Pulaski Day':

> (That I had never had cancer, knew anyone with cancer, didn't believe in a Christian God, was not queer, and have never lived in Michigan didn't matter.) …
> You can attach yourself or your experiences to one of his songs without having to consider too much of the song's original purpose.
>
> (Koul 2018)

The song's lyrics, including 'All the glory that the Lord has made / And the complications you could do without / When I kissed you on the mouth', suggest themes of sexuality, spirituality and death. Although Koul does not directly connect to suggested themes of a 'Christian God', queerness and living in Michigan, she argues the lyrical content is nonetheless presented to openly overlay *her* sadness and personal emotions within the song's musical content.

Fans experiencing and processing their emotions through listening to Stevens's music alongside participating in public discourse about his biography and performance styles are elements for fans in cultivating Stevens as their celebrity. Further, fans weave together Stevens's biographical background, lyrical compositions and performance elements to make a template upon which to inflect a Christian hipster celebrity identity.

Considering the Tumblr web page and reddit blogs dedicated to identifying Stevens's anointing qualities, Stevens remains private about his personal and romantic life, a public ambiguity which leads fans to seek answers within his musical output. Hence, a plethora of internet articles and blog postings focus on the relationship between Stevens, his music and his sexual orientation. Similar to http://fuckyeahsufjanstevens.tumblr.com, the Facebook page titled 'Is this Sufjan Stevens song gay or just about God?' is a web page dedicated to contributors posting links and information related to the title's question.[12]

In a spin-off article titled 'We Can't Stop Wondering if Sufjan Stevens Sings About God or Being Gay', writer Jared Richards goes a step further by analysing song lyrics to provide an answer to this Facebook question, using his 'The Predatory Wasp of the Palisades Is Out to Get Us!' to illustrate its queerness (Richards 2017). Lyrical phrases including 'Touch his back with my hand I kiss him' and 'I can tell you I love him each day' suggest a same-sex romance. Of course, considering the title of the post, 'We Can't Stop Wondering if Sufjan Stevens Sings About God or Being Gay', this lyrical phrase may simultaneously suggest Stevens's reverence to Christ.

Likewise, the songs 'Mystery of Love' and 'Visions of Gideon', for the 2017 film *Call Me By Your Name*, a same-sex romantic drama, further fan conversations about Stevens's sexuality. Specifically, commentators on this topic often reference Stevens's 'Mystery of Love', nominated for an Oscar in 2018; for example, writer Michael Cuby's post titled 'Sufjan Stevens' Music Is Queer – And He Deserves an Oscar Tonight' (Cuby 2018). Photographs of Stevens in wings alternate between Cuby's commentary about Stevens, the film and queerness. Cuby writes:

> Speaking in no uncertain terms, Sufjan Stevens acted as a vessel for my queerness. Without being openly queer himself (which isn't to say the questions pertaining to his sexuality haven't been speculated about endlessly), he made me feel like I deserved happiness – and more importantly, that I would eventually find it.
> (Cuby 2018)

Cuby sees Stevens and his musical works as mediums for a mode of self-expression. Indeed, approaching Stevens and his works as malleable vessels for fans allows them to anoint Stevens as a hipster Christian and, in this case, speculate about Stevens's sexuality alongside his Christianity for collective fandom expression.

Conclusion

Sufjan Stevens was and continues to be an icon and subject for speculation for fans. Indeed, his public performances and music are vessels for fans to express their own views and personal identities. In this essay, I showed how Stevens's celebrity identity is cultivated and performed both by his regular use of wings in performance and how fans draw from these performances to provide rationale for personal and celebrity narratives. Further, I illustrated how the artist is anointed as a celebrity both for hipster versions of Christian identification and how his celebrity identity is constituted in discourses surrounding gender, sexuality and Christianity. Through an analysis of blogs and websites themed around Stevens and his music, fans draw from Stevens's performances, interviews and lyrical content to construct a biographical sketch allowing them to project personal agendas and conversations through discussions in social media. In this process, fans project their personal agendas and conversations through discussions about Stevens.

Notes

1 Stevens has additionally worked on collaborative projects including choreographer Justin Peck and the New York City Ballet's ballet *Everywhere We Go* (2014) and with the Brooklyn Academy of Music for the multimedia composition *The BQE* (2007).

2 The label first started in Holland, Michigan, and now has locations in Lander, Wyoming, Indianapolis, Indiana, and in New York City. Visit http://asthmatickitty.com for more information about sponsored artists and news related to this label. In 1999, Stevens left Marzuki band and moved to New York City to pursue a full-time solo career. *Sun Came* (2000) is his first of many albums as a solo artist. In 2003, Stevens achieved mainstream recognition with his *Greetings from Michigan* album, the first of his declared 'Fifty States Project', a long-term project producing a full-length album for each state in the United States. Although Stevens abandoned this project, he ultimately produced two full-length albums, *Greetings from Michigan* (2004) and *Illinoise* (2005) as odes to each state.

3 Scholars who focus on contemporary (1960s to present) Protestant Christian music have documented and theorized about an industry commonly referred to as 'contemporary Christian music' (CCM) – a broad genre or category that draws from elements of pop-rock (instrumentation, chord progression, performer's physical appearance, etc.) with biblically themed lyrics whose performers and song writers publically identify as Christian. Indeed, scholars have additionally worked

to make distinctions between Christian music genres (e.g. 'contemporary Christian music' verses 'Christian worship music') according to use (see Ingalls et al. 2013 and Wagner 2014).

4. One example of a distinctly Christian outlet is GodTube, 'a video sharing platform offering online Christian videos with faith-based, family friendly content'. Although GodTube's interface is similar to YouTube, GodTube's platform specifically promotes Christian-based cultural artifacts. Conducting a search of 'Sufjan Stevens' in GodTube's search box yields twelve video results with titles including 'Come Thou Fount of Every Blessing' and 'Sufjan Stevens-Abraham'. On YouTube's web page, this search phrase yields 415,000 results, each post containing extensive comment threads. On GodTube, each 'Sufjan Stevens' post contains explicit Christian content. For example, after clicking on a chosen video, near the bottom of the web page under the heading 'ABOUT GODTUBE.COM', the opening text reads: 'You are watching Sufjan Stevens-Abraham on Godtube.com the largest video sharing platform offering online Christian videos with faith-based, family friendly content.' Unlike YouTube, where participants can post comment threads corresponding to videos, GodTube does not programme discussion space; rather it curates its platform to only disseminate exclusively Christian videos.

5. This organization is so big that the word 'Hillsong' may refer to any of the following: Hillsong Church, Hillsong Conference, Hillsong Global Project, Hillsong International Leadership College, Hillsong Music Australia, Hillsong United and Hillsong United (the band). The sub-organizations of Hillsong allow this industry to disseminate their production model in a myriad of Christian-based avenues. See http://myhillsong.com and https://www.hillsong.com/en/ for more about this church, and https://hillsong.com/en/store/ to learn more about Hillsong Music (all accessed 12 November 2013).

6. *Silver & Gold* by Sufjan Stevens (2012). Available online: http://music.sufjan.com/album/silver-gold (accessed 14 April 2013).

7. https://www.reddit.com/r/Sufjan/comments/3oim14/casimir_pulaski_day/ (accessed 8 January 2018).

8. While *Christianity Today* put Stevens's autobiographical album within a Christian framework, more secular reviews consider this aspect one of many themes in Stevens's album. For example, *Pitchfork*'s review of Stevens's *Carrie & Lowell* notes that '[t]here are Biblical references, and reference to mythology, but most of it is squarely about Stevens and his family' (Stosuy 2015).

9. Whiteness is absent in the descriptions of hipster Christians. In Stevens's aesthetics (music, dress, social media pages, etc.), I do see his brand as a white 'hip' aesthetic. However, I will not focus on how race performativity, specifically white performances, is imbedded in this case study.

10 A similar hipster fan fiction Tumblr web page exists featuring Bon Iver, an indie band featuring lead singer-songwriter Justin Vernon, titled 'Bon Iver Erotic Stories'. Here, contributors post satirical fan fiction related to Justin Vernon and his broad musical themes of nature and spirituality. One writer posts: '[excerpt] I drive the truck (Bon Iver has been sampling the wine for several hours) and he sings O Magnum Mysterium to me in his falsetto, breath visible in the night air: a tipsy angel' (Anonymous, http://boniverotica.Tumblr.com/).

11 In an interview with Selman, the designer explains the inception for Stevens's wings: 'I said [Selman], "Oh, I actually know these guys who make the Victoria's Secret wings"' (Eckardt 2016). Victoria's Secret's models wearing wings down runways has become an iconic feature for the lingerie brand since it's launch of the 'Angels' bra line in the late 1990s. Since this debut, angels are integrated throughout the company's brand expressed in model hierarchy, bra lines, social media, credit cards, etc. (Victoriassecret.com).

12 https://www.facebook.com/Is-this-Sufjan-Stevens-song-gay-or-just-about-God-1462192820689584/ (accessed 8 January 2018).

References

Beaty, K. (2010), 'The Age of Adz' review, *ChristianityToday*.com, 12 October. Available online: http://www.christianitytoday.com/ct/2010/octoberweb-only/ageadz.html (accessed 29 March 2018).

Beaujon, A. (2006), *Body Piercing Saved My Life: Inside the Phenomenon of Christian Rock*, Cambridge, MA: Da Capo Press.

'Between Hipsters and God There is Sufjan Stevens'. Available online: http://fuckyeahsufjanstevens.tumblr.com/ (accessed 1 August 2018).

Boilen, B. (2017), 'Sufjan Stevens, Nico Muhly and Bryce Dessner on Creating "Planetarium"', NPR, 8 June. All songs considered. Available online: https://www.npr.org/sections/allsongs/2017/06/08/531946097/sufjan-stevens-nico-muhly-and-bryce-dessner-on-creating-planetarium (accessed 17 September 2020).

'Bon Iver Erotic Stories' (n.d.), Available online: http://boniverotica.tumblr.com/ (accessed 1 August 2018).

Breimeier, R. (2005), 'Illinois' review, *ChristianityToday*.com, 1 January. Available online: http://www.christianitytoday.com/ct/2005/januaryweb-only/illinois.html (accessed 29 March 2018).

Busman, J. K. (2015), '(Re)Sounding Passion: Listening to American Evangelical Worship Music, 1997-2015', thesis, The University of North Carolina at Chapel Hill. In PROQUESTMS ProQuest Dissertations and Theses A&I. Available online: http://login.ezproxy.lib.umn.edu/login?url=https://search-proquest-com.ezp3.lib.umn.edu/docview/1689691201?accountid=14586 (accessed 5 September 2020).

Cashmore, E. (2006), *Celebrity Culture*, New York: Routledge.
Cuby, M. (2018), 'Sufjan Stevens' Music is Queer – And He Deserves an Oscar Tonight', *them*. Available online: https://www.them.us/story/sufjan-stevens-music-is-queer-and-he-deserves-an-oscar-tonight (accessed 1 August 2018).
Dombal, R. (2015), 'True Myth: A Conversation With Sufjan Stevens', Pitchfork.com. Available online: https://pitchfork.com/features/interview/9595-true-myth-a-conversation-with-sufjan-stevens/ (accessed 1 August 2018).
Dunham, D. (2010), 'Hipster Christianity: Did You Know That You're a Hipster?', *Christ and Popular Culture*, 6 September. Available online: https://christandpopculture.com/hipster-christianity-did-you-know-that-youre-a-hipster (accessed 30 March 2018).
Dyer, R. (1986), *Heavenly Bodies: Film Stars and Society*, 2nd edn, New York: Routledge Taylor & Francis Group.
Eckardt, S. (2016), 'How Sufjan Stevens Got His Victoria's Secret Wings', *WMagazine*. Available online: https://www.wmagazine.com/story/sufjan-stevens-adam-selman-costumes-panorama (accessed 18 November 2018).
Farias, A. (2004), 'Seven Swans', review, *ChristianityToday*.com, 1 January. Available online: http://www.christianitytoday.com/ct/2004/januaryweb-only/sevenswans.html (accessed 29 March 2018).
Farias, A. (2006), 'The Avalanche: Outtakes and Extras from the Illinios Album', *ChristianityToday*.com, 1 July. Available online: http://www.christianitytoday.com/ct/2006/julyweb-only/theavalanche.html (accessed 29 March 2018).
Faris, M. (2004), '"That Chicago Sound": Playing with (Local) Identity in Underground Rock', *Popular Music and Society*, 27 (4): 429–54.
Grimes, I. (2017), 'Sufjan Stevens and the Plight of the Christian Hipster', *Dappled Things*. Available online: https://dappledthings.org/12772/sufjan-stevens-and-the-plight-of-the-christian-hipster/ (accessed 1 August 2018).
Haynes, M. (2014), 'Heaven, Hell, and Hipsters', *Ecclesial Practices*, 1 (2): 207–28.
Hendershot, H. (2004), *Shaking the World for Jesus: Media and Conservative Evangelical Culture*, Chicago, IL: University of Chicago Press.
Heng Hartse, J. (2015), 'How Not to Listen to the New Sufjan Stevens Album: Can We Avoid Turning the Brooklyn-based Artist and Christian into a Poster Boy?', *ChristianityToday*.com, 15 April. Available online: http://www.christianitytoday.com/ct/2015/april-web-only/how-not-to-listen-to-new-sufjan-stevens-album.html (accessed 29 March 2018).
Holmes, S. and S. Redmond, eds (2006), *Framing Celebrity: New Directions in Celebrity Culture*, New York: Routledge.
Ingalls, M. M. (2008), 'Awesome in this Place: Sound, Space, and Identity in Contemporary North American Evangelical Worship', thesis, University of Pennsylvania. IN PROQUESTMS ProQuest Dissertations and Theses A&I. Available online: http://login.ezproxy.lib.umn.edu/login?url=https://search-proquest-com.ezp2.lib.umn.edu/docview/304494371?accountid=14586 (accessed 5 September 2020).

Ingalls, M. M., C. Landau and T. Wagner (2013), *Christian Congregational Music: Performance, Identity, and Experience*, London: Ashgate.

Ingalls, M. M., M. S. Reigersberg and Z. C. Sherinian (2018), *Making Congregational Music Local in Christian Communities Worldwide*, New York: Routledge.

Jones, A. L. (2014), 'Pole Dancing for Jesus: Negotiating Masculinity and Sexual Ambiguity Gospel Performance', in S. Finley, M. S. Guillory and H. R. Page, Jr (eds), *Esotericism in the Africana Religious Experience: There is a Mystery*, London: Brill.

Justice, D. (2014), 'When Church and Cinema Combine: Blurring Boundaries through Media-Savvy Evangelicalism', *Journal of Religion, Media and Digital Culture*, 3 (1): 84–119.

Koul, S. (2018), 'The Sexy Sadness of Sufjan Stevens', BuzzFeedNews. Available online: https://www.buzzfeednews.com/article/scaachikoul/the-sexy-sadness-of-sufjan-stevens (accessed 1 August 2018).

Mall, A. T. (2012) '"The Stars are Underground": Undergrounds, Mainstreams, and Christian Popular Music', thesis, The University of Chicago. In PROQUESTMS Dissertations and Theses A&I. Available online: http://login.ezproxy.lib.umn.edu/login?url=https://search-proquest-com.ezp2.lib.umn.edu/docview/955176168?accountid=14586 (accessed 5 September 2020).

McCracken, B. (2010), *Hipster Christianity: When Church and Cool Collide*, Grand Rapids, MI: Baker Books.

Miller, V. J. (2004), *Consuming Religion: Christian Faith and Practice in a Consumer Culture*, New York: Continuum.

Porter, M. J. (2017), *Contemporary Worship Music and Everyday Musical Lives*, London: Ashgate.

Richards, J. (2017), 'We Can't Stop Wondering if Sufjan Stevens Sings About God or Being Gay', *noisey*. Available online: https://noisey.vice.com/en_au/article/599j3d/we-cant-stop-wondering-if-sufjan-stevens-sings-about-god-or-being-gay (accessed 1 August 2018).

Saunders, M. (2015), 'Sufjan Stevens - Carrie & Lowell Review', *ChristianityToday*.com, 31 March. Available online: https://www.christiantoday.com/article/sufjan-stevens-carrie-lowell-review/51124.htm (accessed 29 March 2018).

Spinks, C. (2017), 'Sufjan Stevens' "Planetarium" Charts a God-Sustained Cosmos: The Singer-Songwriter's Latest Collaboration Sets a Distinctly Biblical Course through the Created Order', *ChristianityToday*.com, 31 August. Available online: http://www.christianitytoday.com/ct/2017/august-web-only/sufjan-stevens-planterium-charts-god-sustained-cosmos.html (accessed 29 March 2018).

Stosuy, B. (2015), 'Sufjan Steven: *Carrie & Lowell*', Pitchfork.com. Available online: https://pitchfork.com/reviews/albums/20218-carrie-lowell/ (accessed 1 August 2018).

u/Headstreams (2016), 'Why does Sufjan wear wings in concert?', reddit. Available online: https://www.reddit.com/r/Sufjan/comments/4pqlpb/question_why_does_sufjan_wear_wings_in_concert/ (accessed 1 August 2018).

Wagner, T. (2014), 'No Other Name? Authenticity, Authority, and Anointing in Christian Popular Music', *Journal of World Popular Music*, 1 (2): 324–42.

Welk, B. (2018), 'What Should Sufjan Stevens Wear to the Oscars? We Have Ideas (Photos)', TheWrap. Available online: https://www.thewrap.com/what-should-sufjan-stevens-wear-to-the-oscars-photos/ (accessed 18 November 2018).

Whitman, A. (2012), 'Sufjan Stevens's Conflicted Christmas: 100 Songs In, Stevens Understands the Joys, Pains, and Ironies of Christmas Like No Other Artist', *ChristianityToday*. com, 18 December. Available online: https://www.christianitytoday.com/ct/2012/december-web-only/sufjan-stevenss-conflicted-christmas.html (accessed 29 March 2018).

Part Three

Alternative Religions

'Save My Soul From the Poisons of This World': Straight Edge Punk and Religious Re-Enchantment

Francis Stewart

Introduction

In 1966 John Lennon famously stated 'Christianity will go. It will vanish and shrink. I needn't argue about that; I know I'm right and I will be proved right. We're more popular than Jesus right now' (*London Evening Standard*, 4 March 1966). This was a time when the secularization thesis – the idea that traditional religions are in terminal decline in the industrialized world – was perhaps the central debate in the sociology of religion and in religious studies (Berger 1967; Parsons 1966). As a theory, it was capturing the attention of the wider public, being featured in national newspapers and televised debates and on early Open University television programmes from 1971 onwards (ER1).[1] This occurred at a time of huge social upheaval and change – civil rights movement, the availability of the pill for many women, continuing women's rights movement and the ending of global empires as they had traditionally existed. Therefore, an assertion that religious institutions and teaching would continue to decline in their social significance and influence until it became a private matter that occurred in the domestic rather than public sphere did not seem unrealistic (McLeod 2007).

Lennon articulated the same ideas of the time in his infamous statement noted above. He was not speaking directly of the Beatles, but rather of popular culture in general, as having more influence and significance than Christianity or even the figure of Christ. In other words, he was articulating the notion that religion as a concept (in his thinking, notably Christianity) was diminishing in power, influence, purpose and public positions. Religion was believed to be, for Lennon like so many others, shrinking to the private realm through 'the pervasive influence of science' (Berger 1967: 110) resulting in what Charles Taylor refers to as 'the automization of the different spheres driven by a process of rationalization' (2007: 779). This is not to say that Lennon was not spiritual, or even religious in his own way – he absolutely was, very publically so – rather that this was the emergence of new ways of thinking about religion as an identity and its public influence.

In reality, those who put forward the secularization thesis were ultimately wrong, as Berger came to acknowledge (1999). Religion has not become wholly private, it remains an influence within various parts of the public sphere such as education, politics and welfare. However, the articulation of the secularization and its prominence has given credence to the notion that religion is insufficient as a means of an identity marker, or of fully understanding the spectrum of how people are articulating and locating their individual approaches to it. Increasingly, we are finding that people in the West are turning to or utilizing aspects of popular culture, especially popular music, as part of their 'religious' identity construction or approach. Therefore, when we consider the notion of popular music as being sacred, we are also interested in how it can be utilized as an individualized form of faith.

It is important to note that some theorists have argued that these types of individualized religions are, in fact, a confirmation of secularization. Bryan Wilson (1976) has argued that, far from being a resurgence of religion, they are actually evidence of the trivialization of religion. Similarly, Steve Bruce has argued that they are little more than the dying embers of religion in the concluding stages of the history of the secularization of the West (2000). I would respond to such approaches by noting that they have ignored the power of popular culture, especially music, and so cannot, or will not, see that Western culture is increasingly characterized by forms of religion that do not claim absolute truth, do not require devotion to one religious leader, do not insist on the authority of a single set of teachings, but rather encourage exploration, eclecticism, an understanding of the self as divine and, consequently, a belief in the final authority of the self. This chapter is drawing upon Christopher Partridge's notion of occulture and re-enchantment and Edward Bailey's notion of Implicit Religion to demonstrate that sXe is functioning, for many of its adherents as an individualized religion or an implicit religion that helps to re-enchant the world for its adherents. It will do this by examining the rise of individualized religions from a theoretical perspective, giving a brief note on the methodological approach of the case study before focusing in detail on sXe as an example of the arguments being put forward.

Individualized religions

When Max Weber ([1904] 2005) borrowed the expression 'the disenchantment of the world' from Schiller, he was offering a sociological provocation, which still resonates today as it continues to lie at the very heart of modernity (or indeed postmodernity). Weber understood disenchantment to mean two distinct but interrelated processes: the first, the removal of religion from public spaces and influence and thus a removal of a sense of magic, wonder or inexplicableness from those spaces; and the second, the continually increasing scale, scope and power of the formal means–ends rationalities of science, bureaucracy, the law and policy-making ([1904] 2005: 18–31). For the most part, Weber was ambivalent in his assessment of the disenchantment process, seeing both positive and negative in it, with the most negative consequence being that of the development of anomie, which Durkheim considered to be 'an un-mooring of the individual from the ties that bind in society' (Bell 1997: 26).

The mechanizing processes and increased bureaucracy did not result in some 'glorious' secular world, and instead we are in the midst of a growing desire for a re-enchantment of the world. This desire is feeding into current attempts to individualize religion and the rise of spirituality as both a marker of identity and a means of 'believing without belonging' to traditional religious institutions (Davie 1990). Primarily, what is being witnessed or created are personally tailored forms of 'self-religion' that seek in various ways to reinvigorate the sense of wonder and magic that connect with and seek to preserve nature (especially in relation to climate change) and somehow transcend the mundane without denying the empirical aspect of human life. For example, Gordon Lynch notes that the increase in Wiccans and Pagans (self-designated and designated by the Covenant of the Goddess) as a religious designation on census data and other official forms is increasingly detached from covens or other group structures because of the proliferation of information and resources available elsewhere and the conviction that one can shape this as best suits the self (2007: 72).

Christopher Partridge argues that such attempts at re-enchantment are often defined against traditional religion and are thus articulated by those involved with them in ways that either reduce or remove the baggage of traditional religion.

Drawing instead upon and simultaneously shaping popular culture provides a large constantly replenishing reservoir of ideas, practices and methodologies to utilize, that he refers to as occulture (2005). One need look no further than the pilgrimage and religious devotion of the dead heads who followed The Grateful Dead, or the site of Graceland as sacred place of pilgrimage for those heavily invested in the religiosity of Elvis. In particular, those fans who believe Elvis had mystical power and his apparent resurrection after death, and call upon him in prayer or devotion to perform miracles for them (Tharpe 1983: 11; Windsor 1997: 58). King and Stewart note of Elvis: '[h]is image encompasses issues of myth, modernity as well as identity' (2016: 98). Within the fandom of Elvis, some are using his life, legacy and music to re-enchant or to give sacred/spiritual/religious meaning and structure to their lives.

This re-enchantment and drawing upon popular culture should not be seen as a superficial secondary development in the shadow of Christianity, nor dismissed as fandom taken to extreme lengths. In many ways, it is a religious phenomenon in its own right driven by fundamental questions of what it means to be a human being, often manifesting as new versions of what Charles Taylor refers to as 'modern social imaginaries' (2003). Partridge notes that:

> [P]eople are, from their own particular perspectives, developing religious and metaphysical ideas by reflecting on themes explored in literature, film and music. ... Popular culture both reflects and informs ideas, values and meanings within society as well as providing a site for the exploration of ideas, values and meaning. Hence the relationship is rather a complex one.
>
> (2004: 121)

Such meaning and exploration should not, therefore, be dismissed simply because of its complex relationship with popular culture. Likewise, it should not be assumed to be suitable for analysis or understanding through a standard lens applied to the study of more traditional or institutional-based religions. It necessitates an approach that can take seriously the meaning and value of popular culture as a site for learning about or developing new understandings and approaches to the concept of religion; and this is where Edward Bailey's Implicit Religion is most apt.

Implicit Religion is a set of analytical tools developed by Edward Bailey that aims to provide a means to consider seriously and comprehensively, emically and etically, that which is often dismissed, in other studies, as simply a form of popular culture rather than a site of meaning or meaning-making. It seeks to see and understand 'the sacred-in-the-secular/the secular-in-the-sacred' (Keenan 2016: 41). It is based on three areas of focus:

- 'Commitment(s) – to what do people, groups, communities, professions, institutions, corporations commit themselves and why? What meaning does that commitment provide for them?
- Integrating foci – what do people, groups, communities, professions, institutions, and corporations use to integrate their commitment into the rest of their life and its vagaries? In what ways are the integrating foci related to or born from the commitment?
- Intensive Concerns with Extensive Effects – what arises from the commitment that matters / excites / stimulates / moves the individual, group, community, business, or corporation to such an extent that it changes and shapes their actions, behaviours, attitudes and opinions?' (Stewart 2017: 12)

It is important to be clear that this is not a set of tools intended to enable the scholar to artificially layer existing understandings of religion as traditionally understood over an apparently secular activity or pursuit in such a way that the people involved would not recognize or accept it, or in such a way as to demonstrate that 'true' or 'authentic' faith can only be located within a narrowly defined conception of religion. For example, Implicit Religion should not be used to look for indicators of Christianity within football or hip hop, but it should be used to meaning, value and purpose of football or hip hop for its respective participants and creators.

Implicit Religion directly refutes, then, the viewpoint noted above by Bruce and Wilson that the rise of popular culture derived, or secular-based faiths and spiritualties reveal no more than the dying embers of religion. To take the approach to Bruce and Wilson is to assume that religion can have a fixed definition of what it actually is and therefore its texts have a static, unilateral meaning. If one applies such an approach to something of meaning outside of traditionally defined religions (such as those linked with an institution), one quickly finds that the static, unilateral meaning is either contorted as to be unrecognizable by its followers or is entirely inapplicable. Consequently, the very thing being examined is reduced in status and its importance to the individual or community is disregarded or dismissed. It is not taken seriously because it has failed to reach some mythic (and specious) level of being 'a religion'. In contrast, Implicit Religion takes the approach that religion is not a distinct, singular category that is, or indeed must be, separate/different from the secular or popular culture. The 'religion' within the term Implicit Religion cannot be seen as coterminous with Christianity or any other religion, and that as a consequence 'the secular is thus no less viable at helping us to understand the nature and location of contemporary religious debate than the traditionally religious' (Deacy 2016: 126). Likewise, 'the implicit should not be conceived of as subordinate to or as a substitute for explicit religion. Just because someone's religion is not as explicit does not mean that they don't have one. All it may mean is that the main force of their commitment is directed elsewhere' (Deacy 2016: 138).

A brief note on methodology

The case study will draw on nine years of interviews undertaken by the author, an insider participant within sXe, from across the USA, the UK and Ireland, with a small number from Europe. All interviewees are between the ages of twenty-five and sixty, male, female, transgender, genderqueer and non-binary, most self-identify as working class with no higher education qualifications and most identify as white. They were interviewed in person as much as possible but some interviews were conducted online via Skype, Google Hangout and other similar means due to time or funding constraints. All interviewees are given the choice as to how they want to be identified in their quote attribution, their choices have been honoured here so the reader will see that some have more details than others, and that those who choose a pseudonym are marked by '…' around the name they created. All interview quotes are as articulated; they are not tidied up or edited. Hesitations, repetitions, pauses, colloquial terms, self-corrections and emotional reactions are all a necessary component of human interaction and cognitive processes. To fully understand what someone is saying it is important that we listen to how they say it as much as to what they say. In part, this approach is a direct response to the criticism of subcultural studies put forward by scholars such as Chambers (1985), Bennett (1999) and Miles (1995: 35) who notes that specific theory was fronted 'at the expense of the actual meanings' for participants. However, in part, it is also a response to my own experiences as a female, disabled, working-class academic who was frequently spoken over and for in academic settings in part because I have a regional accent, a working-class vocabulary and my disability makes articulation difficult at times. These experiences led to a realization of the importance of how people articulate, confirmed by the work of Jackson on storytelling among refugees, asylum seekers and displaced persons in which he notes that language and how we tell our own story directly disrupts the power relation between the public and private spheres (2013: 67).

What is sXe?

'I'm a person just like you, but I've got better things to do, than sit around and fuck my head ... I've got the straight edge' (Minor Threat, 'Straight Edge', 1981).

The above song was penned in 1981 by Ian MacKaye, lead singer and lyricist for Washington DC hardcore punk band Minor Threat. Intended as a statement of personal philosophy and his own lifestyle choices, it became a rallying cry for those within the hardcore scene who either recognized themselves and their choices in the lyrics or saw within them the life they wanted to live. Taking their inspiration from the title of the song, these individuals began to self-identify as straight edge punks. This spread to bands using it as a descriptor and eventually it became its own community within a community. Today, it is estimated that sXe has a worldwide membership in the tens of thousands (Haenfler 2006: 10). These bands and individuals took on the symbol of the X as a marker of that identity. At the time, an X was stamped onto the hands of underage patrons of bars and clubs to prevent them from purchasing alcohol. Using it as a symbol was a reclaiming of the mark, a statement of intent (of abstinence) and a means of demonstrating that punk is supposed to be for all, including the youth. Typically, the X is drawn on both hands in strong marker pen, but it is also common for sXe adherents to have it tattooed on their bodies as either a single X or a triple XXX.

The XXX symbol marks the 'code' or behaviours of being sXe which all adherents commit to and self-monitor, this is called 'claiming edge'. Each of the X's represent one of the three things that adherents abstain from: drugs (including tobacco), alcohol and casual sex. Some adherents will also add veganism, caffeine or even pharmaceutical drugs. The purpose of abstaining is two-fold; first to have a clear or better understanding of the world, the belief being that intoxicants prevent you from paying full attention and the second to ensure that one does not contribute to the profit and power of companies who exist solely to make money from products that are considered poisonous or harmful, or who profit from toxic representations of sex, the pursuit of sex and gender expectations. Claiming edge can only be undertaken once in a lifetime: akin to a wedding vow it is irreparable if not adhered to (called breaking edge), although breaking it will seldom result in ostracism from the community. Although the claiming of edge is often talked of in regards to resistance, anti-captialism and taking responsibility for one's actions and choices, it is often, though not always, also connected with long family histories of alcohol and/or drug addiction and the abuse that can be a part of that. It is also not uncommon to have sXe adherents talk about being sXe as part of their own recovery plan from addiction (Stewart 2017: 111):

> Addiction runs in my family; my great grandmother died of an opium overdose, my grandmother spent her life an alcoholic. I was 14 when I discovered that my mother, who raised me and my sister as a single parent, is a drug addict ... I don't remember what time of year it was, but I remember the day I became straightedge. As I was clearing empty bottles and drug remnants [after an unauthorized party] out of the garage, all of a sudden, it struck me that I actually was all alone, and I wasn't happy with or proud of the life I'd found myself living. I realized at that moment that no one else is going to change the course of my life for me – no one else was even around to notice what the course of my life had become. I knew that something needed to change and that I needed to be the one to change it. I didn't really know then how to do that, but I did know that if I chose to live without the poisons that had destroyed my mom's life and her mother's before her (and so on), and that if I coupled that with cutting ties with the unhealthy people I'd chosen to surround myself with, that a healthy path would become more clear and that my decision making would improve. Essentially, I had to become my own parent and I couldn't do that unless I dedicated myself to a clean and sober lifestyle.
>
> (S.G. New York 2010)

The sXe rejection of intoxicants and what it conceives of as individually and socially destructive sexualities, with its corresponding praise of addressing life's challenges with sobriety and responsibility echoes Taylor's (2007: 9) description of the ideologies of modern reason, 'contemplating the world and human life without illusion, and of acting lucidly for the best in the interests of human flourishing'. sXe desires nothing beyond 'human flourishing' and invokes no supernatural assistance or sanction to that end (Taylor 2007: 84). Yet it is not entirely self-sufficient nor immune from the same patterns as the rest of society in regards to notions of religion and secular disenchantment and re-enchantment. This can be evidenced in the relationship between sXe and religion.

sXe and religion

From its beginnings, punk, both as a musical genre and a social movement, positioned itself as the voice of the disenfranchised and potentially uncommercial (Unterberger and Hicks 1999: 433). A positioning solidified by the anti-establishment actions and demeanour of its members, some of whom stole their instruments, played without ability or embarrassment, supported one another in local scenes, created their own record labels, created their own means of internal communication and promoted to the point of idolization the concept of D.I.Y. Punk, did not emerge with the purpose or intention of being 'religious' in any sense, nor did it have any interest in engaging with traditional religious institutions and teachings beyond challenging, critiquing, arguing or dismissing them. Yet, in the 1990s a shift occurred and there was a growing sense of disillusion and disappointment with a disenchanted world within the sXe scenes in particular. Individuals and bands began expressing a desire for something that would help them re-enchant the world as they experienced it through connections with the Hare Krishnas and later Buddhism and Islam which became known respectively as Krishnacore, Dharma Punx and Taqwacore (all three groups have been examined in much greater depth in Stewart 2017: Chapter 3 of this volume; Abraham and Stewart 2017; Stewart 2015).

While there had been a previous connection between punk and Christianity, and to a much lesser extent punk and Judaism, that sought to use the music in a missional, cynical or playful way, it seldom stepped outside of evangelical norms. For example, the call to proselytize is understood as fulfilled through their lyrics, performance and band names (The City in Crisis, The City HE Loves and Ekklesia, for example), the conviction that Christianity is the means to prevent moral degradation and crisis, holding to conservative doctrines, and behavioural codes being set and enforced by the church (Abraham 2014: 92–3). Christian punk functioned on the premise that 'punk provides an amenable youthful template for evangelicalism's encouragement of exuberantly embodied religious celebration, and the sharing of one's beliefs with one's peers through often church-supported creative self-expression' (Abraham and Stewart 2017: 243). However, this is a contested group within punk in relation to their status as 'authentic' punks (variously understood) due to their refusal to move away from the belief that the answers to all or almost all questions about life are ultimately to be found in the Protestant biblical scriptures and therefore that truth can only be conceived of as ultimately biblical (Stewart 2017: 49). Ibrahim Abraham's work on evangelical and Christian punks demonstrates that many who participated within the Christian punk scenes saw themselves as authentically punk (Abraham 2017; Abraham and Stewart 2014). Many of my interviewees struggled to accept them as 'authentic punks' because they understood them as deriving answers and social structures that were still biblically orientated and saw them as little more than marginalia:

> I dunno, I can't say if they are or aren't punks can I? I mean who am I to say that, but I don't think they are, in my opinion, you know. How can you call yourself a punk and be tied to an institution that hates on women, gays, people of colour and basically anyone who isn't a male WASP because of a book? That doesn't make sense to me at all.
>
> (Dan, 39, Manchester, 2010)

> What are they doing but peddling someone else's lies, agendas or prejudice in the name of a God who, if he exists, probably hates how they think and act. These so called Christian punk bands challenge nothing, offer no solution beyond trust and obey; if anything they fucking promote the neoliberal capitalist structures that only profit the powerful and the wealthy.
>
> (Phil, 49, Belfast, 2012)

While there is not space here to examine the issues of authenticity at the core of this dispute over the 'right' to call oneself a 'punk', it is worth noting that Christianity has had a significant influence over the development and shape of punk, especially in the West. sXe emerged at a time in which there was the rise of the new Christian right, fundamentalism was on the rise as global migration increased, there were a number of youth evangelical movements and the launch of Nancy Reagan's 'Just Say No' anti-drugs campaign. According to Haenfler, 'Straight Edge's unyielding, black-and-white strictures on behaviour were similar to fundamentalist religion's rigid clear-cut beliefs' (2006: 10). The response of some sXe adherents was to seek out new ways of engaging with religion by aligning themselves with religions that they felt, for various reasons, did not carry the same baggage or problematic teachings as Christianity – namely Hinduism and Buddhism, and post 9/11 Muslim teenagers began to seek ways to articulate their own Islamic punk identities (Donaghey 2015; Fiscella 2012). Realistically, some of the interest in these groups was driven by an unaware orientalist perspective on what those religions or philosophies were, especially in relation to Hinduism and Buddhism. Partridge elaborates:

It is also important to understand that Eastern spirituality is not parachuted into Western culture – it is inhistorized, inculturated, contextualized. It should therefore come as no surprise to learn that the spirituality taught by Western gurus and masters is distinct from that taught by their Eastern counterparts … because Eastern thought is being processed in Western minds, shaped as they are by a late modern context, an eclectic, bricolage approach to religion and neo-Romanticism.

(2004: 106)

Interviewees were explicit in regards to the extent of musical content, lyrical content and 'preaching' of bands in their introduction to these religions and making them want to explore them further – not all were happy with what they found, as they explained.

> First I knew of it I heard Shelter, 108 and all. I asked those who had been around longer than me all about it and discovered it was called Krishnacore. I read up on it in fanzines and then one day my friend invited me to go to the temple. I wrote out a bunch of questions to ask the monks and they sat and talked with me for ages. No gods, no masters. I stand by that but that doesn't mean I can't have spirituality – I just gotta always think it through for me.
>
> (Chris, 33, Boston, 2016)

> It was appealing but I was suspicious. I talked to Porcelly and all and got their ideas, then I talked to my friends. Finally I started going to the temples and watching what was what. Eventually I talked to the monks. Some of it I choose to take on for me, some of it I discarded as religious, misogynist bullshit.
>
> (C-Ann, 38, New York, 2015)

These groups, especially Krishnacore, were the beginning point of sXe engaging with and taking seriously the concepts of religion, secular, sacred but also of many of the adherents beginning the process of finding ways to re-enchant their lives. A significant proportion of interviewees talked about this in a very interesting way, by describing sXe as their religion, by locating spirituality (sometimes referred to as faith in the UK) within sXe, and in so doing noting the centrality of the music for the success, longevity and potentiality of a re-enchantment.

> An essential component of hardcore is the spirit invested in the music. Every form of music comes from within, but the passion displayed at a hardcore show can be similar to what is seen at a religious ritual. At nearly every hardcore show,

bands play their songs with the utmost intensity, singers testify to an issue that is close to their hearts, and fans struggle to reach the stage in an effort to be a part of the experience. To many, hardcore is a religion – it can have its own values and belief systems (e.g. Straight Edge, vegetarianism / veganism, D.I.Y), classic texts (e.g. records, zines), and leaders (e.g. band members, zine writers, show promoters) who speak their minds and sometimes find themselves wrapped in controversy.

(Peterson 2009: 109)

What the interviewees were expressing and thinking through was their own notions of what is sacred, and whether their commitment to sXe punk was providing a new means to re-enchant their world or personal experiences. A significant number of interviewees referred to Straight Edge punk as their religion or their faith because it enabled them to be their authentic self and forced them to be held to account for their own actions or inactions.

> I guess punk is like a new religion, well I wouldn't say religion maybe but it is something that people put their trust in, have hope in, I do. So definitely I think punk rock is a faith. Like I said everything I have done has been influenced by it … The more people that get influenced by punk rock as a faith the better! [laughs] … like a lot of people I know their whole lives have been changed by punk rock. It's too much of a coincidence; it's too many people for it not to be something real.
>
> (Ewan, 28, tattoo artist, Glasgow, 2010)

> Straight edge is absolutely mint [laughs] I don't know any other way of lifestyle now, cause it seems to be that long now so, I seriously would not go back … to me it's a personal thing … if anything I find it kinda is a religion, cause like, well it's just my way of an upbringing, the way I brought myself up.
>
> (Karl, 28, tattoo artist and drummer, Durham, 2010)

It is worth noting, however, that not all interviewees agreed with this sentiment or perspective.

> I am a full blooded atheist. Have been ever since early high school, around the time I became Straight Edge. So, for me, the two are pretty closely related. Spirituality is just a weak willed way of saying you want a religion, but you're not sure which one works for you. Straight Edge is not a religion. It's a way of life, and a way of thinking, but you're not blindly following someone else.
>
> (Nate, USA, interviewed via email, 2010)

A key feature of the positive life view of much of Straight Edge is the continued attempts to associate consumption and production with the relentlessly 'civilizing' process. Many Straight Edge punks believe that production and consumption is inherently linked with the norms, rationale and desired behaviours of corporate capitalism and imperialism. Therefore, resisting the consumption of alcohol, drugs and casual sex is a means of resisting corporate capitalist dominance and searching for a more authentic way to live. Such resistance and authenticity is mediated through the music, the live performances in particular and further accessed through the fanzines, clothing, tattoos, websites and books. Ultimately, they all lead to the community of Straight Edge; a community of like-minded individuals which participants often frame as a brotherhood (the hyper-masculinity of sXe is dealt with in detail in Stewart 2017).

> Listen to 'Hurts to Ask' [by Chain of Strength] in a crowd and everyone sings along and it is a real moment of solidarity. When I listen to it by myself it forces me to confront the negative feelings and depression that I sometimes struggle with a little bit. It challenges me to not wallow in it or allow it to take me under. That I have to be better than that, stronger than that.
>
> (Sarah, 39, Chicago, 2011)

> Everyone singing along, united through this music. You feel your heart beating in time with the music, it's like we all beat as one, em, you know. We become this mass that for those minutes has a singular purpose, em, like a real brotherhood. It's what I imagine people used to get at those like, em, things, oh what where they called, you know the old like church meetings in a big tent? ... Yeah, yeah, revival meetings. Like them.
>
> ('Chloe', 33, Edinburgh, 2017)

When the music of the sXe subculture was talked about by interviewees (often the longest part of the interview) it was done so in terms that made it evident they considered the music sacred in a Durkheimian sense, in that it is a rising above the ordinary to the super-ordinary (Durkheim 2001: 160). Attendance or performance at a sXe show gives them an opportunity to leave aside the everyday and become a part of something much larger than themselves. It affords an opportunity to see themselves in a new way, to realize new potential and connections as part of their search for an authentic self. It is important to understand that they are not undertaking or partaking in this musical experience with the express purpose of obtaining a rapturous experience or connecting with the divine or spiritual in some way, but to enhance their own emotional state and satiate a deep longing to connect with the communal dimension of music. Consequently, what they connect with as extra-ordinary is not the divine but the Straight Edge community, the belief that punk rock can achieve more than some songs to dance to, and an opportunity to develop an authentic self (Stewart 2017: 90). In other words, sXe as a musical subculture is functioning as a means of re-enchanting the world through the implicit religion of sXe punk rock.

> You can go to a gig and feel like you are on top of the world when you leave, like you've had a religious experience, how can you beat that? Go and see Stiff Little Fingers or Toxic Waste and we would come out saying 'that was like going to church'. It was like having your faith revived, your strength renewed.
> (Patrick, 44, Belfast, addiction counsellor, 2013)

> Religion is the human effort to understand and order the self, society, the world and transcendent reality. Faith is different, it doesn't try to understand in order to control, rather faith is about beliefs which are concepts that are too deep to be called ideas. What's my faith? My faith is me, my faith is my sXe community, it's the music, it is sXe, sXe is my faith. D'ya know what I mean?
> (Dylan, 36, Belfast, teacher and musician, 2012)

Accepting sXe as an implicit religion means acknowledging that the importance of the subculture is far beyond what it is often assumed to be. It functions on a collective level enabling adherents to create a familial bond they often experienced as fractured within their own home lives. Furthermore, it is linked with political and social issues in a way that encourages action and enables them to see beyond a selfish view of the world. It promotes thought and justification that, spurred by their suspicion of authority, in turn promotes the challenging of one another and of themselves, in no small way through the music of their subculture.

> The music of sXe demonstrates a struggle with, promotion and expression of modern Western ideals and society. It contains a strong emphasis on challenging oneself, a desire for improvement, and a call for action that necessitates commitment with cost. There is a refusal to back away from uncomfortable issues such as domestic violence, suicide, rape, child abuse and self-harm. Lyrically and in images, concepts such as acceptance, community and referring to the local scene as one's family abound. Furthermore, there is a transcendent and salvific accent with many artists and adherents declaring that 'I didn't choose punk, punk chose me' or 'punk saved my life'. These are all markers of what is often traditionally considered important to a number of 'religions' and 'religious' communities. sXe music could arguably be understood as an attempt

to reintegrate or unite body and soul [in a world that increasingly calls for a new understanding of what religion is or could be and seeks to find new ways to challenge the perception of an a priori religious – secular binary].

(Stewart 2017: 94)

It is important to note that this is by no means unique to sXe communities and individuals. Similar objections and priorities are among the many of those who identify as belonging to or practising new puritanism, or progressive spirituality as Gordon Lynch terms it (2007). Lynch notes that they are responding to four perceived needs: credible understandings of faith that are compatible with a modern, scientific, technological age and provide a more inclusive experience for women, and focused on the environmental crisis (2007: 22). This could be viewed as both their commitment to changing religion and their intensive concerns for the encroaching potential environmental disaster as worked out through their actions and behaviours of abstinence, self-sustainability instead of consumption and reliance upon industrial production.

Outro

Christianity is on the decline in the UK and in many parts of Europe is a headline grabber that we have become used to seeing in recent years when new census data is released or polls are taken. Since the twentieth century, the credibility of Christianity has declined (in direct correlation with the rise of technology and instantaneous access to knowledge) and in more recent years has markedly lost its influence. The declining influence of Christianity is often tacitly assumed to mean a decline in religion writ large, which does not bear true in ethnographic-based work or even broader statistical analysis. One of the reasons for this is that too often such an assumption not only correlates Christianity as *the* marker of religion but also fails to account for the rise of non-traditional understandings of what religion could be within the lived experiences of individuals and communities. Heelas et al. note that traditionally understood religious designations and identities are in decline, whereas designations such as spiritual, holistic and quest are increasingly being used by a range of people and communities (Heelas et al. 2017: 2), Such markers are as likely to be driven or catered for by high-street consumption and availability as they are by religious or spiritual yearning. Not every religious expression fits within identifiable borders or boundaries. There is an increasing popularity for individualized approaches to our understandings of faith, religion or spirituality; this chapter drew upon a case study of the music-based punk subculture of sXe to illustrate such approaches by focusing on why they are seeking to re-enchant their world, and using the tools of Implicit Religion to outline how they are achieving it.

Within sXe there was a move towards embracing carefully chosen aspects or traditions such as Hare Krishna, Buddhism, Islam and Christianity by a minority of adherents, while many others sought some way to create a sense of wonder, awe, mystery, community, identity and even the numinous through sXe itself. Interviewees often explained this as wanting to find something that would help them find or recapture something larger than themselves, or something they couldn't easily explain. Their implicit religion of sXe is a re-enchantment understood as something which enables them to be caught up, either momentarily or for longer, both within the moment and in an acute awareness that they are a part of something larger than themselves. It is the animation of nature and the cosmos that delights and charms us in a way nothing else can and that leaves us altered from the experience. A significant number of interviewees referred to Straight Edge punk as their religion or their faith because it enabled them to be their authentic self and forced them to be held to account for their own actions or inactions.

This chapter has sought to demonstrate that when we consider communities such as sXe and their desire to re-enchant the world to varying degrees, critically and consciously, it is more productive to move outside of traditionally bound notions of what religion is, can be or how it should be studied. Instead, it demonstrates how valuable approaches such as Implicit Religion can enable a more nuanced understanding of what sXe adherents are doing and why.

Note

1 https://www3.open.ac.uk/media/fullstory.aspx?id=9898.

References

Abraham, I. (2014), 'Respecting Religion in Youth Music Subcultures', *International Journal of Children's Spirituality*, 19 (2): 83–96.

Abraham, I. (2017), *Evangelical Youth Culture: Alternative Music and Extreme Sports Subcultures*, London: Bloomsbury.

Abraham, I. and F. Stewart (2014), 'Desacralizing Salvation in Straight Edge Christianity and Holistic Spirituality', International *Journal for the Study of New Religions*, 5 (1): 77–102.

Abraham, I. and F. Stewart (2017), 'Punk and Hardcore', in C. Partridge and M. Moberg (eds), *The Bloomsbury Handbook of Religion and Popular Music*, 241–50, London: Bloomsbury.

Bell, C. (1997), *Ritual: Perspectives and Dimensions*, Oxford: Oxford University Press.

Bennett, A. (1999), 'Subcultures or Neo-tribes? Rethinking the Relationship Between Youth, Style and Musical Taste', *Sociology*, 33 (3): 599–617.

Berger, P. L. (1967), *The Sacred Canopy: Elements of a Social Theory of Religion*, Garden City, NY: DoubleDay.

Berger, P. L. (1999), *The Desecurlarization of the World: The Resurgence of Religion in World Politics*, Grand Rapids, MI: Eerdmans.

Berger, P. L. and T. Luckman (1966), *The Social Construction of Reality: A Treatise in the Sociology of Knowledge*, Garden City, NY: Anchor.

Bruce, S. (2000), 'The New Age and Secularization', in S. Sutcliffe and M. Bowman (eds), *Beyond New Age: Exploring Alternative spirituality*, 220–36, Edinburgh: Edinburgh University Press.

Carrette, J. and R. King (2005), *Selling Spirituality: The Silent Takeover of Religion*, Abingdon: Routledge.

Chambers, I. (1985), *Urban Rhythms: Pop Music and Popular Culture*, London: Macmillan.

Davie, G. (1990), 'Believing without Belonging: Is This The Future of Religion in Britain?', *Social Compass*, 37 (4): 455–69.

Davie, G. (2013), *The Sociology of Religion: A Critical Agenda*, 2nd edn, London: Sage.

Deacey, C. (2016), *Christmas as Religion: Rethinking Santa, the Secular and the Sacred*, Oxford: Oxford University Press.

Donaghey, J. (2015), '"Shariah don't like it … ?" Punk and Religion in Indonesia', *Journal of Punk & Post Punk*, 4 (1): 29–50.

Doss, E. (1999), *Elvis Culture: Fans, Faith and Image*, Lawrence, KA: University of Kansas Press.

Durkheim, E. (2001), *The Elementary Forms of Religious Life*, Carol Cosman translation, London: Penguin.

Fiscella, A. (2012), 'From Muslim Punks to Taqwacore: An Incomplete History of Punk Islam', *Contemporary Islam*, 6 (3): 255–81.

Haenfler, R. (2006), *Straight Edge*, New Brunswick, NJ: Rutgers University Press.

Heelas, P., G. Davies and L. Woodhead, eds (2017), *Predicting Religion: Christian, Secular and Alternative Futures*, Abingdon: Routledge.

Jackson, M. (2013), *The Politics of Storytelling*, Copenhagen: Museum Tusculanum Press.

Keenan, W. (2016), 'The Sacramental Thought-World of Implicit Religion', *Implicit Religion*, 19 (1): 11–47.

King, C. and F. Stewart (2016), 'Blue Suede Shoes to Doc Marten Boots: Music, Protest and Implicit Religion', *Implicit Religion*, 19 (1): 95–115.
Lynch, G. (2007), *The New Spirituality*, London: I.B. Tauris.
McLeod, H. (2007), *The Religious Crisis of the 1960s*, Oxford: Oxford University Press.
Miles, S. (1995) 'Towards an Understanding of the Relationship Between Youth Identities and Consumer Culture', *Youth and Policy*, 51: 35–45.
Parsons, T. (1966), 'Religion in a Modern Pluralistic Society', *Review of Religious Research*, 7 (3): 125–46.
Partridge, C. (2004 and 2005), *The Re-Enchantment of The West*, Vols 1 and 2, Edinburgh: T&T Clark.
Peterson, B. (2009), *Burning Fight: The Nineties Hardcore Revolution In Ethics, Politics, Spirit, And Sound*, Huntington Beach, CA: Revelation Books.
Stewart, F. (2015), 'The Anarchist, the Punk Rocker and the Buddha Walk into a Bar(n): Dharma Punx and Rebel Dharma', *Journal of Punk & Post Punk*, 4 (1): 71–89.
Stewart, F. (2017), *Punk Rock is my Religion: Straight Edge Punk and 'Religious' Identity*, Abingdon: Routledge.
Taylor, C. (2003), *Modern Social Imaginaries*, Durham, NC: Duke University Press.
Taylor, C. (2007), *A Secular Age*, Cambridge, MA: Harvard University Press.
Tharpe J. L. (1983), *Elvis Images and Fancies*, Jackson, MS: University of Mississippi.
Unterberger, R. and S. Hicks (1999), *Music USA: The Rough Guide*, London: Rough Guides.
Weber, M. ([1904] 2005), *The Protestant Ethic and the Spirit of Capitalism*, trans. T. Parsons, Abingdon: Routledge.
Weber, M. (1981), *General Economic History*, New Brunswick, NJ: Transaction.
Wilson, B. (1966), *Religion in Secular Society*, Oxford: Oxford University Press.
Wilson, B. (1976), *Contemporary Transformations of Religion*, London: Oxford University Press.
Windsor, J. (1997), 'Identity Parades', in J. Elsner and R. Cardinal (eds), *Cultures of Collecting*, London: Reaktion Books.

Discography

Carpathian, 'Monochrome'. On *Wanderlust* (2010), Deathwish Records. Minor Threat, 'Straight Edge'. On *Minor Threat* (1981), Dischord Records.
Rancid, 'You Want It, You Got It'. On *Let the Domino's Fall* (2009), Epitaph Records.
Shelter, 'In Defense of Reality'. On *Eternal* (2006), Dockyard 1 Records.
The Faith, 'Aware', On the EP *Subject to Change* (1983), Dischord Records.

10

'Message From Thee Temple': Magick, Occultism, Mysticism and Psychic TV

Mike Dines and Matt Grimes

> A reality that cannot face itself becoums an illusion. Cannot be real. We must reject totally the concept and use of faith, that sham. We must emasculate religion. The 'universe of magick' is within the mind of mankind. The setting is but illusion even to the thinker. The Temple is committed to building a modern network where people are given back pride in themselves, where destruction becoums a laughable absurdity to a brain aware of its infinite and immeasurable potential. (P-Orridge 2006: 58–9)

> Thee Temple strives to end personal laziness and engender discipline. To focus the Will on one's true desires, in the belief, gathered from experience, that this maximizes and makes happen all those things that one wants in every area of Life. (P-Orridge 2006: 39)

Writing in *The Psychick Bible* (2006) Genesis P-Orridge notes how 'Thee Temple ov Psychick Youth has been convened in order to act as a catalyst and focus for the Individual [sic] development of all those who wish to reach inwards and strike out. Maybe you are one of these', he continues, 'already feeling different, dissatisfied, separate from the mass around you, instinctive and alert? You are already one of us' (P-Orridge 2006: 33). Founded after the disbanding of Throbbing Gristle, Psychic TV was formed in 1981 by the performance artist Genesis Breyer P-Orridge, musician and video director Peter 'Sleazy' Christopherson and musician/producer Alex Fergusson. Over a period of more than thirty years, Psychic TV have produced a vast oeuvre of mixed media work including recordings, moving image, art installations and literature. As a band and performing arts group, they have embodied various incarnations, working collaboratively with over thirty musicians, writers, artists and philosophers, with P-Orridge remaining the one constant core member of the band.

P-Orridge's awareness of the occult and pagan ritual was integral to forming Psychic TV, and was also central to the simultaneous formation of the Thee Temple ov Psychick Youth (TOPY), an organization that was to become the magickal and philosophical wing of Psychic TV, and which subsequently led to the incorporation of magick, occultism and ritual into their music and multimedia productions. Using the Psychic TV's debut album, *Force the Hand of Chance* (1982) as an investigative framework, this chapter seeks to investigate, scrutinize and illuminate Psychic TV's past and ongoing relationship with magick, occultism, mysticism and paganism. Through a semiotic and discursive analysis of Psychic TV and TOPY's multimedia texts, performances, rituals and interviews, this chapter unpacks the significance of magick, occultism and ritual in asserting Psychic TV's occupying of an interesting '*cult*'ural and philosophical space between music, performance art and the practice and exposition of '*chaos magick*'.

Thee Infinite Beat: The magickal mileu of TOPY

It is commonly thought that Genesis P-Orridge coined the term 'Occulture' (see Partridge 2004: 68). 'Probably no word does better justice to the TOPY phenomenon that "Occulture"', notes Carl Abrahamson, 'meshing "Occult" with "Culture", there's a prefixed trace of "Occident" if you will. The defined concept as such was integrated in the inter-TOPY-"lingo" in the late 1980s, and then grew to become a readily accepted term for anything cultural yet decidedly occult/spiritual' (P-Orridge 2006: 11). As Abrahamson explains, 'occulture' was never really about occultism as such, but instead 'consisted of interchangeability where the clear cut borders were gently erased'. In other words, he notes how

> [b]ooks, pamphlets, newsletters, film and video screenings, record and cassette releases and other manifestations could certainly contain more or less blatant esoteric form or content, but is in no way a prerequisite. The literal meaning of 'occult' (as in 'hidden') was given a wider perspective than the merely 'magical' one.
>
> (P-Orridge 2006: 11)

Further to Abrahamson, Christopher Partridge emphasizes the *confidential* nature of occulture, noting how 'occulture includes those often *hidden*, *rejected* and *oppositional* beliefs and practices associated with esotercism, theosophy, mysticism, New Age, Paganism, and a range of other subcultural beliefs and practices' (Partridge 2004: 68). For Partridge, occulture 'refers to the environment within which, and the social process by which, particular meanings are disseminated and become influential in the lives of individuals and in societies in which they live' (Partridge 2014: 191). For Partridge, these meanings 'typically relate to spiritual, esoteric, paranormal and conspiratorial ideas', and whose core vessels are popular culture (he pulls upon television series such as *The Twilight Zone* and films such as *The Wicker Man* (1973) and *The Omen* (1976)), noting how 'popular (oc)culture provides a space within which there is an openness to the possibility of metaphysical interpretation' (Partridge 2014: 191). Importantly for Partridge – and this chapter – P-Orridge's concern was not following one particular tradition, that being either occult traditions or paganism, but instead to 'challenge tradition, question received ways of thinking, unravel established moralities, and subvert political and religious hegemonies' (2014: 194). In other words, P-Orridge's occultism 'focused on change and the future: it is confrontational, subversive, experimental and, to a large extent, dystopian' (2014: 192).

P-orridge's reclamation of magical elements therefore not only reached back to the 1960s where he notes how 'some people were prepared to live on the edge and explore what happens' (Morin 1994: 74), but more importantly were influenced by an occult lineage, and primarily by the work of the English occultist Aleister Crowley. Crowley's influences were eclectic, drawing upon ideas from, among others, the Thelemite, Gnostic, Occultist and eastern traditions (he had travelled through India in his late twenties). Born in 1875, and from parents who were members of the repressive Christian sect known as the Plymouth Brethren, Crowley was living at a time when both America and Europe 'had become fascinated by mediums, séances and hypnotism', and where the Theosophical Society 'had stimulated an interest in magical and esoteric doctrines from both the East and West' (Carr-Gomm and Heygate 2009: 431). It was a time of time, therefore, since,

> Until the twentieth century, magic had been a practice that moved between the worlds of science, medicine, philosophy and religion. The great magicians of the past had been sages, had pioneered the experimental method, particularly with alchemy, and had been concerned with healing as well as finding ways of communicating with other worlds and the Divine.
>
> (2009: 432)

Thus, Crowley's influence cannot be underestimated, not least in his writings informing modern paganism, the Ordo Templi Orientis (OTO), Gardnerian witchcraft and the development of modern Satanic thought and philosophy (espoused by Anton LaVey who established the Church of Satan in 1966 and who later worked with P-Orridge). Crowley also became a figure that fed into popular culture, including works by the novelists John Buchan, Dennis Wheatley and Dion Fortune; as well as an inclusion on the front of the Beatles's album *Sgt Peppers Lonely Hearts Club Band* (1967), an inclusion of Crowley's motto 'Do What Thou Will' on Led Zeppelin's album *Led Zeppelin III* (1970) and the song 'Mr Crowley' (1980) written by Ozzy Osbourne.

Furthermore, P-Orridge also acknowledged the power of sexual magic as purveyed by Crowley. 'There's no question in my mind', he notes, 'that one of the most important traditions in human history that's worked in terms of that power is sexual magick in various forms' (Morin 1994: 74). Further elaborated below, P-Orridge believed that the power of sexual magic embodied 'a sacred forbidden place, quite literally where the spirit flowed like sexual fluid for our beings … a chantry ov our minds chanting thee same human desire to breaks the bounds of temporality' (P-Orridge 2006: 66): thoughts reflected in P-Orridge's fascination with the artistic/magickal presentation of body modification.

Calling this practice 'a response to a deeper sense of alienation' (Morin 1994: 75), P-Orridge describes the skin and the surface of the body as a boundary between certain means of communication, and, thus, working with the skin draws in notions of the primitive nature and shamanistic quality of body modification, embodying a sense of power and control of one's body. For P-Orridge, therefore, body modification allows us to connect 'with older traditions and an older lineage that's been hidden in our society' (1994: 75), and thus allows us to challenge an illusion of experience and feeling. In conclusion, P-Orridge, as provocateur, performance artist, exhibitor of outrage and demonstrator of mystical depths somehow mirrored the lifestyle and predilection for the obscene and forbidden as Crowley did at the turn of the twentieth century.

Just Drifting: An investigation into *Force the Hand of Chance*

Released in 1982, *Force the Hand of Chance* was Psychic TV's debut album,[1] filling the immediate creative space after P-Orridge's earlier musical endeavour, Throbbing Gristle. Interestingly, John Encarnacao notes how Throbbing Gristle were symptomatic of the 'freethinking and political struggles of the late 1960s' (2019: 71). Comparing the band to the likes of US artists Patti Smith, Devo and Suicide, Encarnacao explores the aesthetics, political standpoint and cultural expression of that time between post-hippie and punk: an aesthetics of 'confrontation, amateurism and disruption' (2019: 76). For many, Psychic TV continued the countercultural path seen in the Throbbing Gristle's punk-like attitude. Musical styles are juxtaposed within a debut album that, again like Throbbing Gristle, struggles with a balance between content and style. As Encarnacao quite rightly suggests (2019: 74), there is a complex relationship between the conceptual background of P-Orridge's work (what that work is *trying to say*), and the form of that expression. In other words, musical style becomes the antithesis of a disinterested aesthetic, and is instead bound up by external meaning and motive.

Examples of this can be seen in the uneasy juxtaposition of 'Just Drifting (For Caresse)', whose diatonicism and conventional instrumentation underpins the subject matter (it was written for the birth of P-Orridge's daughter, Caresse); 'Ov Power', a track reminiscent of 1980s pop, with its mantra-like lyrical content, brass interludes and bass line; and the meandering and often discordant 'Guiltless', a track conjuring up influences from Throbbing Gristle. Arguably, the album is pulled together by the manifesto-style declaration of the track 'Message of Thee Temple', especially through its ethereal aesthetic and meditative-style vocal delivery. Indeed, Psychic TV's renown for their use of intertextuality in the production of their work gave credence to the track, in this case producing a video to accompany the narration of the audio (Psychic TV 1982). The narrator is filmmaker Derek Jarman, who had previously referenced paganism in his 1972 film *Journey to Avebury*, and collaborated with P-Orridge on the filmmaker's quasi-psychedelic *In the Shadow Of The Sun* (1981), with Throbbing Gristle providing the soundtrack. The mise en scène and delivery of the narration is visually and aurally/sonically confrontational and challenging; the viewer is presented with a male, business-like figure in dark suit and tie positioned behind a lectern. The setting is one of a plain white background with the TOPY 'cross' symbol to the right of the narrator.

A beam of white light rises from behind the narrator, resting on the right-hand side of his face, illuminating cheek, nose and eye. The rest of his face is mostly in the dark including his mouth. The visual impact remains rather unnerving, especially in the context of receiving an authoritative, 'forceful' and persuasive delivery reminiscent of an evangelical minister or religious cult-like spokesperson. The vocals are prominent throughout, a friendly, almost trustworthy tone, but monotone and instructional. 'Thee Temple strives to end personal laziness and to engender discipline', begins the narrator, 'to focus thee Will on one's true desires.' During the video the camera moves between close-ups of the side of the face or back of the head (3:45), and a close up of the face (3:40) focussing on the eye area that is lit by a side light. Not once do we see the narrator's face in full light, giving an air of mystery and distance.

At 4:03 the camera scene shifts to the narrator sitting behind an altar-like desk, with the TOPY cross placed beside him. With the white light beam behind him, the narrator remains shrouded in dim half-light, thus adding to the religiosity and enigmatic setting. At 6:16 he picks up the cross and thrusts it towards the viewer while continuing with his narration. 'It is up to everyone to accept the power that their bodies are endowed with', he notes, with the next camera shot showing the cross back on the table next to the narrator as if it returned there without assistance. At the end of the address the narrator promptly stands from behind the 'altar' and exits stage left with the music still playing in the background.

Written in the form of a manifesto, 'Message from Thee Temple' creates an esoteric foundation from which Psychic TV and TOPY go on to further develop in their later productions.[2] Interestingly, the track was allegedly written by P-Orridge 'after consideration of sexual magic and L-OV-E under Will', (Cope 2010) perhaps highlighting P-Orridge's familiarity of the techniques of the Ordo Templi Orientis as regenerated by the occultist Aleister Crowley, and evident within the latter's *The Book of the Law* (1909). For Crowley, each individual has a 'True Will', as distinct to the desires of the ego. 'True Will', therefore, has an almost divine character, a 'purpose' of one's life that an individual can only truly uncover through deconditioning, a process by which one can free the subconscious mind from the conscious mind.

What remains within *Force the Hand of Chance*, therefore, is the delicate balance between concept and style, the ever-present otherness that accompanies the musical object. With P-Orridge's reputation as a performance artist already established, one is immediately aware of the intertextuality of imagery, performance art and music. Although referred to as 'Message from Thee Temple' on the track listing, it is, however, referred to as 'Message from Thee Temple of Psychic Youth', on the lyric sheet. Despite TOPY/PTV claiming an almost anti-cult status, it soon became apparent among adherents that the structure and aesthetic of the organization had become increasingly cult-like, not least in the individual/single acts of sigils feeding into a group/collective/cult-like dynamic.

For the German theologian Ernst Troeltsch, mystical cultism 'had no desire for organized fellowship; all it cared for was freedom for interchange of ideas, a pure fellowship of thought', and where interestingly through the 'invention of printing … [t]he isolated individual, and psychological abstraction and analysis become everything' (Partridge 2004: 62). For Troeltsch, therefore, cultic spirituality is essentially 'self-oriented, eclectic and epistemologically individualistic' (Partridge 2004: 62), traits that resonate in the lack of complex hierarchy in cultic organizations (they are often led by a charismatic leader) and their membership of marginalized groups (where the group demands almost total commitment). The sociologist Roy Wallis developed Troeltsch's ideas surrounding mystical religion, noting in *The Road to Total Freedom* (1977) and *The Elementary Forms of the New Religious Life* (1984) that cults are loosely organized, individualistic and with a rapid turnover of membership. Of key interest to this discussion, however, is Wallis's unpacking of membership, in that cults do not adhere to a rigid overarching authority, being 'epistemologically individualistic' instead of being 'epistemologically authoritarian' (Partridge 2004: 25). Moreover, Wallis believes that

> [i]n constructing the typology, several key questions are asked. On the one hand, what is the self-understanding of the insiders? In particular, do they understand their organization to be *uniquely legitimate*? In other words, is the organization to be the sole repository of truth and the only path to salvation? Or is it *pluralistically legitimate*? … On the other hand, what conception do *outsiders* have? Specifically, is it generally understood to be a *respectable* or a *deviant* organization?
>
> (2004: 24–5)

As an aside, Wallis's typology of cult – whether the organization can be regarded as 'respectable' or 'deviant' – allows for a socio-cultural reading of the cult in question. Moreover, Wallis's work allows for an analysis of cults and their schismatic (where a smaller group may break away from a larger group) or evolutionary beginnings (2004: 26), a framework useful in the examination of TOPY and its belonging within a further subcultural space.

Wallis's critique of the historical/social contextualization of the cult is further explored through the work of the sociologist Colin Campbell. Turning to the structure of the cult, Campbell believes that there is a unifying set of belief values that Troeltsch and Wallis overlook. Indeed, for Campbell, cultic writing and definition has often been centred around what it is '*not*, a sect, church or denomination', and how the cult 'comes closest to resembling a *non*-group' (1977: 377). For Campbell, cultic organizations arise out of what he terms as the 'cultic milieu', which 'can be regarded as the cultural underground of society. Much broader, deeper and historically based than the contemporary movement known as *the* underground, it includes all deviant belief-systems and their associated practices' (Partridge 2004: 66).

An overview of writing around cultic formation and organization is useful in furthering an understanding of the practices of TOPY, not least in uncovering the complex relationship between established forms of religious practice and those formed from Campbell's 'underground', and echoed by Simon O'Sullivan. The latter uses a framework of 'performance fictions' highlighting how TOPY 'had a mythopoetic character (they produced – or *fictioned* – their own world), perhaps most evident in the emphasis on performance and collective participation' (O'Sullivan 2017: 1). For O'Sullivan, the work of the writer William Burroughs and performance artist Brion Gysin (especially in the use of the 'cut up' as method), and Aleister Crowley and Austin Osman Spare (especially in relation to sigil magick) are key to unlocking the complexities of Psychic TV's music and framework of religiosity. O'Sullivan also turns to the notion of ethics, not in the framework of any particular morality, but instead as instigating a 'way of life':

> Exploring what, precisely, a body was capable of and in developing a programme, involving certain disciplines and discipline more generally ... A central aspect of this ethics was the will to self-determination – 'to become oneself' – and, with that, the refusal of any transcendent enunciators, in particular Christianity.
>
> (O'Sullivan 2017: 5)

Highlighting the complex, interwoven relationship between the individual and the collective (not least in the sharing of experiences, the sharing of performance space and philosophical/religious ideas), O'Sullivan therefore notes how collectivism 'provided both a context and a legitimization for this other way of life' (2017: 5), thus echoing Troeltsch's and Wallis's ideas surrounding cultic religiosity. As is further noted in *Thee Psychick Bible*,

> Don't think we are going to tell you what to do, what to be. The world is full of institutions that would be delighted if you thought and did exactly what they told you. Thee Temple ov Psychick Youth is not and NEVER WILL BE one of them. We offer no dogmas, and no promises of comfort or easy answers. You are going to have to find out your Self, we offer only the method of survival as a True Being, we give you back to yourself, we support your Individuality in which the Spirit and Will united burn with passion & pride. Our function is to direct and support. Work that is needlessly repeated is simply wasteful.
>
> (P-Orridge 2006: 33)

That said, there are still questions that arise over the role of the individual and its relationship with TOPY. 'No matter how often we stress that thee Temple seeks to create a sense ov fierce individuality', it notes in the document entitled

'TOPY Is …', 'that it is for each Individual to redefine and redesign TOPY within themselves to meet their own needs, thee question still arise: what is TOPY?'. The piece continues:

> As we have said before, and no doubt will say again, TOPY exists to promote a system ov functional, demystified magick, utilising both pagan and modern techniques. It is a process ov individual and collective experimentation and research with no finite answers, dogmas or unchallengeable truths. It is for each to discover his or her own understanding ov thee questions that suggest themselves, and through that voyage ov discovery to find their personal and true identity, thee True Will.
>
> (T.O.P.Y n.d.)

A perfect example of this can be seen in 'Thee Sigil Ov Three Liquids', a ritual developed by TOPY 'to strengthen and refine [initiates] inner objectives, both sexual and practical, but also to provide a fertile basis for those objectives to grow and becoum real' (P-Orridge 2006: 47). The ritual is performed alone on the twenty-third of the month at 23.00 hours. If at all possible, the only source of light should be a candle and the ritual should be performed naked. The initiate must first write down their most 'intense sexual fantasy', and one that would 'generate … the maximum possible excitement, pleasure and fulfilment, regardless of the identity, sex or age of those who take part with you, alive and guiltless' (2006: 48).

From here, the initiate must make the piece of paper 'special', by being touched by 'the three liquids of the body – that is spit, blood and OV, which is the Temple name for the fluids obtained by masturbation, semen from the male and lubrication from the female' (2006: 48). During this process, the individual should not only concentrate on their chosen fantasy, but 'also on the idea of the Temple and the fact that doing this Sigil is inevitably bringing closer what you really want' (2006: 48). The individual must then attach a lock of hair from their head as well as pubic hair to the paper. Furthermore, twenty-three monthly rituals qualifies one as a full Initiate of the Temple.

In accompanied commentary, P-Orridge provides a brief historical overview of religious practice, noting how 'most religious and political groups of the last two centuries have stressed, among other things, the superiority of their leaders and the inferiority of the individual' (2006: 49). As such, and through the recognition of a growing disinterestedness in religion, P-Orridge concludes that 'if we are to be able to suggest even guidelines in this area, it must be done without dogma and in ways that people will understand' (2006: 49).

To further unpack P-Orridge's work, one must look in the most incomprehensible of places, and in this case it could be Coldplay and Lori Burns's article on the transmedial storyworld of the band's concept album *MyloXyloto* (2011). Burns looks at Gérard Genette's model of intertexuality, noting how the 'paratext' are materials that 'surround [the text] and extend it, precisely in order to *present* it, in the usual sense of this verb but also in the strongest sense: to *make present*, to ensure the text's presence in the world' (Burns 2016: 96). Burns then draws upon the work of Serge Lacasse (see Lacasse 2000: 35–58) looking at the transferring of Genette's model of intertextuality towards the concept of 'paraphonography', to illuminate those materials whose purpose is to both accompany and inform the music object. For Burns, these may be the artwork (album covers, liner notes and digital media), film footage, including music videos, documentaries and concert footage, as well as stage persona and performance practices. As the author notes, 'adopting the perspective that … meaning … emerges through a potentially complex network of materials' we can receive a multitude of meanings via the 'multimedial, intermedial and transmedial contexts' (Burns 2016: 96).

Drawing upon the work of Gunther Kress and Theo Van Leeuwen for their use of multimodality (see Kress and Leeuwen (2001), and Irina O. Rajewsky (see Rajewsky 2010), Burns notes how multimediality can 'comprise the artistic integration of multiple semiotic modes within one media' (2016: 96), while intermediality is a relationship that exists between different media texts. In other words, multimediality consists of video footage, live performance, musical genre and lyrical content, while intermediality consists of the live performance (and its links towards occulture and religious practices).

It is not difficult to see how Burns's work can inform the study of Psychic TV's *Force the Hand of Chance*, not least in the intersectionality of the popular music aesthetic and notions of spirituality and religiosity. Not only in the complex interplay of albums, books, newsletters and film screenings, but more so in the function and liminal musical experience. As such, Burns's conception of intertextuality extends towards a spritual, transcendent phenomenography of musical experience, of blurring the lines between 'audience' and 'congregation'. As June Boyce-Tillman notes, 'the totality of music experience' is one of

> encounter with the natural world through the body and Materials of the musical instruments, with the Expressive domain of another self or selves, with the mind in the ways in which musical ideas are debated through musical Construction and another culture in the domain of Values (whether that is geographical or historical).
>
> (Boyce-Tillman 2019: 51–2)

For Boyce-Tillman, the musical experience becomes a negotiation of experience, of Expression (anOther self), Values (anOther culture), Construction (the world of abstract ideas) and Materials (the environment), whereby the listener enters into 'another way of knowing' (2019: 52). In other words, through notions of liminality and ritual, music experience makes contact with the transpersonal, and thus 'tak[ing] the form of a change of consciousness' (2019: 53). Drawing upon the work of Isabel Clarke, Boyce-Tillman notes how 'the transliminal way of way of knowing' is primarily related with a 'porous' relationship with others, and where the crossing of 'an internal "limen" or threshold … opens up the possibility of transformation – both social and personal' (2019: 53).

Notions around intertexuality and the phenomenography of musical experience echo P-Orridge's own thoughts that the music accompanies a wider agenda for listeners to 'get interested in the ideas and the theories and the philosophies or the attitudes or just the engagement to try to wake up'. He notes the frustrations around the traditional relationship between a fanbase (particularly in exchanging of letters, etc.) and an artist, noting how 'people feel the need to probe us more and there always has been a ritual need – A [*sic*] need for ritual and celebration and so on'. For P-Orridge, therefore, Psychic TV are not there to be 'rock 'n' roll', but instead to 'get the effect, through the instrumentation, of a ceremony or an initiation or a ritual or a celebration or an ecstatic state – It [*sic*] can vary, we're not sure always what state it is – or a sexual arousal state.' Key for P-Orridge, then, is the *function* of sound, and not merely its ability to entertain. In terms of Psychic TV, he continues,

> That's the big difference with us, and they go, 'I wasn't entertained, it wasn't rock 'n' roll.' We don't want to do that. We want it to further function and effect people and it does – they go away and talk about their mental state having changed and their physical state having changed and the way and the way it made them feel or whether it was like such a drug! They don't go, 'really good songs,' they talk about the effect it had. The music is functional. This is the big thing that everyone seems to have forgotten. It's [*sic*] primary use and it's [*sic*] origination was function. It was to celebrate or to initiate certain states of mind or physical states and that's what it's for and that's what people have completely forgotten and that's why we use it in such a thrusting and tribal way.
>
> (P-Orridge n.d.)

P-Orridge's relationship with performance art has a long lineage dating back to his earliest work with COUM. Similarly Psychic TV's early live performances, such as those that debuted the album, *Force Thee Hand of Chance* often combined electronic and ethno-acoustic instruments, subdued lighting and banks of TV screens showing visual collages of still and moving images: all of which create a sensory multimedia intertextual experience for the audience. P-Orridge was a close friend of William Burroughs and, as noted above, was influenced by his approach to 'cut up as method'. Burroughs had initially used this approach in written text but later developed a similar process for film and video, contributing to a series of films directed by Antony Balch, including *Towers Open Fire* (1963) and *The Cut-Ups* (1966), which used occult and esoteric imagery and explored the overlap between aesthetics and the experiential through the deployment of the cut up as method or technique. As a useful referent, William Fowler discusses in detail how 'Scratch Video', a British video art movement from the 1980s inspired pop videos where 'the phenomena centred on the recycling of found materials, exploring non narrative, associational and sometimes musical connections, between disparate images' (Fowler 2017: 71). Writing in *City Limits* magazine in 1984 Andy Lipman suggested that Scratch Video as a form positions the TV screen as 'a crystal ball, triggering the subconscious. TV as the Dream Machine' (2017: 71).

P-Orridge who was familiar with these styles and methods of video mash-up/cut up, predated Scratch Video by actively deploying these approaches in the video and multimedia productions of Psychic TV; where images of sexual transgression, occult-like symbols and rituals, live performances of Psychic TV, ethereal landscapes, time-lapse films of flowers blossoming and decaying and cultural icons were looped, overlayed and juxtaposed against contradictory, conflicting and disparate images; creating unusual connections and a fragmented narrative held together by a musical soundtrack that was equally sonically challenging. Psychic TV's earliest foray into this approach to visual texts was the aforementioned *First Transmission*, a collection of experimental short films that include magick rituals, sexual transgression, pornography, body cutting, footage of cult leader Jim Jones and the Jonestown massacre, and members of Psychic TV discussing the importance of its philosophies and aims, among other dreamlike and surreal scenes.

In the live performance environment these visual productions would be either shown on banks of television screens arranged in the shape of the Psychic TV tri-cross at each side of the stage or projected on to a large screen behind the band. This multimedia experience created a sense of what one may term as 'hypnotic otherworldliness', where multimedia experiences become representative of the 'DreamMachine' that Lipman earlier referred to, where visually there is a sense of hyperreality at work. It is no surprise that the DreamMachine was a creation of Ian Sommerville (William Burroughs's 'systems advisor') and visual artist Brion

Gysin, long-term collaborator and friend of William Burroughs and devotee and friend of P-Orridge. The DreamMachine is a stroboscopic flicker device that is set at the frequency range that corresponds with the human brain's alpha waves, related to REM sleep/wake period. P-Orridge was aware of the potential relationship between alpha waves, dreams, hypnosis and trance-like states.

One could argue that one of the later defining moments for Psychic TV was the emergence of the acid house subcultural scene of the late 1980s and early 1990s. At this time P-Orridge was severing his relationship with TOPY and moving towards developing a new project called The Process, an art and philosophy collective that utilized the internet, which was in its early developments, as a platform for artistic and philosophical collaborations unrestricted by geographic location. While in America in the mid-1980s P-Orridge experienced the emergence and development of house music and acid house, including via one party organization, Mr Floppy's, who was affiliated to TOPY. Following a 1992 Channel 4 investigation and programme that claimed that Psychic TV and TOPY were involved in satanic ritual abuse,[3] P-Orridge, who was at the time in America, decided to exile himself after the authorities threatened to take his children into custody if he returned to the UK. The sound and structure of acid house, where electronic synthesizers and drum machines deployed to create trance-like repetitive beats, combined with mind-altering drugs, such as LSD and MDMA that created a euphoric, empathic and connected feeling towards others, presented Psychic TV with another medium and audience in which to explore ideas of ritual and magick, in a form of 'technopaganism' and 'cyberdelics'. As Reynolds notes, during this period P-Orridge disseminated a number of ideas including:

> Psychedelia/sampladelia as the creative abuse of technology; house's 125bpm as the primordial trance inducing, alpha-wave-triggering tempo that connects Arab, Indian and aboriginal music; [and] the manipulation of sonic frequencies to achieve 'metabolic engineering', à la Aleister Crowley's dictum 'our method is science, our aim is religion.
>
> (Reynolds 1999: 150)

Performances during this period, such as one at the London club Subterania in 1991, captured the essence of how Psychic TV's exposition of acid house music tapped into a collective euphoric form of ritual practice through sound, light, visuals and body movement. Again, cut-up visuals and collages were projected behind the band, with stroboscopic lights creating a sense of fracture and disorientation. Further, members of the audience are seen on stage dancing, trance like to the beat. As O'Sullivan notes (2017: 7) one of the key technologies deployed by Psychic TV was trance; but not only to engender a trance-like state of being but also as a means of creating a space for people to let go of fear, social division and form a collective energy that holds individual and collective power (Psychic TV 1990). Historically, music and dance that engender trance-like states and which create a euphoric state and space that transcends reality and allows mystical and spiritual connections and experiences have been well documented, such as the whirling Sufi dancers of Konya and other forms of ancient shamanic trance-inducing dances. Psychic TV's *Toward Thee Infinite Beat* (1990) and their 'fake' 1991 album *Ultrahouse-The LA Connection* capture the essence of this period of their musical output in terms of acid house and related electronic dance/trance music.

Conclusion

Using Psychic TV's debut album, *Force the Hand of Chance* as an investigative framework, this chapter has explored the band's past and ongoing relationship with magick, occultism, mysticism and paganism. By drawing upon a semiotic and discursive analysis of Psychic TV and TOPY's multimedia texts, performances, rituals and interviews, this chapter has examined the significance of magick, occultism and ritual in asserting Psychic TV's occupying of an interesting '*cult*'ural and philosophical space between music, performance art and the practice and exposition of '*chaos magick*'. Without a doubt, P-Orridge's oeuvre remains one of the most complex in popular culture, drawing upon a plethora of philosophical and religious ideas, and often resulting in groundbreaking musical styles. 'Clean out the trappings and debris of compromise, of what you've been told is reasonable for a person in your circumstances' (P-Orridge 2006: 39), writes P-Orridge in *Thee Psychick Bible*; a quote fitting for the study and investigation of the work of Psychic TV and TOPY.

Notes

Special thanks to Stephen Spencer-Fleet for his guidance during the writing of this chapter.

1   The first 5,000 pressings of *Force the Hand of Chance* were accompanied by the album *Themes* (1982).

2   Given that P-Orridge's previous band grounded their music in electronics and industrial noise, there is a notable shift in the use of instrumentation for *Force the Hand* and *Themes*, almost denoting a metaphor for rebirth and a new musical direction. Throughout *Themes*, in particular, PTV deploy the use of various folk/ethnic instruments such as drones, African initiation drums, joujouka, bells and twenty-three Tibetan human thigh bone flutes/trumpets and gongs: instruments used in Indian and Tibetan tantric Buddhism temple rituals. Included as (perhaps) a nod to the emerging and developing 'cultism' of TOPY was a recording made at cult figure Jimmy Jones's Jonestown settlement at the time of the mass suicides in 1978.

3   The producers of the programme 'Beyond Belief', an episode of the Channel 4 series *Dispatches*, believed that footage they had acquired of an experimental film titled *First Transmission,* and produced by Psychic TV, was evidence of satanic ritual abuse by Psychic TV and TOPY members (see Kirby 2011).

References

Boyce-Tillman, J. (2019), 'The Western Audience as Congregation', in J. Boyce-Tillman, S. Roberts and J. Erricker (eds), *Enlivening Faith: Music, Spirituality and Christian Theology*, 45–65, Oxford: Peter Lang.

Burns, L. (2016), 'The Concept Album as Visual-Sonic-Textual Spectacle: The Transmedial Storyworld of Coldplay's Mylo Xyloto', *IASPM@Journal*, 6 (2): 96.

Campbell, C. (1977), 'Clarifying the Cult', *The British Journal of Sociology*, 28 (3): 375–88.

Carr-Gomm, P. and R. Heygate, eds (2009), *The Book of English Magic*, London: John Murray.

Cope, J. (2010), 'Unsung Reviews: Psychic TV *Force the Hand of Change*'. Available online: https://www.headheritage.co.uk/unsung/review/2121/ (accessed 4 November 2019).

Crowley, A. (1909), *The Book of the Law*. Available online: https://www.sacred-texts.com/oto/engccxx.htm (accessed 1 November 2019).

Encarnacao, J. (2019), 'Throbbing Gristle's Early Records: Post-Hippie/Pre-Punk/Post-Punk', in Z. Beaven, M. O'Dair and R. Osborne (eds), *Mute Records: Artists, Business, History*, 71–86, London: Bloomsbury.

Fowler, W. (2017), 'The Occult Roots of MTV: British Music Video and Underground Film-Making in the 1980s', *Music Sound and The Moving Image*, 11 (1): 63–77.

Kirby, D. (2011), 'Transgressive Representations: Satanic Ritual Abuse, Thee Temple ov Psychick Youth, and *First Transmission*', *Literature and Aesthetics*, 21 (2): 134–49.

Kress, G. and T. Leeuwen (2001), *Multimodal Discourse: The Modes and Media of Contemporary Communication*, London: Arnold Publishing.

Lacasse, S. (2000), 'Intertextuality and Hypertextuality in Recorded Popular Music', in M. Talbot (ed.), *The Musical Work: Reality or Invention?*, 35–58, Liverpool: Liverpool University Press.

Morin, A. (1994), 'Genesis P-Orridge: Psychic Conspirator Steps Beyond the Infinite Beat', *Seconds Magazine*, 29: 74–83.

O'Sullivan, S. (2017), 'Mythopoesis, Scenes and Performance Fictions: Two Case Studies (Crass and Thee Temple ov Psychick Youth)'. Available online: https://www.simonosullivan.net/articles/Mythopoesis_Scenes_and_Performance_Fiction.pdf (accessed 1 November 2019).

Partridge, C. (2004), *The Re-Enchantment of the West Volume 1: Alternative Spiritualities, Sacralization, Popular Culture and Occulture*, London: T & T Clark International.

Partridge, C. (2014), 'Esoterrorism and the Wrecking of Civilization: Genesis P-Orridge and the Rise of Industrial Paganism,' in D. Weston and A. Bennett (eds), *Pop Pagans: Paganism and Popular Music*, 189–230, London: Routledge.

P-Orridge, G. (2006), *The Psychick Bible*, Port Townsend, Washington: Feral House.

P-Orridge, G. (n.d.), 'That's the Big Difference With Us', personal collection of Stephen Spencer-Fleet (accessed 1 November 2019).

Psychic TV (1982), 'Psychic TV First Transmission 1982 1 4 VHSRip XviD Z Com'. Available online: https://www.youtube.com/watch?v=ybv60hPAdpU&list=PLSEqKTzAsOwkbe9rD0ed9XrDltcWb76Yj&index=2&t=0s (accessed 16 September 2020).

Psychic TV (1990), 'Psychic TV: Interview and Live Toronto 1990'. Available online: https://www.youtube.com/watch?v=OUWyyDUSTXk (accessed 1 November 2019).

Rajewsky, I. O. (2010), 'Border Talks: The Problematic Status of Media Borders in the Current Debate about Intermediality', in L. Elleström (ed.), *Media Borders, Multimodality and Intermediality*, 51–68, New York: Palgrave Macmillan.

Reynolds, S. (1999), *Generation Ecstasy: Into The World Of Techno and Rave Culture*, New York: Routledge.

Reynolds, S. (2005), *Rip It Up and Start Again: Postpunk 1978–84*, London: Faber.

T.O.P.Y (n.d.), 'TOPY Is …'. Available online: http://www.ain23.com/topy.net/topy_is_1.html (accessed 1 November 2019).

Wallis, R. (1977), *The Road to Total Freedom: A Sociological Analysis of Scientology*, New York: Columbia University Press.

Wallis, R. (1984), *The Elementary Forms of the New Religious Life*, London: Routledge.

I am God! The Transference of Musical Fandom as Religion to Worshipping the Self

Javier Campos Calvo-Sotelo

Introduction: *I am God!*

Few topics have raised more academic interest in the last years than the digital age and its impact on everyday life, particularly on youth culture. Popular music shapes and echoes the aesthetic and ideological engagements of each generation and rather than disappearing altogether, religion seems to evolve, sometimes shrouded either in declared neo-pagan rites/beliefs, or in unconscious formulas of de-secularization and re-enchantment of the world. The intersection of digital culture, popular music and religion have created hybrid cultural spaces demanding specific analytical tools. As Fung (2017) notes, cultural identity is formed through the arts, and the spirituality in music is a medium through which people explore their identities. The ensuing cross-cultural field of investigation is fertile and currently under-explored: '[t]he relationship between religion and popular music has been a somewhat under-researched subfield within the broader interdisciplinary study of religion and popular culture' (Moberg and Partridge 2017: 1).

This study is based upon literature concerning the threefold amalgam of music, religion and the digital era. It also relies on several fieldworks and theoretical research carried out by the author especially for this study in the form of a written survey undertaken in 2018 at the Department of Music of the UAM (Autónoma University of Madrid) with thirty-six volunteers from the degree programme. The central hypothesis is that recently there has been a subtle but outstanding transference of the mechanisms of adoration away from the musical idol towards worshipping the self. Most notably, through creating public profiles on social networking sites (SNSs); in online games; adopting the culture of the *selfie*; with remarkable presence of concrete musical styles; or relying on performative practices and rites. In fact, for many adolescents the membership of their first SNS becomes a true rite of passage (Lincoln and Robards 2017). The current supremacy of electronic dance music (EDM) is meaningful here, because it might be a rather depersonalized and de-ideologized genre, where both the creator/performer and the songs will serve only the party purpose, lacking the magnetism and moral leadership of old rock demigods (Cohen 2016; Gilmour 2009).

Within their personal and collective context, the so-called Web 2.0 generation no longer worship an *external* figure (e.g. God or a famous artist) because with a click they can make almost anything available, making them masters of the (virtual) world. In fact, many research interviews underline personal empowerment as the main sensation of participants when making use of digital devices. Anchored in an online tower, isolated from their surroundings, modern adolescents see reality from a dominant bubble, falling into an emotional and, in many ways, spiritual celebration of the self. Sophie, a marketing manager from London, described her iPod experience as 'making the world look smaller – I am much bigger and more powerful listening to music' (cited in Bull 2007: 48). Another user (Zuni) declared: 'I [used the iPod] to control my environment and desensitise myself to everything around me' (Bull 2007: 53). Ignoring the surrounding world creates an environment for a divine self, one who is not affected by external events, thus feeling progressively stronger: 'So it's just fun over all to like to know that you have that power almost.' 'Overall it was just powerful feeling' (participants in Bull 2007: 53). Krause, North and Hewitt underline the 'control' that earphones offer listeners, extensive to the surrounding milieu: 'self-selected music [offers] a greater sense of control over the situation' (2015: 158). Similarly, Park highlights the autonomy provided by the mobile phone to teenagers from the very title of his article: 'My whole world's in my palm!' (2015).

The current 'amplification of the self' (Squire and Dikkers 2012: 453) has important spiritual connotations. Cyberspace becomes a holy space, where immortality is achievable for digital natives (Geraci 2010; Wertheim 1999), bringing the 'sacred ego' closer to the condition of divinity. Flawless and devoid of unwanted appearances which can be immediately removed with Ctrl+W, representing a metaphorical encounter with the lost Eden – unencumbered, playful and far from evil and pain.

According to the results of the UAM survey (see below) and the literature examined in this chapter, the current cult to the self could be viewed as an *implosion of sacredness* making a historical break towards the self in terms of adoration. Rather than egomania it represents a deep sociological trend where individuals replace external deity by concentrating spiritual energy within the self and immediate milieu. The rejection of God is not always a deliberated decision, and goes far beyond the religious realm, involving solipsism and self-enclosure.[1] 'Real' world vanishes, turned into cyberspace for many adolescents, who will construct public avatars replacing the real person: online images of the self gradually become *the self*; and online life, *life*. Absorption and addiction come to the fore: '[M]any of these youth have spent more of their lives connected to the internet, and digital technologies, than not' (Avdeeff 2014: 138).

This generational turn is visible with respect to religious stances in that modern reifications of religion generally consist of a psycho-emotional assumption and complementary semiotics, not stable theology or elaborate dogmas and rituals. That is the case of neo-pagan movements, wherein popular music can play a crucial role (Weston and Bennett 2013). Following art theorist Carl Einstein, Ezzy explains the decline of dogmatic religions based on the body–soul duality:

> Religious transcendence, and with it a collective understanding of reality, is not founded on the belief of the viewer but is the result of aesthetic experience … Embodied experiences such as dancing are the primary source of experiences of religious transcendence. Religious narratives, including formal dogmas, play a secondary supporting role. It is the Dionysian experience of openness and transformation that is primary …
>
> (2013: 124–5)

Nonetheless, new spiritual tendencies have not taken over from orthodox religions in the same way. A controversial representative of the countercultural rejection of formal religion was John Lennon; despite taking an oppositional stance and dabbling with Christianity and other religions, some of his statements have long lingered as symbols of resistance, challenging the hypocrisy of conventional religions:

> For him, religion is part of the establishment and its abuses, and he is characteristically blunt when asserting freedom from its control, as heard on John Lennon/*Plastic Ono Band* (1970): 'There ain't no Jesus gonna come/from the sky … ' ('I Found Out'); '[They] Keep you doped with religion' ('Working Class Hero'); 'I don't believe in Bible/ … /I don't believe in Jesus' ('God').
>
> (Gilmour 2017: 67)

Current youths do not rebel against God – as the Boomers did; instead, many live in an era of post-Christian spirituality that triggers countless cultural forms of underground religious contents (Campos 2016; 2019; Coleman and Arrowood 2015). It seems God has died or is an indifferent, false and distant figure, paving the way for alternative spiritual configurations. Lipovetsky notes that the recent revolution of individualism is characterized by narcissism, where the knowledge of oneself is central (1993: 91). As Heelas states: 'with nothing else to believe in, one is forced to come to believe in oneself and what that has to offer' (1996: 143). This notion of 'self-spirituality' is key to the study, as it condenses its main thesis:

> New age is a difficult term, as it has been applied indiscriminately to a range of disparate groups, alternative spiritualities emerging as a response to the re-enchantment of society ... A more accurate term is self-spirituality, in which the self, rather than the divine is the ultimate source.
>
> (Till 2017: 334)

No less important is Lynch's concept of the 'sacralization of the self', describing contemporary de-secularization where the individual's ego acquires a divine dimension:

> [In the] sacralization of the self ... the struggles, growth and interior life of the individual have developed a sacred quality without any necessary reference to a transcendent sacred or external religious authority.
>
> (Lynch 2007: 136)[2]

Among other reifications, the social online rush constitutes a culture of 'constant self-celebritization', within which people reveal 'far more about themselves than is necessary or, indeed, desirable' (Waugh 2017: 241). A key causal element to explain these processes is globalization, which induces both the de-localization and de-identification of the individual, provoking a disassociation with the milieu and enclosure in the ego even physically, within the set of smartphone, earphones and loud music; wearing a hood, which hides the head, became fashionable with musicians like Eminem. From this instinctive strategy of defence – building a bodily and psychological fortress – the self is inwardly elevated to the category of absolute being, due to the lack of reliable anchor points outside (Furth 2017).[3] The current culture of exacerbated consumption – based on obvious falsehoods – accentuates the feeling of affective insecurity and need for self-reinforcement before the surrounding world. For instance, on Twitter the more numerous the tweets the more they are appreciated: 'greater information quantity in tweets in the form of a greater number of words predicted being perceived more positively' (Orehek and Human 2017: 67). Hence an entire generation look feverishly in their phones for 'likes', constructing a super-ego able to resist the critical and disaffected surrounding environment, and attractive enough to maintain the superior/divine status. Yet this 'more self-focused language has been linked to negative psychological states and outcomes, including depression ... and suicidal tendencies' (Orehek and Human 2017: 67).

Absorption in the smartphone (an umbrella of earphones, cables, manipulation and full attention) makes it an isolating device (Livingstone 2008). As Bull states, the iPod (comparable to the smartphone a decade ago) 'works as a kind of territorial preserve, a boundary marker for others' (2007: 112). The silencing of the 'other' becomes thus a 'strategy of control' (2007: 32), representing a refusal to communicate with others in public and a 'filtering mechanism' (2007: 36), producing 'islands of undisturbed peace' (2007: 51). But this self-immersion can also act as an invitation to other youngsters to meet online where failure to participate invites social death: 'Smartphone-oriented sociability also tends to isolate non-iPhone users' (Lee 2013: 78). Thus, the bubble is also a social bubble, although invisible to strangers, who will only notice confinement (Layder 2004; Moshman 2005). Communicativeness and interactive options through the smartphone in fact involve a 'media orgy' (Kellner 2014: 8).

Another destiny of the people's spiritual disquiet are certain fashionable brands, which are worshipped by a faithful community who believe that the highest technology and most attractive goods will provide with a virtual paradise in this life. It is a phenomenon complementary of self-adoration, as the individual will demand the best for him/her. A passion for fashion brands and commercial labels increasingly exerts a religious role, for example in the case of Apple-as-religion:

> Apple is also somewhat similar to New Age movements in its millenialistic expectations ... Apple followers are expecting a transition to a new technological era where humanity and technology will live in perfect harmony, and Steve Jobs plays an important role in such a vision. He is attributed the role of the messiah leading humanity into a better future via developments in computer technology ... [Jobs is] a superhuman, hero, and prophet.
> (Pogačnik and Črnič 2014: 358)

Furthermore, the alias of the iPhone is 'Jesus phone', a fetish-object for the users; and Apple stores act like 'Apple temples' (Pogačnik and Črnič 2014: 358) with their corresponding high priests (the experts), worshippers (the clients) and adequate atmosphere of lights, colours and background music (Atkin 2004). Apple seems to take advantage of egomania even in the very names of their products (see below). Concerning youth specifically, there is a dense concentration of spiritual bias around fashionable brands: 'media consumption nowadays feeds, formats and mediates teenagers' beliefs in the supernatural' (Van Otterloo, Aupers and Houtman 2012: 253).

Life offline and online

As anticipated above, for many young people digital culture is 'more than a way of life, it *is* life' (Avdeeff 2014: 138;[4] Quelhas 2011; Thulin and Vilhemson 2007). The internet offers youths 'a realm where one's yearnings for community can at last find their realization', constituting a kind of 'extended family, a virtual village' (Gelder 2007: 147). Furthermore '[t]eens' online social behaviour has been found to be associated with a level of loneliness and need to belong' (Seo et al. 2014: 886). Consequently, contemporary youth are not interested in *the* world, but in *their* world, an ephemeral place with no credible afterlife (Campos 2014a; Zorzanello 2017). To some degree this results in a disconnection with reality: 'contemporary youth do not feel themselves embedded in a living reality that will endure over time, because youth are taught to concentrate on their personal status and wellbeing' (McLaren 2014: 154).

In social life online the public image reflects the sacralization of the ego in the selfie (see the Results of the UAM survey below), an image of the self that represents 'transformations of everyday figural representation as an instrument of mediated, embodied sociability' (Frosh 2015: 1624; Tiindenberg and Gómez 2015). Selfies mirror the virtual world where images, music and effects are bright, suggestive and flawless, courtesy of Photoshop. Following this semantic language, the names of some SNSs like *Face*book, *My*Space, About.*me* and the website *You*Tube reference image and self-adoration (my emphasis). Similarly, Apple products such as the iPhone, iPad and iTunes privilege the self in the initial 'I', whereas Instagram and Twitter allude to the immediacy and brevity of the content conveyed.

In the construction of the MySpace alter ego 'persona becomes a continually updatable identity, which exists independently of the person who created it' (Booth 2016: 118). Hence, the online image of the self will gradually become *the self*, and it is unclear which and where are the boundaries between offline and online existence. In 'My laptop is an extension of my memory and self', Waugh (2017) locates SNSs as 'real' part of life as that outside the internet; both dimensions (online and face-to-face) would coexist in constant interaction.

As Jurgenson writes, '*Facebook* is real life', and very demanding: '[i]t's not real unless it's on *Google* pics or it didn't happen. We aren't friends until we are *Facebook* friends. … Social media is more than something we log into; it is something we carry within us. We can't log off' (2012).

Cyberspace is a sacred space: the lost Eden

We might ask 'why is it that music of the last fifty or so years constantly draws on language, themes and imagery from the Christian Bible? And it is everywhere' (Gilmour 2017: 67). Since the Enlightenment, massive secularization provoked the abandonment of institutional religions leading to alternative myths such as Celtic spiritual fantasy and ancestral invocations (Campos 2016). The revived figure of Ossian, a remote bard of the third century AD, 'offered welcome opium from the deadly reason and intellect of the Enlightenment' (Sawyers 2001: 127). Other desecularizing mythologies were generated, based on the construction of fictional worlds and characters that harboured neo-pagan connotations, as happened with Frankenstein (Mary Shelley, 1818) and Dracula the vampire (Bram Stoker, 1897).[5] Authors like H. G. Wells, E. A. Poe and J. Verne consolidated science fiction in the general public; and among the first silent films were *Le Voyage dans la Lune* (Georges Méliès, 1902), *Nosferatu* (Friedrich Willhelm Murnau, 1922) and Fritz Lang's *Metropolis* (1927).

Perhaps human spirituality remains active in new formulas and neo-pagan tendencies designed to recover the lost paradise from which humans were expelled. McAvan describes the postmodern sacred as 'pastiched together from the fragments of spiritual traditions that *do* have that ontological foundation' (2010). In everyday life 'salvation, or analogues of salvation, are sought, found, or unconsciously implied in the everyday, in the vernacular' (Bacon, Dossett and Knowles 2015: 5). That religious forms may belong to ordinary life has been already explored in terms of 'implicit religion' (Edward Bailey), 'invisible religion' (Thomas Luckmann), 'surrogate religion' (Roland Robertson), 'quasi-religion' (Arthur L. Griel and Thomas Robbins), 'alternative spiritualities' (Rupert Till), 'popular magic' (Paula Eleta), 'religion/spirituality à la carte' (Adam Possamai), and 'hidden religiosity' (Helen Kommers).

For Western youth, cyberspace becomes a holy space where immortality is achievable (Geraci 2010) and in some games the virtual world may develop into a polytheistic cosmology, providing an alternative religion: 'cyberspace is not the product of any formal theological system, yet for many of its champions its appeal is decidedly religious' (Wertheim 1999: 24; see also McNamara et al. 2010). For Wertheim the digital world takes on a sacred aura precisely because people need to locate spiritual impulses somewhere. According to Geraci, 'Cyberspace is sacred space. Cyberspace allows us to build paradise in ways previously unimaginable' (2010: 13). Moreover: '[t]he desire to escape alienation, suffering, and impotence has promoted the relocation of the sacred to the digital realm' (2010: 76).

The dialectic between real and virtual can involve a spiritual challenge, with virtual realities (VR) provoking a sensorial catharsis, strongly connected to the notion of online embodied transcendence, or 'techno-spirituality' (Davis 2015):

> Davis's notion of techno-spirituality [is] a gnostic variation of spirituality. Davis coined the hybrid term 'techgnosis' to identify technologies like VR that provide a transcendent experience or ineffable ecstasy, a sensation akin to 'electronic LSD'.
>
> (Heim 2017: 163)

It is important to separate the subliminal search of spiritual compensation in modern societies, and the deliberated interest on religion itself. Concerning the latter, Kale's locution 'techno-pagan' (2004: 98) defines internet users who find a new religious experience in cyberspace (although dogma-less and with no resident theology). These new faiths depart from the collective rites of conventional religions, locating themselves in internet technology. George Barna predicted that by 2010 more than fifty million Americans might be using the internet as their sole means of having religious experiences.

> [There are] more than 19 million Web pages for the word Christian, 2,130,000 for Islam, 660,000 for Hindu, 461,000 for Wicca, and just fewer than 5 million for New Age. [And] more than 3 million pages for the word spirituality and one and a half times as many for the word religion.
>
> (Kale 2004: 101)

Émile Durkheim's work illuminates how the sanctity of a thing is due to the collective sentiment, not to any inherent divine nature. The transition from a straightforward digital-religious interest into social platforms cult implies a metamorphosis of the religious ontology. Walker's first title – 'My[Sacred]Space' (2010) – summarizes his central hypothesis: MySpace and other SNSs are a cult phenomena; relying upon Durkheim, he establishes their constitutive elements:

> [T]he typing of a username and password, along with the click of the 'Login' button, are clearly ritualized and routine activities that transport the individual

into another 'time'; the actual creation of an account and profile is also ritualistic in the sense that it 'initiates' the user into the world of MySpace, and serves as an act of 'consecration.' The 'Login Screen' also functions in a way that is analogous to an Eliadean 'threshold' …

(Walker 2010)

Likewise, the interactor may be self-represented with an avatar, without impurities or physical defects, as in online games where users embody heroes, gods, sages or warriors.[6] Finally, digital assiduity can become an end in itself, an autotelic experience detached from physical reality: '[w]e don't *want* to look at flesh and blood people – we want to watch their shadows on a screen. We don't *want* to hear their actual voices: only transmitted through a machine' (MacMillen 2011: 1). Cyberspace, by dissociating from corporality, is returning somehow to the Platonic body-soul dualism that presided over western philosophy for twenty-five centuries.

Electronic dance music (EDM)

Popular music is the 'global language' of the 'Now Generation' (Wang 2005: 187), constituting an irreplaceable catalyst to forge identity: 'music is a central element in adolescence and beyond … to master developmental tasks … regulate emotions, manage difficulties and provide points of reference in the process of constructing personal and social identities' (Kuntsche, Le Mével and Berson 2016: 219–20; Mulder et al. 2010; Schäfer and Sedlmeier 2009). Portable devices manage 'the listener's impression of the environment' (Yamasaki, Yamada and Laukka 2015: 61) allowing them to 'aestheticize' their surroundings by 'sound tracking' them (2015: 62). It also helps to 'mask unwanted sounds and environmental noises' (2015: 71). In the resultant acoustic *identityscape* (Appadurai 1996) teenagers ignore the contextual and aesthetic substrate of the music channelling their preferences without borders or defined locations. Personalized lists are organized for different moments of the day as the smartphone becomes 'a literal extension of the self' (Avdeeff 2014: 136).[7]

It is worth considering whether popular music conveys any inherent religious ontology (Sylvan 2002). In effect, it may become both a vehicle and a destiny of adoration, acting as a catalyst in the existential search for meaning. As Led Zeppelin frontman Robert Plant argues, it may be 'a better religion than religion itself, or a different kind of religion, or an alternative to traditional religion' (cited in Gilmour 2017: 70). There are other testimonies of interest:

'I've found grace inside a sound/I found grace, it's all that 1 found,' sings Bono ('Breathe', *No Line on the Horizon*, 2009). Rock and roll 'is my religion and my law,' sings Ozzy Osbourne ('You Can't Kill Rock and Roll', *Diary of a Madman*, 1981). In such cases, music is sacrosanct. Art becomes religion. Here too, songwriters often borrow the discourses of religion, including the Bible, to express that high praise of the music and musicians they prize.

(Gilmour 2017: 69. See Marsh 2017; Partridge 2017)

However, the last generations of young Westerners are deviating from such committed orientation, turning the affective and spiritual experience into a playful expansion. Assuming that music is fundamental for youth, among the immense variety of current styles EDM[8] is the most popular and better reflects their temperament, disposition and aesthetics:

As I write (September 2016), the week's top 100 most played Spotify tracks are almost entirely dominated by electronic music production. ... Even most traditionally rock-based acts that were in this selection such as Ed Sheeran and Coldplay utilize electronic production styles in order to orientate themselves towards the mainstream market.

(Strachan 2017: 12)[9]

Formally, EDM is condensed around bass-pitched sounds, fast *tempi*, timbre nuances and rhythmic variation: melodically, harmonically and structurally, most pieces are elementary and standardized. It is also described as 'Technology obsessive ... Texture and rhythm promoted above melody and harmony ... Mass communion for dancing crowds ... Showy if shallow ...' (Collins, Schedel and Wilson 2013: 112).

Dynamics are normally constant, high or very high with occasional drops to enhance the return to the dominant intensity. However, despite EDM's emphasis on the beat, its accents regularly fall on each quarter note pulse, thereby following a simpler and more linear pattern than in rock, where syncopation is fundamental (like in jazz and blues, its forerunners). Furthermore, unlike rock, EDM is more habitually instrumental, as if it did not need to think/say/ convince with oral language. Accordingly, the listener will not need to make any special effort to 'understand' or 'think', but be swept up. In contrast 'old' rock has superior formal density in almost every morphological parameter, perhaps mirroring the wider aesthetic and intellectual scope of its generation.

Among EDM followers the phenomenon of fandom is rare. Whereas Grateful Dead fandom 'went far beyond music, to become an integral part of their identity and vision of self', allowing them to 'make sense of the world' (Smith and Inglis 2013: 321–2), in EDM there is a 'primacy of sound over visuals, and crowd over any specific artist', which develops into a 'facelessness, anti-personality cult' (Collins, Schedel and Wilson 2013: 112). The musician thus fades away as high priest, moral and ideological leader, and while leading DJs are famous, they do not generally propound critical content or alternative ideologies within lyrics. Rock musicians passionately brandished guitars, the singer sang until hoarse, drummers lost several kilos in a form of self-surrender imbued with notions of a purifying sacrifice. Indeed, the deaths of Jimi Hendrix, Janis Joplin and Jim Morrison were likely assumed as alter Christy martyrdom (Middleton 2015). In rock concerts the stage becomes a shrine, and the musician a god-made man, radiating magnetism and demanding veneration. The DJ does not perform similarly because followers don't need a god to venerate – acting instead as a de-ideologized operator, generating and embodying a self-enclosed musical language.[10]

Finally, EDM is somewhat egocentric 'a culture of immediate gratification' (Takahashi 2018: 196) – the equivalent of smartphones use in isolation, aiming for individual pleasure although shared in social performances. With its scarce communication out of direct sensoriality,[11] lack of compromise with social causes, meaningless ideology and aspects like expensive festival tickets, EDM musically enacts the current ego cult, signifying the collapse of traditional forms of solidarity and community within a progressively atomistic society.

The 2018 UAM survey

Method

For this research we carried out a survey in March 2018 at the Department of Music of the UAM, with students from the second year of the degree. It consisted of a written questionnaire integrated by thirty-one questions (some of them with one or more sub-items), in four blocks: *Music / Digital Immersion / Personal Image / Religion*. Questions were both closed and open-ended, to obtain both statistical results and broader responses.

The survey was proposed as a voluntary exercise at the beginning of a class where all thirty-six students accepted the proposal. No compensation was offered or demanded. Anonymity was verbally granted; a single name was asked for, not necessarily the real one. Ages ranged from 19 to 27 years; mean age was

21.43 years old. There was a female majority: twenty-one respondents (58.33 per cent) against 14 (38.88 per cent); one of them showed no gender.

The sample was chosen because a group of music students was deemed likely to feel extreme admiration towards one or more musicians of one or another epoch (see below the surprising results). Furthermore, their socio-economic status granted them access to ample digital media. As young people in higher education with significant cultural capital they would be familiar with classical religions, displaying perhaps new religious tendencies. Convenience was a factor as personal knowledge of the UAM's musicology staff eased the task.

Almost all the closed questions had five options, ranging from the lesser to the higher, following the Likert-type scale. Thus, there were two 'negative' responses, a neutral one in the middle, and two 'affirmative' responses. Several comments in the following epigraph (see Results and discussion below) are based on the organization of these responses. Respondents' culled cites were in Spanish original, my translation.

Note that this survey has limits: first, the sample was rather reduced and some issues received insufficient responses to reach reliable conclusions. Second, the participants belonged mainly to a homogeneous milieu, and other populations should be studied to achieve more universal results. Finally, the fluctuating nature of musical taste is subject to change and the work may be either corroborated or outdated in the future.

Results and discussion

As expected, the students showed broad and refined musical preferences. For example, the category of 'Classical Music' received seventeen affirmative responses (47.22 per cent), sixteen neutrals (44.44 per cent), and only three negative (8.33 per cent; none of them 'very' negative). The category of EDM, got ten positive responses (27.78 per cent), nine neutrals (25 per cent) and no less than seventeen negative (47.22 per cent, half of them 'very' negative). Although music experts tend to prefer other styles, this must not undermine the study as the genre is nowadays at the top of youth preferences. Further, the questionnaire asked if the respondent identified him/herself with EDM and it is noticeable that from the eight participants who replied affirmatively (22.22 per cent) only two stated that their favourite DJ was an idol for them; the other six responded that they were not at all. This and other information gathered from the survey suggests that fandom and personal identification with the preferred artist may be diminishing among modern youth.

Interesting data arose from the questions about earphone use, proving that it is almost universal (see Table 1 below). We are facing a new generation regarding the audience habits: independent, web-oriented and isolated/isolating. Music therefore becomes an inner experience, not perceived through the whole body (including skin and bones), but as a secret voice that goes directly to the brain, ignoring the material and social environment. Rather than universal, music becomes the private and non-transferable life soundtrack of the sacred self. Since the listener can manipulate, transform, intensify and interrupt at will, the ensuing soundtrack becomes less the composer/performer's production, and increasingly an individual elaboration detached from its initial context. More a humble server of the ego: much appreciated but ontologically impoverished.

Listening to music with earphones triggered important reactions in the participants. Answering the question 'Sensations produced by the use of headphones' (see Table 2 below), most of the sixteen participants responding to the category 'None in particular' checked the Null box. For them, wearing a headset significantly affects their sensations and perception of reality. Perceived 'Isolation before the surrounding world' received 47.22 per cent positive responses, 44.44 per cent neutral and only 8.33 per cent negative, indicating that the psycho-emotional fortress may be a full reality in this generation. However, the highest valued response to the use of earphones was overwhelmingly 'Musical pleasure', which suggests that the intensification of pleasure is an aspect of self-worship in the digital era.[12] Certainly, users can currently control the overall experience of sound in ways that were not possible pre-digitally, listening to their favourite pieces where and when they wish, thereby emphasizing the cohesiveness and synergistic potential of the threefold amalgam music, digitization and personal deification. Other interesting sensations described in Table 2 – 'See the outside as a movie'; 'Control of the surroundings'; 'Feel better' – received rather scattered responses worthy of further research.

Concerning personal image, participants displayed a constrictive consciousness (moral correction): most responses avoided any kind of self-congratulation or self-adoration. For example, one question inquired how physically attractive they saw themselves compared to average; neutral responses

Table 11.1 Use of earphones. Total figures and percentages

	Never	Rarely	Sometimes	Frequently	Always
Total	0	0	4	10	22
Percentage	0%	0%	11.11%	27.78%	61.11%

Table 11.2 Sensations produced by the use of headphones. Total figures[13]

	Null	Low	Medium	High	Highest
Isolation before the world	0	3	16	11	6
See the outside as a movie	6	7	11	7	5
Musical pleasure	0	1	3	11	21
Control of the surroundings	11	5	12	4	1
Feel better, more secure	5	7	8	11	4
None in particular	11	2	1	2	0

Table 11.3 Self-image of the participants. Total figures and percentages

	Very bad	Bad	Medium	Good	Excellent
Total	1	1	8	21	5
Percentage	2.77%	2.77%	22.22%	58.33%	18.89%

were significant. Despite the 'moral correction' described, direct responses of personal image were clearly positive: 26 students (72.22 per cent) had a 'good' (21) or 'very good' (5) image of themselves, 8 (22.22 per cent) a neutral one and 2 were negative (5.56 per cent) (Table 3 shows the trend towards a high self-esteem).

In the item regarding succeeding in SNSs, almost nobody appeared to care; instead, these traits surfaced in the 'hidden' contents of certain questions. For example, selfish tendencies were visible in an inquiry about future priorities: 'Personal hobbies' were selected most (even ahead of professional future and family). Respondents showed some solidarity regarding wars and poverty, although clearly below the realm of the self (see Table 4 and Graphic 1 below). Rather than ignoring the main troubles of humanity, they seem absorbed in their own enclosed world, outside of which nothing is significant.

A key topic was religion. Of the thirty-six participants, twenty-eight of them (77.78 per cent) plainly espoused atheism, confirming the collapse of traditional religions and triumph of rationality in modern societies (Margry 2008; Steffen, Jöhncke and Raahauge 2015). Significantly, they had no true musical idols either, and did not wish to changes places with them. Yet an ample majority expressed a preference for science fiction and fantasy film, perhaps as a substitute for the spiritual cosmologies conveyed by formal religions. Asking for their three favourite films hoped to elicit whether non-believers directed their religious impulse towards other formulas to re-enchant the world. Very possibly they do, and the mechanism develops into cinematographic sagas, novels and series, websites oriented towards the supernatural, certain festivals and musical styles, mysticism, and other voluntary or involuntary spiritualties.

From that group of twenty-eight atheists, 88.46 per cent included at least one fantasy or science fiction movie, and no less than 65.39 per cent preferred two or three films of 'unrealistic style'. Among these were *The Shining* (Stanley Kubrick, 1980), *The Hunger Games* (Gary Ross, 2012), *Blade Runner* (Ridley Scott, 1982), *Batman* (Tim Burton, 1989), *Back to the Future Part II* (Robert Zemeckis, 1989), *Harry Potter and the Philosopher's Stone* (Chris Columbus, 2001), *Star Wars* (George Lucas, 1977), the *Lord of the Rings* trilogy (Peter Jackson, 2001 and on), and *The Nightmare Before Christmas* (Henry Selick, 1993). In fact, the list of fantasy and science fiction movies preferred by atheists was huge. Other favourite movies were based on the figure of the hero-demigod, which possibly replaces the 'lost God' in a film construction, like *Rocky* (John Guilbert Avildsen, 1976), *Raiders of the Lost Ark* (Stephen Spielberg, 1981) and *Forrest Gump* (Robert Zemeckis, 1994), whose main character directly embodies Jesus Christ in several episodes (Campos 2014b; Chumo 1995). Also interesting were the preferences for *Tarzan* (Kevin Lima and Chris Buck, 1999) and *The Lion King* (Rob Minkoff and Roger Allers, 1994); both movies involve pantheistic connotations, with animals talking and supernatural heroes. *The Avengers* (Joseph Hill Whedon, 2012) is also based on superheroes. Some preferred movies echoed a radical evasion from the real world, like *Into the Wild* (Sean Penn, 2007), of a pantheistic substrate and ending in death as liberation. *Moulin Rouge* (Baz Luhrmann, 2001) was selected by several females. It is an ultra-romantic and fatalistic recreation, with appreciable doses of unrealistic elements in the realization, audio-visual whirl and anachronistic soundtrack.

Some individual responses were noteworthy; P-11/M-20[14] claimed to be an atheist, not superstitious at all, and never consulting the zodiac, tarot or similar, but his favourite movie was *Blade Runner*, he by far preferred the science fiction movie genre and also appreciated terror films (which usually invoke the supernatural). P-1/M-22 presented the same non-believer profile, and also loved science fiction films above the rest (like six more participants), while his two favourite movies were hero-based *Rocky* and *Raiders of the Lost Ark*. P-30/F-20 adored terror movies and liked *Forrest Gump* the most. P-29/M-20, also a full non-believer, preferred science fiction movies, and his three favourites were Disney cartoon fictions. P-27/F-20, another self-reporting atheist, believed that it is possible to communicate with the dead, and travel to other worlds 'via meditation and imagination'. Atheist and totally sceptical, P-3/F-27 believed, too, that it is possible to make contact the dead. These media productions influence social behaviours via hidden-religion language, creating fictions that transcend this world. These fictions invite reinterpretation while offering re-enchantment of everyday life, increasing well-being in the audience, as they compensate the extreme materialism and technological domination of our time (McAvan 2010).

Are the film preferences and other personal tendencies sufficient to conclude that the convinced non-believers are unconsciously searching for religious alternatives by those means? Although an empirical demonstration is not currently feasible, there is a plausible correlation between both facts, and the literature on the topic seems to corroborate it. For instance, according to the classic volume on religion and popular music by Sylvan: 'for millions of people … religion and God are not dead … ; the religious impulse has simply migrated to another sector of the culture …' (2002: 3). In the words of Kommers, 'Even after the "death of God," even if there is no longer "worship," religion will persist as an individual and communal phenomenon' (2011: 20). Deepening further into the topic, neo-pagans (either declared or subliminal) subjectively construct reality as a set of 'poetic truths'; hence, modern myths are born in the individual rather than in churches and spiritual leaders: '[i]n this sense, myths can be understood as a set of images known primarily to the self' (Possamai 2002: 204–5). This phenomenon would be happening in the mass consumption of science fiction and horror novels, video games, movies and music (Sutton and Sutton 2019). Concretely, some movies convey a dense metaphorical symbology concerning the dialectics analysed:

> The *Star Wars* mythos is also idiosyncratically borrowed by individuals to support their spirituality … In Australia, the Star Wars Appreciation Society is attempting to establish Jedi as an officially recognized religion and even planned to ambush the 2001 national census.
>
> (Possamai 2002: 205)

Possamai also cites the *Star Trek* series, *ET*, *The X-Files* and *Buffy the Vampire Slayer* as sources of inspiration for neo-pagan groups. Another cult film, *2001: A Space Odyssey* (mentioned by several atheist UAM participants), is essentially a religious film according to Williams (1984), and is described by many viewers as a religious experience (DeMet 2001).

Regarding having 'musical idols', ten participants (27.78 per cent) – being themselves music students – lacked a single one. Even more importantly for the present study, half of those twenty-six who did mention one or more idols would not exchange themselves for any of them (the most negative response), eleven (42.30 per cent) would exchange 'maybe for a while' and only two responded affirmatively (7.70 per cent, just one the most favourable response). It seems clear that participants esteem decidedly their own existence. The final one of this group of questions was whether their musical idols were role models for them outside of the musical space, with open responses: of the twenty-six 'idolaters', nine (34.62 per cent) replied with a simple 'no', and seventeen (65.37 per cent) replied affirmatively. Nevertheless – and this point is fundamental – all but two in the latter group (who answered just 'yes') responded with quite a few nuances, evincing that their admiration was under control and constrained to specific features of their models (i.e. far from passionate fandom). Moreover, a subtle personal bias frequently emerged: for example, P-8/F-22 wrote: 'At most their motivation to reach what I want.' P-11/M-20: 'Perhaps in the areas that affect my own musical career, but not personally.' The selection of just one specific positive feature was another widespread answer, like P-3/F-27: 'It depends. Michael Jackson, for example, regarding humanitarian aid … but there are things of him I do not agree with.' P-12/M-20: 'Only as artistic models.'

Figures regarding digital immersion were striking, with an average of 8.56 hours per day of combined use of computer (or tablet) and smartphone, and no single participant under 5 hours per day. They were also massively connected to the internet. Around smartphones usage, one of the most surprising results came in the open-ended question 'What would your life be like without a mobile phone?' Thirteen responses were neutral or indifferent (36.11 per cent), but only eight were averse (pointing to a worse life; 22.22 per cent); while fifteen declared their life would be better or much better (41.67 per cent). Among the latter, quite a few expressed a deep joy and relief about the idea; their lives would be 'healthier' (P-36/F-19); 'more social and active' (P-6/M-22); 'with more free time to meet and read' (P-7/M-19); 'very peaceful' (P-8/F-22, and one more); 'better' (P-11/M-20, and three more); 'good' (P-12/M-20, and one more); 'more productive' (P-19/M-23); 'unstressed and undisturbed' (P-20/F-21); 'more personal' (P-27/F-20); 'more independent' (P-22/F-19); and so on. Significantly, almost all of those who opined their lives would worsen without a mobile phone referred to practical reasons (mostly unable to be on the phone with relatives). These responses evince a meaningful divorce between youth's perception and behaviour: many can abhor the smartphone, but all of them will use it massively, either because they are trapped by the advantages of digitization or because they enjoy the practice more than they are willing to acknowledge.

The questions about social media profiles had especial interest. The average was 3.24 SNSs profiles per respondent, and only one respondent lacked a single membership. An open question asked what their main use of personal profiles was; in the following order, replies were: to keep up with news; to contact people; for music and entertainment; and to view videos and pictures. Only a few avowedly used these profiles for self-promotion; participants declared a clear lack of interest in succeeding on social media: twenty-seven (77.14 per cent) were negative responses, and among them seventeen (almost half of the sample) the null option; there were five neutral responses, and only three positive ones. However, the average time spent on online social life was 2.03 hours per day, which is a significant amount. But most importantly, no less than twenty-nine participants (80.56 per cent) described more than one use of their SNSs. It was the open-ended question most extensively responded to in the whole questionnaire, which is particularly significant as it might prove that online sociality is highly motivational for them. Here, there is possibly another divergence between what respondents believe and reality, like the case of P-36/F-19 who gave 'little' importance to SNSs, but used them 'to vent, reflect, think. In the case of Instagram as an album' and spent three to four hours a day on them.

Another question dealt with the importance that diverse elements had for the student; the results provided essential information (Table 4 and Graphic 1).

To tabulate the results of Table 4, zero points were assigned to the Null reply; one to the Low; two to the Medium; three to the High; and four to the Highest.

Table 11.4 Esteemed importance of several elements. Total figures and percentage ratio

	Null	Low	Medium	High	Highest	Ratio
Professional future	0	0	6	19	11	78.47%
Family	0	2	4	9	21	79.86%
Friends, couple	0	0	3	18	15	83.33%
Personal hobbies	0	0	0	21	15	85.41%
Fashionable brands	18	14	1	2	1	18.06%
Religion	23	6	4	2	1	16.67%
Political/social problems	0	4	17	10	5	61.11%
Wars, terrorism, violence	0	4	14	15	3	61.81%

I am God!

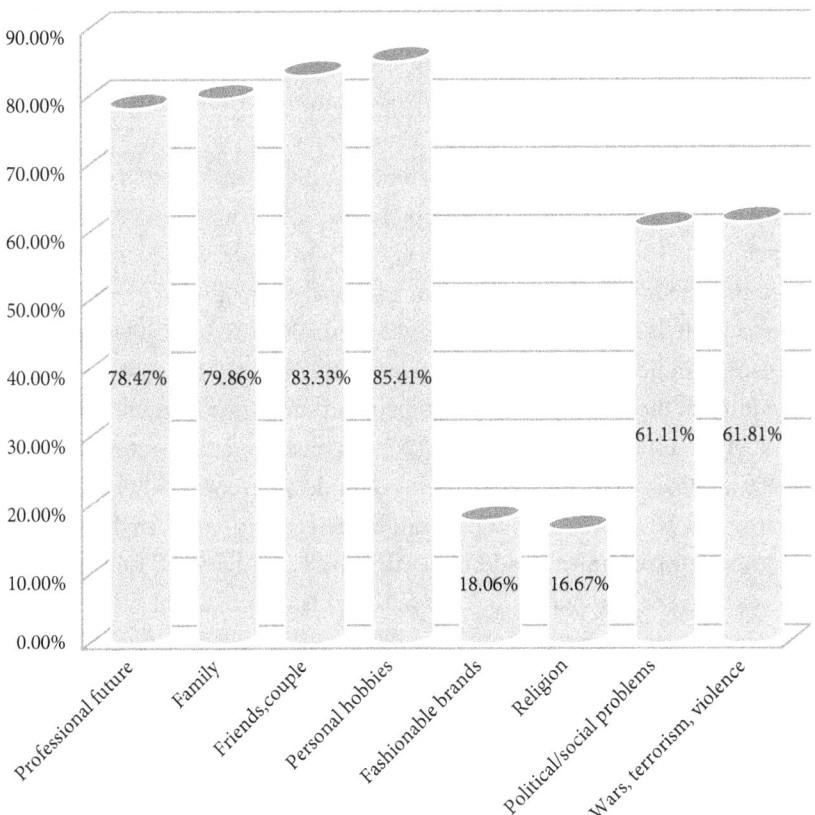

Graphic 11.1 Esteemed importance of several elements, converted into percentage ratio

The ensuing coefficients were converted proportionally out of 144 (maximal ratio), and then out of 100 per cent (Graphic 1).

The category 'Religion' declines visibly. In the past it was a deep assumption of both individuals and the whole society, but nowadays it becomes an out-of-the-self notion, alien to the real-life experience of many young people, at least concerning orthodox rites and doctrines.

On the contrary, it is palpable that the self prevails over the rest, as evinced by a gap between categories concerning the respondents' world and the 'external' world. Regarding fashionable brands there is a possible disjunction as, while they reject giving them importance, in a previous question about future smartphone intentions, several expressed the wish for an iPhone. The list is dominated by 'Personal hobbies', shortly ahead of 'Friends and couple'. 'Family' and 'Professional future' are a step below. 'Personal hobbies' was the only category receiving exclusively positive responses. We have to conclude that modern youngsters are more engaged with enjoying what they like than even with family and working perspectives, while wars and famine, for example, occupy an inferior stage in their worldview. Once more, there may be a meaningful background of egomania and narcissism/self-devotion in these preferences, which point to a 'philosophy of playfulness'. (Booth 2016: 20; Ozimek, Baer and Förster 2017).

Another 'hidden-content' question was inserted to find out real levels of self-esteem. It asked about strengths and weaknesses regarding work. Several respondents indicated one or two positive qualities and a defect. But the majority stated more of the former and some of them did so exaggeratedly, pointing to an overrated self-esteem. For example, P-22/F-19 considered that her qualities were: 'concentration, punctuality, kindness, work in detail, responsibility, willingness to learn, and fellowship', while her unique defect was to be 'shy'. P-23/M-21 only indicated some merits, adding no drawback. In the same vein, also half-disguised was the question of number of selfies taken per week: although many participants stated none or 1–2, some followed the trend unequivocally, like P-32/F-20 (10); P-7/M-19 (10); P-19/M-23 (40); P-26/M-24 (7); P-27/F-20 (10); and P-33/F-20 (30).

The lack of musical idols, together with declared atheism and a high self-appreciation, corroborates the view that some participants may be self-worshipers, and are the only god that exists in their lives. The fact is they prefer their own life to that of a music star with fame and fortune. Here are two synergistically coinciding facets: on the one hand, today's young Western adults are not psycho-emotionally dependent/worshipers of a sacralized external figure, as were the classic fans of rock and the like. On the other hand, the musicians that they admire (not more than that) do not represent for them vital or moral models to imitate. As a whole and in everyday life, their super-ego will reject making any concession to whatever they consider alien but shall be paradoxically tied to the online approval as an umbilical cord necessary to survive.

In the survey no significant gender differences were detected, and no other relevant associations were found.

Conclusions

Institutional religion (the most important monotheistic churches) does not currently arouse major interest, perhaps because of a gap between imposed rites and the sociological reality of our time. But religious impulses have not disappeared; instead they are projected onto alternative formulae, migrating from ontological instances to individual perceptions. God may have 'died' as an omnipotent majesty but the world remains full of potentially transcendent objects and situations that may turn sacred for a specific individual or human group. In this dialectical unsettledness between the sacred and the profane, combined with the existential search for self-meaning, lies the tension of renewing religious discourse and formation of a new *imago mundi* (Eliade). The rejection of God is not always a deliberate decision and goes far beyond the religious realm, involving a deep solipsism and social dismissal while avoiding direct confrontation. We are probably facing the development of a generation strongly tied to sophisticated technology and subtly antisocial, who are transitioning from the old style counterculture to a more elusive and hedonistic consumer cyberculture.

In a world full of uncertainties, cyberspace becomes a logical creation, where virtual realities provide a perfect, happy, untouched universe and whereas orthodox religion is optional, membership of one or more SNSs is nowadays an imposition; as failure to participate provokes social death.

The UAM survey also points out that the students live in a post-fandom era, far from conventional religious devotion. Yet, they haven't lost the human transcendental impulse. The lack of external superior beings or doctrines may be triggering an implosion of sacredness, which ultimately finds expression in the self, with youngsters feeling they have the world in their palm.

EDM is ideologically disembodied to some extent, perhaps reacting dialectically to the countercultural era by exempting meaning and foregrounding vacuity, winning the battle of popularity against rock music.[15] Yet any music can 'convey a complex and multidimensional phenomenon like religion' (Kommers 2011: 16), as is often witnessed at music festivals. The digital invasion of music may also be fostering a wave of rejection, leading to a 'digital indigestion' and diminishing fascination with the computer (Baker 2015: 176). Nevertheless, the cohesiveness and synergistic potential of music, digital media and personal deification must be underlined since they are forming a new and potent culture firmly embedded in modern societies, driving towards an uncertain future.

Every stage of post-medieval Europe has coined its own cultural *diabolus*: books when the printing press was born; comics and film along with the radio about a century ago; TV since the 1950s; and now the risk of computerization of human life. They were/are the 'haunted media' of history, taking the notion from Blackman (2015). While such fears are mostly anachronistic nowadays, according to the results of this study we can conclude that the digital era provides huge advantages for modern life, but may involve serious dangers and the risk of addiction, egocentricity and unawareness of real life.

Acknowledgements

I am grateful to Professor Adela Presas Villalba for her valuable help in carrying out the survey at the UAM Department of Music and the collaboration of the students who participated deserves acknowledgement.

Notes

1. 'Solipsism' comes from the Latin *solus ipse*, which means 'just oneself/only me'. Some expressions have been coined around this idea, like 'the aural solipsism of the iPod' (Bull 2005; Campos 2014a).
2. A locution that might be considered here is *theosis*, which consists of a transformative progression attempting a likeness to or union with God regardless of conventional religion. The concept stems from Eastern Orthodox Catholic theology.
3. The impact of globalization on cultural (collective) identities has received broad scholar attention (e.g. Tomlinson 2003). To a much lesser extent has been the study of its influence on the formation and shaping of individual identities, which is also notable, especially for adolescents (Thompson 2018). For the interaction between religion and globalization, see Dessi (2018).
4. Emphasis is always in the original, except where otherwise indicated.
5. Interestingly, Shelley entitled the book *Frankenstein; or, The Modern Prometheus*; thus referring her creation to Prometheus, a culture hero Titan in Greek mythology. Count Dracula stayed in the rural and remote Transylvania; but in the 1890s, according to the novel, he travelled to London, which was then the capital of the industrial revolution, to find new blood and spread the undead curse.
6. The origin of the term *Avatar* is in the Hindu religion, where it means the bodily manifestation of a deity.
7. Some modern radio stations increase the supply of broadcasting *music à la carte* (where the listeners can select one by one their preferences), like the pioneers Pandora, closely followed by Spotify, Google Play and iTunes.
8. Electronic dance music, techno, dubstep, house, trance and other denominations encompass several interrelated genres.

9   By a narrow margin, in 2009, techno was the preferred genre in the biggest USA cities, ahead of rock and rap (Johansson and Bell 2009: 233).
10 'Essentially the DJ simply has to show up', states Takahashi (2018: 194–5). A contrasting approach to EDM, highlighting its committed and religious values, can be read in St John (2006). It is interesting Maloney's perspective on house music as a cohesive narrative imbued with Christian values (2018).
11 The physical intensity of gatherings like Tomorrowland can reach unusual levels, as if youngsters suddenly discharge all their largely concealed public potential.
12 This interpretation matches consistently with the results of Table 4 and Graphic 1.
13 Note that in this table some categories are integrated by less than thirty-six responses, as some participants left one or more blank. This affects especially the 'None in particular' category. The analysis has been adapted to this imbalance.
14 Hereafter, participants are quoted with the abbreviation P-X (X = survey number of the participant) and gender (M = male; F = female) – and age (e.g. M-21).
15 According to Georgina Gregory, the continuing interest in highly regarded rock auteurs cannot be denied – Paul Weller in the UK, for example, who still has a very large following and high standing. When Bruce Springsteen and The Rolling Stones go on tour, they can still command a very large audience. The same was true of Prince and David Bowie, who were admired by younger fans (personal communication, December 2018).

References

Appadurai, A. (1996), *Modernity at Large: Cultural Dimensions of Globalization*, Minneapolis, MN: University of Minnesota Press.

Atkin, D. (2004), *The Culting of Brands: When Customers Become True Believers*, London: Penguin.

Avdeeff, M. (2014), 'Young People's Musical Engagement and Technologies of Taste', in A. Bennett and B. Robards (eds), *Mediated Youth Cultures: The Internet, Belonging and New Cultural Configurations*, 130–45, New York: Palgrave Macmillan.

Bacon, H., W. Dossett and S. Knowles (2015), 'Introduction', in H. Bacon, W. Dossett and S. Knowles (eds), *Alternative Salvations: Engaging the Sacred and the* Secular, 1–7, London and New York: Bloomsbury.

Baker, G. (2015), '"Digital indigestion": Cumbia, Class and a Post-Digital Ethos in Buenos Aires', *Popular Music*, 34 (2): 175–96.

Blackman, L. (2015), 'The Haunted Life of Data', in G. Langlois, J. Redden and G. Elmer (eds), *Compromised Data: From Social Media to Big Data*, 247–71, London and New York: Bloomsbury.

Booth, P. (2016), *Digital Fandom 2.0. New Media Studies*, New York: Peter Lang.

Bull, M. (2005), 'The Intimate Sounds of Urban Experience: An Auditory Epistemology of Everyday Mobility', in K. Nyíri (ed.), *A Sense of Place: The Global and the Local in Mobile* Communication, 169–78, Vienna: Passagen Verlag.

Bull, M. (2007), *Sound Moves: iPod Culture and Urban Experience*, London and New York: Routledge.

Campos, J. (2014a), '*I Don't Want to Hear You!* Solipsism and Identity Struggle in the MP3 Generation', Paper presented at the Kismif Conference, *Keep It Simple, Make It Fast! Underground Music Scenes and DIY Cultures*, University of Oporto.

Campos, J. (2014b), 'Grease, Forrest Gump y la inducción de identidades sociales en la deconstrucción de la contracultura', in H. Cairo and L. Finkel (eds), *Crisis y cambio: propuestas desde la sociología*, vol. 2, 705–15, Madrid: Universidad Complutense de Madrid

Campos, J. (2016), 'New Gods, New Shrines: Identity and De-secularization Processes in Young Followers of Celtic Music', in A-V. Kärjä and K. Kärki (eds), *Holy Crap! Selected Essays on the Intersections of the Popular and the Sacred in Youth Cultures*, 15–24, Turku: International Institute for Popular Culture, Available online: http://iipc.utu.fi/holycrap/Campos.pdf. Accessed 28/10/2020

Campos, J. (2019), 'Apocalypse as Critical Dystopia in Modern Popular Music', *Journal for Religion, Film and Media*, 5 (2): 69–95.

Chumo, P. (1995), '"You've got to put the past behind you before you can move on": Forrest Gump and National Reconciliation', *Journal of Popular Film and Television*, 23 (1): 2–7.

Cohen, J. D. (2016), 'Rock as Religion', *Intermountain West Journal of Religious Studies*, 7 (1): 45–86.

Coleman, T. and R. Arrowood (2015), 'Only We Can Save Ourselves: An Atheist's "Salvation"' in H. Bacon, W. Dossett and S. Knowles (eds), *Alternative Salvations: Engaging the Sacred and the Secular*, 11–20, London and New York: Bloomsbury.

Collins, N., M. Schedel and S. Wilson (2013), *Electronic Music*, Cambridge: Cambridge University Press.

Davis, E. (2015), *TechGnosis: Myth, Magic, and Mysticism in the Age of Information*, Berkeley, CA: North Atlantic Books.

DeMet, G. (2001), '*2001: A Space Odyssey*. Internet Resource Archive. The Search for Meaning in 2001' (1998 undergraduate honors Thesis revised). Available online: https://bit.ly/2RV06YP (accessed 9 February 2019).

Dessi, U. (2018), 'Religion: Globalization and Glocalization', in M. Middell (ed.), *The Routledge Handbook of Transregional Studies*, 475–81, London and New York: Routledge.

Ezzy, D. (2013), 'Dancing Paganism: Music, Dance and Pagan Identity', in D. Weston and A. Bennett (eds), *Pop Pagans: Paganism and Popular Musicx*, 475–81, Durham: Acumen.

Frosh, P. (2015), 'The Gestural Image: The Selfie, Photography Theory, and Kinesthetic Sociability', *International Journal of Communication*, 9: 1607–28.

Fung, A. (2017), 'Music Enables the Holistic Development and Discovery of Self: A Phenomenological Study of Two Christian Musicians', *Psychology of Music*, 45 (3): 400–16.

Furth, B. (2017), 'Ethnic Neo-Pagan Altars and Ancestors in Texas: An Ethnoreligious Strategy to Reconfigure European Ancestry and Whiteness', *Western Folklore*, 76 (3): 313–45.

Gelder, K. (2007), *Subcultures: Cultural Histories and Social Practice*, London: Routledge.

Geraci, R. (2010), *Apocalyptic AI: Visions of Heaven in Robotics, Artificial Intelligence, and Virtual Reality*, Oxford: Oxford University Press.

Gilmour, M. (2009), *Gods and Guitars: Seeking the Sacred in Post-1960s Popular Music*, Waco, TX: Baylor University Press.

Gilmour, M.l. (2017), 'The Bible and Popular Music', in M. Moberg and C. Partridge (eds), *The Bloomsbury Handbook of Religion and Popular* Music, 67–76, London: Bloomsbury.

Heelas, P. (1996), *The New Age: The Celebration of Self and the Sacralization of Modernity*, Oxford: Blackwell.

Heim, M. (2017), 'Bridging Real and Virtual: A Spiritual Challenge', *Journal for Religion, Film and Media*, 3 (1): 159–81.

Johansson, O. and T. Bell (2009), 'Where are the New US Music Scenes?', in O. Johansson and T. Bell (eds), *Sound, Society and the Geography of Popular Music*, 219–39, Farnham: Ashgate.

Jurgenson, N. (2012), 'The IRL Fetish', *The New Inquiry*. Available online: https://bit.ly/2GBORT1 (accessed 22 September 2018).

Kale, S. (2004), 'Spirituality, Religion, and Globalization', *Journal of Macromarketing*, 24 (2): 92–107.

Kellner, D. (2014), 'Toward a Critical Theory of Youth', in A. Ibrahim and S. Steinberg (eds), *Critical Youth Studies* Reader, 2–14, New York: Peter Lang.

Kommers, H. (2011), 'Hidden in Music: Religious Experience and Pop Festivals', *The Journal of Religion and Popular Culture*, 23 (1): 14–26.

Krause, A., A. North and L. Hewitt (2015), 'Music-Listening in Everyday Life: Devices and Choice', *Psychology of Music*, 43 (2): 155–70.

Kuntsche, E., L. Le Mével and I. Berson (2016), 'Development of the Four-Dimensional Motives for Listening to Music Questionnaire (MLMQ) and Associations with Health and Social Issues Among Adolescents', *Psychology of Music*, 44 (2): 219–33.

Layder, D. (2004), *Social and Personal Identity: Understanding YourSelf*, London: Sage.

Lee, D-H. (2013), '"In bed with the iPhone": The iPhone and Hypersociality in Korea', in L. Hjorth, J. Burgess and I. Richardson (eds), *Studying Mobile Media: Cultural Technologies, Mobile Communication, and the* iPhone, 63–81, Abingdon and New York: Routledge.

Lincoln, S. and B. Robards (2017), 'Editing the Project of the Self: Sustained Facebook Use and Growing Up Online', *Journal of Youth Studies*, 20 (4): 518–31.

Lipovetsky, G. (1993), *L'ère du vide: Essais sur l'individualisme contemporain*, Paris: Gallimard.

Livingstone, S. (2008), 'Taking Risky Opportunities in Youthful Content Creation: Teenagers' Use of Social Networking Sites for Intimacy, Privacy and Self-Expression', *New Media & Society*, 10 (3): 393–411.

Lynch, G. (2007), *Between Sacred and Profane: Researching Religion and Popular Culture*, London: I.B. Tauris.

MacMillen, S. (2011), 'The Virtual Pilgrimage: The Disappearing Body from Place to Space', *Journal of Religion & Society*, 13: 1–19.

Maloney, L. (2018), '… And House Music Was Born: Constructing a Secular Christianity of Otherness', *Popular Music and Society*, 41 (3): 231–49.

Margry, P. J., ed. (2008), *Shrines and Pilgrimage in the Modern World: New Itineraries into the Sacred*, Amsterdam: Amsterdam University Press.

Marsh, C. (2017), 'Pop and Rock', in M. Moberg and C. Partridge (eds), *The Bloomsbury Handbook of Religion and Popular Music*, 232–40, London: Bloomsbury.

McAvan, E. (2010), 'The Postmodern Sacred', *The Journal of Religion and Popular Culture*, 22 (1).

McLaren, P. (2014), 'Contemporary Youth Resistance Culture and the Class Struggle', *Critical Arts*, 28 (1): 152–60.

McNamara, C., L. Nelson, S. Davarya and S. Urry (2010), 'Religiosity and Spirituality During the Transition to Adulthood', *International Journal of Behavioral Development*, 34 (4): 311–24.

Middleton, P. (2015), '"Unlock Paradise with your own Blood": Martyrdom and Salvation in Christianity and Islam', in H. Bacon, W. Dossett and S. Knowles (eds), *Alternative Salvations: Engaging the Sacred and the Secular*, 109–20, London and New York: Bloomsbury.

Moberg, M. and C. Partridge (2017), 'Introduction: Religion and Popular Music', in M. Moberg and C. Partridge (eds), *The Bloomsbury Handbook of Religion and Popular Music*, 1–9, London: Bloomsbury.

Moshman, D. (2005), *Adolescent Psychological Development: Rationality, Morality and Identity*, 2nd edn., Mahwah, NJ: Lawrence Erlbaum.

Mulder, J., T. Ter Bogt, Q. Raaijmakers, S. Gabhainn and P. Sikkema (2010), 'From Death Metal to R&B? Consistency of Music Preferences Among Dutch Adolescents and Young Adults', *Psychology of Music*, 38 (1): 67–83.

Orehek, E. and L. Human (2017), 'Self-Expression on Social Media: Do Tweets Present Accurate and Positive Portraits of Impulsivity, Self-Esteem, and Attachment Style?', *Personality and Social Psychology Bulletin*, 43 (1): 60–70.

Ozimek, P., F. Baer and J. Förster (2017), 'Materialists on Facebook: The Self-Regulatory Role of Social Comparisons and the Objectification of Facebook Friends', *Heliyon*, 3: 1–19.

Park, y. j. (2015), 'My Whole World's in My Palm! The Second-Level Divide of Teenagers' Mobile Use and Skill', *New Media & Society*, 17 (6): 977–95.

Partridge, C. (2017), 'Emotion, Meaning and Popular Music', in M. Moberg and C. Partridge (eds), *The Bloomsbury Handbook of Religion and Popular Music*, 23–32, London: Bloomsbury.

Pogačnik, A. and A. Črnič (2014), 'iReligion: Religious Elements of the Apple Phenomenon', *The Journal of Religion and Popular Culture*, 26 (3): 353–64.
Possamai, A. (2002), 'Cultural Consumption of History and Popular Culture in Alternative Spiritualities', *Journal of Consumer Culture*, 2 (2): 197–218.
Quelhas, P. (2011), 'Teen Conceptualization of Digital Technologies', *New Media & Society*, 14 (3): 513–32.
Sawyers, J. S. (2001), *Celtic Music: A Complete Guide*, Cambridge, MA and New York: Da Capo Press.
Schäfer, T. and P. Sedlmeier (2009), 'From the Functions of Music to Music Preference', *Psychology of Music*, 37 (3): 279–300.
Seo, H., B. Houston, L. Taylor, E. Kennedy and A. Inglish (2014), 'Teens' Social Media Use and Collective Action', *New Media & Society*, 16 (6): 883–902.
Smith, P. and I. Inglis (2013), 'A Long Strange Trip: The Continuing World of European Deadheads', *Popular Music and Society*, 36 (6): 305–26.
Squire, K. and S. Dikkers (2012), 'Amplifications of Learning: Use of Mobile Media Devices Among Youth', *Convergence*, 18 (4): 445–64.
St John, G. (2006), 'Electronic Dance Music Culture and Religion: An Overview', *Culture and Religion*, 7 (1): 1–25.
Steffen, V., S. Jöhncke and K. M. Raahauge, eds (2015), *Between Magic and Rationality. On the Limits of Reason in the Modern World*: Copenhague: Museum Tusculanum Press.
Strachan, R. (2017), *Sonic Technologies: Popular Music, Digital Culture and the Creative Process*, New York and London: Bloomsbury Academic.
Sutton, M. and Sutton, T. (2019 [1969]), 'Science Fiction as Mythology', in J. Miles-Watson and V. Asimos (eds), *The Bloomsbury Reader in the Study of Myth*, 264–70, London and New York: Bloomsbury Academic.
Sylvan, R. (2002), *Traces of the Spirit: The Religious Dimensions of Popular Music*, New York: New York University Press.
Takahashi, M. (2018), 'Theater in Search of a Storyline: The DJ as "Technoshaman" in the Digital Age of EDM', in A. Häger (ed.), *Religion and Popular Music: Artists, Fans, and Cultures*, 185–200, London: Bloomsbury Academic.
Thompson, L. (2018), 'Globalization and its Impact on Individual Identity and Immersion for Special Track on AGIC 2018'. Available online: https://bit.ly/2N039hv (accessed 1 February 2019).
Thulin, E. and B. Vilhemson (2007), 'Mobiles Everywhere: Youth, the Mobile Phone, and Changes in Everyday Practice', *Young*, 15: 235–53.
Tiindenberg, K. and E. Gómez (2015), 'Selfies, Image and the Re-Making of the Body', *Body & Society*, 21 (4): 77–102.
Till, R. (2017), 'Ambient Music', in M. Moberg and C. Partridge (eds), *The Bloomsbury Handbook of Religion and Popular* Music, 327–37, London: Bloomsbury.
Tomlinson, J.n. (2003), 'Globalization and Cultural Identity', in D. Held and A. McGrew (eds), *The Global Transformations Reader: An Introduction to the Globalization Debate*, 2nd edn., 269–77, Cambridge: Blackwell Pub, Polity Press.

Van Otterloo, A., S. Aupers and D. Houtman (2012), 'Trajectories to the New Age: The Spiritual Turn of the First Generation of Dutch New Age Teachers', *Social Compass*, 59 (2): 239–56.

Walker, S. (2010), 'My[Sacred]Space: Discovering Sacred Space in Cyberspace', *The Journal of Religion and Popular Culture*, 22 (2): n.p.

Wang, J. (2005), 'Youth Culture, Music, and Cell Phone Branding in China', *Global Media and Communication*, 1 (2): 185–201.

Waugh, M. (2017), '"My laptop is an extension of my memory and self": Post-Internet Identity, Virtual Intimacy and Digital Queering in Online Popular Music', *Popular Music*, 36 (2): 233–51.

Wertheim, M. (1999), *The Pearly Gates of Cyberspace: A History of Space from Dante to the Internet*, New York and London: Norton.

Weston, D. and A. Bennett, eds (2013), *Pop Pagans: Paganism and Popular Music*, Durham: Acumen.

Williams, D. (1984), '*2001: A Space Odyssey*: A Warning before its Time', *Critical Studies in Mass Communication*, 1: 311–21.

Yamasaki, T., K. Yamada and P. Laukka (2015), 'Viewing the World through the Prism of Music: Effects of Music on Perceptions of the Environment', *Psychology of Music*, 43 (1): 61–74.

Zorzanello, S. (2017), 'Identity and Sound Identity: What are their Relations within the Landscape?', in A. Calanchi and F. Michi (eds), *Soundscapes and Sound Identities*, 294–316, Giulianova: Galaad Edizioni.

Index

108 (band) 185
2001: A Space Odyssey 224

abortion 48, 53
Abraham, Ibrahim 183, 184
Abrahamson, Carl 194
Acid House 205, 206
Acuff, Roy 60
Adam and Eve 35, 40, 155
addiction 128, 182, 188, 211, 230
Adorno, Theodor 125
aesthetics 154, 167, 196, 197, 205, 218
Aitkenhead, Decca 83
Akins, Rhett 62
Aldean, Jason 53
alienation 1, 119, 159, 196
Al-Junyad 31
Allah 36, 44
Allen, Gary 67
Alleyne, Mike 142, 143
alternative religions/spiritualities 4, 6, 10, 17, 98, 101, 112, 132, 173–236
Amen Break, The 140
Anderson, Bill 53
Anglican Church 97
Anttonen, Veikko 18
Appadurai, Arjun 217
Apple (technology company) 213, 214
Argyle, Michael 123
Aristotle 76
Arnold, Matthew 123, 124
Asthmatic Kitty Records 152
atheism 66, 186, 222, 223, 224, 228
Attali, Jacques 125
attendance (church) 2, 102, 119, 120, 121, 122, 131, 187
authenticity 16, 21, 22, 56, 64, 65, 74, 77, 78, 100, 159, 162, 179, 183, 184, 186, 187, 188, 190
Autonoma University of Madrid 209–236
Avdeeff, Melissa 217
Avengers, The 223

B, Katy 129
baby boomers 126, 211
Back to the Future Part II 223
Bailey, Edward 176, 178, 215
Balch, Anthony 204
Bamford, Gord 61
Barth, Karl 157
Batman (film) 223
Battersby, Christine 12
Bay, James 129
Beatles, The 1, 8, 100, 175, 196
Beethoven, Ludwig van 3, 7
Bell, John 109
Bell, Max 80, 81
Bennett, Andy 14, 15, 148, 180, 211
Berger, Peter L. 175, 176
Bible 5, 7, 12, 54, 55, 57, 58, 62, 66, 84, 85, 105, 108, 121, 124, 126, 130, 133, 158, 160, 211, 215, 218
Black Sabbath 12
Blade Runner 223
blasphemy 32, 63
Blues 50, 69, 127, 218
Blur (band) 80
Bock, Alan W. 58
body modification 196
Bonhoeffer, Dietrich 157
Bono 218
Boon, Clint 73
Boulez, Perre 8
Bowie, David 8, 82, 231
Boyce-Tillman, June 202, 203
Bragg, Billy 75
Brain, Chris 97–118
Brain, Winnie 107
Brandt, Paul 67
Brown, Callum 102, 104, 120
Brown, James 130
Brown, Karl 139
Bruce, Steve 176, 179, 120
Bryan, Luke 53, 67, 68
Buchan, John 196

Buddhism 5, 30, 32, 33, 41, 44, 73, 74, 85, 86, 87, 89, 183, 184, 190, 207
Buffy the Vampire Slayer 224
Bull, Michael 210, 213, 230
Burroughs, William 200, 204, 205
Byrds, The 127

Campaign for Nuclear Disarmament (CND) 103
Campbell, Colin 199, 200
Carroll, Jason Michael 66
Carter Family, The (band) 49, 50, 62, 66, 67
Cash, Johnny 58, 63, 64, 69, 129
Castle, Brian 131
celebrity 60, 67, 100, 108, 111, 158, 159, 162, 163, 164, 165, 166
Celtic 59, 215
Chain of Strength (band) 187
Chalkley, Dean 76, 88
Chaos Magick 6, 194, 206
Charles, Ray 4
'chavs' 128, 129, 132
child abuse 19, 188
Children of the Day (band) 126
Chinese Religious Music 3
Christianity 2, 5, 6, 10, 11, 15, 17, 42, 81, 85, 86, 95–171, 175, 176, 178, 179, 180, 183, 184, 189, 190, 200, 211
Christopherson, Peter 193
Church, Eric 5, 48, 61, 62, 63, 64, 65
church of Satan 196
Citron, Marcia 12
Clark, Lynn Schofield 13
Clean Bandit 129
Codone, Susan 121
Cohen, Leonard 5, 29–47
Cohen, Stanley 101
Coldplay 202, 218
communion 30, 33, 40, 97, 100, 218
Contemporary Christian Music (CMM) 14, 126, 129, 154, 166, 167
Cook, Hector 76
Coolio 127
Cope, Andrew L. 52
Correia, Nancy 145
COUM Transmissions 203
Counterculture 126, 159, 229
Country Music 5, 48–71
Cox, Tom 76

Crowley, Aleister 195, 196, 198, 200, 205
Crowley, Gary 73
cults 15, 17, 21, 65, 100, 101, 194, 197, 198, 199–200, 204, 206, 207, 210, 216, 219, 224
cyberspace 210, 211, 215–217, 229

Davie, Grace 177
Davies, Ray 72
DeNiro, Robert 98
DeNora, Tia 51, 130
dervishes 36, 37
Dessner, Bryce 157
Devo 196
Dharma Punx 183
Dickens, Little Jimmy 53
Digital culture 109, 140, 202, 209–236
Disco 107, 109
DIY (do-it-yourself) 61, 99, 108
dogma 13, 200, 201, 211
Donaghey, Jim 184
Dracula (book) 215
Dr John 85
drum and bass 6, 119, 128–129, 144
dub 109, 140, 143, 144, 145, 147
Dunham, Dave 160
Durkheim, Emile 18, 20, 21, 177, 187, 216
Dyer, Richard 59, 158, 163
Dylan, Bob 75, 126

Edwards, Darren 6, 128–132
ego 29, 34, 42, 61, 82, 198, 210, 212, 213, 214, 219, 221, 228, 230
Einstein, Carl 211
electronica 140, 143
Electronic Dance Music (EDM) 17, 97, 206, 210, 217–219, 230
Elgar, Edward 7
Eliade, Mircea 20, 217, 229
Emerson, Keith 8
emotion 74, 76, 78, 79, 80, 81, 82, 84, 111, 130, 131, 139, 164, 180, 187, 210, 211, 217, 221, 228
enlightenment 87, 124, 215
erotic/eroticism 32, 107, 168
escapism 138, 140, 147
esotericism/esoteric 36, 129, 132, 194, 195, 198, 204
ET (film) 224
ethics 10, 62, 76, 200

evangelicalism 5, 58, 97–118, 119–137, 153, 155, 156, 157, 159, 161, 162, 183, 184, 197
Evans, Sara 54
existentialism 4, 15, 82, 130, 155, 217, 229

Facebook 7, 121, 165, 168, 214, 215
faith 4, 5, 6, 30, 32, 33, 51, 52, 54, 57, 58, 62, 72, 79, 80, 81, 82, 84, 85, 89, 90, 103, 105, 106, 120, 122, 123, 126, 132, 133, 143, 145, 156, 159, 167, 176, 179, 185, 186, 188, 199, 190, 193, 213, 216
Falklands War, The 103
fandom 6, 19, 60, 159–162, 165, 178, 209–236
fanzines 186, 187
Farr, Tyler 62
Fergusson, Alex 193
femininity 12, 40, 43, 65, 103, 106, 164, 180, 201, 223
festivals 21, 99, 105, 120, 154, 223, 229
Fillingim, David 57
Fiscella, Anthony 184
Foley, Red 60
folk 3, 16, 20, 49, 109, 125, 126, 152, 153, 159, 207
football 64, 179
Forrest Gump 223
Fortune, Dion 196
Frankenstein (book) 215
Frith, Simon 9, 52, 53, 127
Frosh, Paul 214
Fung, Annabella 209
funk 83, 84, 140

Gallagher, Noel 80
Garbarini, Vic 76, 77
Garden of Eden 37, 40, 155
Garvey, Marcus 142, 143
Gaye, Marvin 130
Gelder, Ken 214
gender 12, 22, 32, 49, 104, 166, 180, 181, 220, 228, 231
genre 1, 3, 4, 5, 10, 12, 13, 14, 16, 18, 21, 48–61, 63, 65, 66, 67, 68, 69, 97, 101, 108, 119, 126, 128, 129, 138, 139, 140, 153, 154, 166, 183, 202, 210, 220, 223, 231
George, Iestyn 84
Gilbert, Brantley 62

Gill, Vince 66
Gilmour, Michael 3, 52, 210, 211, 215, 217, 218
Gilroy, Paul 141, 148
Glam Metal 127
Glastonbury festival 88, 99
globalization 1, 212, 230
Goldie 138
gospel music 2, 3, 4, 9, 13, 14, 49, 50, 51, 52, 55, 56, 57, 58, 60, 61, 63, 64, 67, 68, 77, 83, 84, 103, 109, 126, 131, 145, 154
goth music 3
Goulding, Ellie 129
Graceland 178
Grateful Dead, The 178
Green, Al 130
Greenbelt festival 100, 107
Greenham Common 103
Griel, Arthur L. 215
Grimes, Ivy 160, 161
Grossman, Maxine L. 50, 57
Guest, Matthew 120
guru 185
Gysin, Brion 200, 204–205

Haenfler, Ross 181, 184
Hadith, The 32, 44
Haggard, Merle 8, 63, 64, 66
Hall, Stuart 122
Handel, George Frideric 7
Harrison, George 2
Harry Potter and the Philosopher's Stone 223
Hart, Samuel 74
heaven 3, 8, 32, 43, 50, 55, 59, 62, 68, 81, 85, 86, 87, 152
heavy metal 1, 16, 52
Heim, Michael 216
Heng Hartse, Joel 156, 159
Hesmondhalgh, David 10, 17
Hebdige, Dick 100, 141
Heelas, Paul 1, 121, 189, 212
Hewitt, Paolo 83, 84–85
hell 3, 32, 43, 44, 60, 62, 64, 69, 75, 85, 86, 87, 127, 144, 145, 146
Hendrix, Jimi 219
Hilton, Walter 40
HIM (band) 12
Hinduism 14, 60, 184, 216, 230
hip hop 108, 138, 140, 179

hipsters 6, 152–171
Hoskyns, Barney 58
house music 98, 107, 139, 205, 206, 231
Hunger Games, The 223
hymns 3, 4, 9, 18, 54, 55, 57, 58, 67, 119–137

Ibiza 109
Ibn Arabi 30, 34
iconography 57, 97, 110
identity 17, 18, 52, 54, 77, 78–80, 100, 103, 139, 147, 160, 163, 165, 166, 176, 177, 178, 181, 190, 201, 209, 214, 217, 218
ideology 5, 9, 14, 15, 19, 20, 22, 50, 75, 78, 85, 90, 101, 124, 142, 182, 209, 210, 219, 229
implicit religion 176, 178, 179, 180, 188, 190, 215
incense 39, 97
indie 108, 153, 159, 168
individualism 104, 212
individualized religion 176, 177–180
iPhone 213, 214, 227
iPod 210, 213, 230
Instagram 7, 57, 159, 214, 226
intertextuality 197, 198, 202
Into the Wild 223
invisible religion 215
Iona community 109
Islam 3, 11, 29–47, 86, 183, 184, 190, 216

Jackson, Alan 5, 48, 55, 56, 69
Jackson, Cecil 61
Jackson, Michael 225
Jam, The 72, 73, 74, 75, 76, 77, 78, 79, 80, 81, 85, 87, 90
Jamaica 139, 142, 143, 147, 148
Jarman, Derek 197
Jazz 16, 78, 127, 138, 218
Jehovah's witnesses 103
Jennings, Waylon 60, 63, 64, 66
Jesus 2, 4, 5, 12, 35, 40, 48–71, 105, 126, 132, 175, 211, 213, 223
Jewish 36, 39, 41, 42, 43, 44
Jones, Bob 109
Jones, George 53, 61, 64
Jones, Owen 133
Joplin, Janis 219
Joyner, David Lee 50, 52, 57, 58
Judaism 42, 126, 183

Judas Priest 12
Jungle 6, 138–151

Kabbalah 5, 32, 33, 42, 44
Kale, Sudhir 216
Kalra, Virinder S. 51, 52, 126
Kansas City Prophets 111
Kantner, Paul 8
Keenan, William 179
Keep Sunday Special 103, 132
Kent, Bruce 103
Kessler, Ted 85
Khalifa, Wiz 129, 130
Kincheloe, Joe L. 63
King, Ben E. 3
King, B.B. 130
Kinks, The 72
Knowles, Mark 37–38
Kotarba, Joseph A. 14–15
Koul, Scaachi 164
Koyaanisqatsi (film) 110
Krauss, Alison 54, 55
Krishna consciousness 2, 183, 185, 190
Krishnacore 2, 183, 185

Lambert, Miranda 67
latin america 110
LaVey, Anton 196
Led Zeppelin 196, 217
Lee, Dee C 88
Lennon, John 1, 72, 175, 176, 211
Lewis, Jerry Lee 129
Life of Brian, The 127
liminality 203
Line, Florida Georgia 53, 68, 69
Lion King, The 223
liturgy 18, 97, 108, 125, 127, 131
Lorca, Federico Garcia 37
Lord of the Rings, The (film) 223
LSD 205, 216
Luckmann, Thomas 215
Lunch, Lydia 12
Lydon, John 75
Lynch, Gordon 13, 14, 19, 102, 112, 177, 189, 212
Lyons, William John 102, 104

MacKaye, Ian 181
MacMillen, Sarah 217
Malone, Andrew 81

Malone, Bill C. 56–57, 58, 60
Marley, Bob 140, 142, 143, 145
Martin, George 8
Marzuki (band) 152
Masculinity 40, 48, 62, 65, 111, 164, 187
Matsuoka, Mikio 86
Maule, Graham 109
Mayfield, Curtis 126
Mayhew, Henry 128
McAlister, James 157
McBride, Martina 66
McClary, Susan 11
McCracken, Brett 159, 160
McDannell, Colleen 101
McLaren, Peter 214
McRobbie, Angela 53, 101
MDMA 205
meditation 30, 107, 224
Melody Maker 78
Menson, Michael 139
Methodist Church 124, 158
Metropolis (film) 215
migration 1, 10, 15, 21, 184
Miller, Vincent J 154
Mind, Body, Spirit Festival 120, 132
miners' strike 103
Minor Threat (band) 179
Moberg, Marcus 19, 209
Monroe, Ashley 61
Moody, Paul 79, 83, 84
Moore, Justin 62
Moore, R. Lawrence 101
moral panic 100, 101, 113
Morgan, Craig 52
Morgan, David 14, 101
Mormon Church 103
Morrison, Jim 219
Morrison, Van 126–127
Morrissey 75
Mohammad (Prophet of Islam) 38
Moulin Rouge 223
Mraz, Jason 129
Muhly, Nico 157
multiculturalism 10, 21, 108
multimediality 202
music halls 124
MySpace 7, 214, 216, 217
mysticism 5, 6, 33, 40, 43, 44, 153, 193–208, 223

Natty, Congo 6, 138–151
Naughty Boy 129
Nayar, Sheila J. 49, 62
Neal, Jocelyn R. 50, 51, 67
Nelson, Willie 63
neoliberalism 122, 123, 184
newage 103, 194, 212, 213, 216
Nightmare Before Christmas, The 223
Nine O'clock Service (NOS) 97–118
northern soul 1
Nosferatu (film) 215

Oasis (band) 80
occultism 6, 193–208
occulture 13, 54, 176, 178, 194, 195, 212
Ocean Colour Scene 80
Omen, The 195
omnism 5, 72–93
Ordo Templi Orientis (OTO) 195
Osbourne, Ozzy 196, 218
Ottoman, Joanna 65
Owen, Jake 53
Oxfam 123

paganism 1, 3, 6, 15, 21, 155, 177, 194, 195, 197, 201, 205, 206, 209, 211, 215, 216, 224
Paisley, Brad 5, 48, 51, 52, 53, 54, 55, 67, 68
Partridge, Christopher 6, 15, 16, 19, 49, 54, 58, 60, 64, 101, 176, 177, 178, 184, 194, 195, 199, 209, 218
Parton, Dolly 54, 69
pentacostal church 5–6, 119–137
personal spirituality 29–93, 120, 121, 126, 130, 132, 153, 162, 164, 166, 181, 186, 201, 203, 210, 214, 217, 219–229
Peter, Paul and Mary (band) 12
phenomenography 201, 203
Piller, Eddie 78
pilgrimage 3, 61, 69, 178
planetary mass 98, 107
Plant, Robert 217
Plastic Ono Band 212
Plymouth Brethren, The 195
Poe, Edgar Allan 215
pop 2, 3, 5, 6, 15, 17, 50, 67, 75, 77, 105, 107, 119–137, 153, 154, 166, 197, 204
popular culture (definition of) Aug-25
P-Orridge, Genesis 193–208

Porter, Mark 154
Possamai, Adam 215, 224
postcolonialism 9–11, 15, 21
postmodernism 1, 17, 20, 109, 131, 177, 215
Prayer Book Society 103
Presley, Elvis 58, 129
Prince 8, 231
profane 18, 54, 62, 64, 98, 100, 104–111, 112, 229
psychedelic/psychedelia 3, 15, 197, 205
Psychic TV 6, 193–208
Psychick Bible, The 193
punk 6, 105, 108, 175–192, 193–208

Quantick, David 77
quasi-religion 215
Quran 30, 32, 42, 44

Radio 1 129
Radio 4 97
Raiders of the Lost Ark 223
rap 3, 21, 127, 154, 231
Rasky, Harry 38, 39
rastafarianism 6, 138–151
rave 1, 5, 97–118, 138, 140
Ray, Keith 138
Reagan, Nancy 184
redemption 55, 62, 105–108
Reed, John 75
Reed, Teresa L. 57
re-enchantment 6, 13, 21, 175–192, 209, 224
Reformation, The 124
reggae 139, 140, 141, 142, 143, 144, 145, 147, 148
Reggio, Godfrey 110
reincarnation 87
Religion and Popular Music in Europe: New Expressions of Sacred and Secular Identity 15
Reynolds, Simon 78, 141, 148, 205
Rhett, Thomas 62
Riethmuller, Albrecht 76
Rimmer, Dave 78
Robbins, Thomas 215
Robertson, 'Eck' 50
Robertson, Roland 215
rock 1, 2, 3, 8, 9, 12, 14, 17, 52, 53, 58, 62, 63, 77, 105, 107, 113, 125, 126, 127, 152, 154, 155, 156, 159, 162, 166, 203, 210, 218, 219, 228, 229, 231
Rocky 223
Rodgers, Jimmie 49, 50, 51, 59, 67
Rogerson, John 102
Rojek, Chris 59
Rolling Stone 153
Rolling Stones, The 231
Roman Catholicism 103, 106, 110, 160, 230
Romanowski, William D. 4
Roosevelt, Franklin 35
Rūmī 32, 36, 38, 39, 41, 42, 43, 45
Runcie, Robert 103

sampling 79, 108–110, 112, 141, 168
Sande, Emeli 129, 131
Satan 64, 66, 131, 196, 205, 207
Schiller, Friedrich 177
Schmidt, Leigh Eric 101
Scott, Darrell 61
Scott, Derek 124
Second World War 126
Selassie, Haile 140, 143
selfies 7, 209, 214, 228
Selman, Adam 164
sexual abuse 99, 100, 101, 102, 107, 112, 205
shamanism 111, 196, 206
Sheeran, Ed 218
Shelley, Mary 215
Shelter (band) 185
Shelton, Blake 53, 62, 67, 68
Shepherd, David 103
Sherwood, Adrian 143
Simon and Garfunkel 127
Shogo-mujo 86
Shuker, Roy 14
Sigils 198, 200, 201
Sinatra, Frank 127
Small Faces, The 79
Smith, Carl 60
Smith, Patti 196
solipsism 211, 229, 230
Spare, Austin Osman 200
spirituality 1, 3, 5, 6, 13, 15, 72, 73, 74, 83, 84, 85, 89, 90, 121, 122, 126, 130, 131, 132, 138, 142, 143, 145, 147, 153, 164, 168, 177, 185, 186, 189, 190, 199, 202, 209, 211, 212, 215, 216, 224

Star Trek 224
Star Wars 223, 224
Statement Quartet, The 60
Stefani, Gwen 67
Stevens, Sufjan 6, 152–171
Stiff Little Fingers 188
St. John, Graham 101
Stone, Sly 130
Storey, John 16, 17, 20
Stott, John 104
Straight Edge punk 6, 14, 16, 175–192
Strait, George 66
Stryper 127
Stuart, Marty 69
Style Council, The 72, 73, 74, 75, 77, 78, 79, 88, 90
subcultures 2, 5, 6, 16, 18, 20, 22, 64, 75, 99–105, 108, 111, 112, 113, 114, 159, 180, 187, 188, 190, 194, 199, 205
Sufism 5, 29–47, 206
Suicide (band) 196
Supergrass (band) 80
surrogate religion 215
Swift, Taylor 67
Sylvan, Robin 217, 224
Sylvia, Robin 64

Taize Community 109
Taqwacore 183
Tallis, Thomas 109
Tarzan (film) 223
Taylor, Charles 176, 178, 182
Tearfund (charity) 120, 121
techngnosis 216
Teenage Jesus and The Jerks 12
Thatcher, Margaret 73, 103, 105, 113, 122
Thee Psychick Bible 200, 206
Thee Temple ov Psychick Youth (TOPY) 6, 193–208
Theosophical Society, The 195
Thompson, Kenneth 18
Thornton, Sarah 101
Throbbing Gristle 193, 196, 197
Tiainen, Milla 11, 12
Till, Rupert 15, 17, 21, 97, 100, 102, 104, 121, 212, 215
Toxic Waste (band) 188
transcendence 1, 3, 5, 8, 10, 11, 12, 15, 59, 72, 97–118, 126, 177, 188, 200, 202, 206, 211, 212, 216, 224, 229

Travis, Randy 66
Tribal Bass (label) 139
Tribal Gathering (festival) 108
Troeltsch, Ernst 198, 199, 200
Tubb, Ernst 60
Tumblr 153, 161, 162, 163, 165, 168
Turner, Tina 130
Turner, Victor 101
Twilight Zone, The 195
Twitter 121, 159, 212, 214

Underwood, Carrie 52
Urban, Keith 62
Urbanski, Dave 63

Vannini, Phillip 14–15
Verne, Jules 215
Voyage dans la Lune, Le (film) 215

Wagner, Tom 153, 154, 155, 158, 162, 167
Wall, Tim 14
Wallis, Roy 199, 200
Walser, Robert 1, 11
Warren, Robert 98, 99, 102
Washington, George 35
Watson, David 104
Watts, Issac 124
Waugh, Michael 214
Weber, Max 177
Weller, Paul 5, 72–93, 231
Wertheim, Margaret 216
Wells, H.G. 215
Wesley, Charles 104, 124
Wheatley, Dennis 196
White, Maurice 8
White, Steve 77, 88
Whiteley, Sheila 149
Who, The 79
Wicca 177, 216
Wicker Man, The 195
Wigglesworth, Smith 125
Wilberforce, William 104
Williams Jnr, Hank 60
Williams Snr, Hank 5, 48–71
Williams, Michael 59–60
Wilson, Bryan 176, 179
Wilson, Colin 132
witchcraft 177, 196
Wolfe, Charles K. 57
Wonder, Stevie 126

Woodhead, Linda 1, 121
world music 17
Wren, Brian 131

X-Files, The 224

Yoga 30
Yom Kippur War 35

Young, Jock 101
Young, Neil 63
YouTube 51, 67, 121, 153, 167, 214

Zappa, Frank 8
Zen Buddhism 5, 32, 43, 44
Zorn, John 16

www.ingramcontent.com/pod-product-compliance
Lightning Source LLC
Chambersburg PA
CBHW072139290426
44111CB00012B/1925